# BEST-LOVED
# POEMS

# BEST=LOVED
# POEMS

Edited by John Boyes

ARCTURUS

ARCTURUS

This edition published in 2014 by Arcturus Publishing Limited
26/27 Bickels Yard, 151–153 Bermondsey Street,
London SE1 3HA

Copyright © Arcturus Holdings Limited

ISBN: 978-1-84837-296-2
AD000070UK

Printed in the UK

# CONTENTS

# INTRODUCTION

Any book titled *Best-Loved Poems* cannot help but encourage the obvious question: '"Best loved" by whom?' Eyes naturally turn to the anthologist. While I admit that there was temptation to include the nursery rhyme that once brought fits of giggles from my infant daughter, personal preferences have been ignored. This book consists not of the classic verse best-loved by the anthologist, rather it is a gathering of English-language verse that is held dear by others, poetry for which many readers have an affection. Some of the verse featured is known to readers throughout the English-speaking world, while other poems extend their reaches no further than the borders of the nation in which they were written. As such, some verse may seem unfamiliar and unexpected. The poetry of the British Isles, that with the longest tradition, forms the greatest percentage of work included in this collection. Beginning with the seventeenth-century poet Anne Bradstreet, American poetry, too, forms a large percentage. These, too, are met with significant contributions by poets from Canada, Australia and New Zealand.

More than any other, an anthology of best-loved, traditional verse is conditioned by contemporary bias. After all, the intent is not to present poems that were once extremely popular, nor is it a goal to promote poetry that deserves more notice. This is a collection of verse that has withstood what we call, through cliché, the 'test of time'. It is an unsparing trial that has reduced the profile of many poems and poets. In the middle of the nineteenth century, for example, the status of Henry Wadsworth Longfellow was such that his place as America's pre-eminent poet seemed unassailable. While Longfellow's poetry continues to be read and appreciated – eight of his poems are included in this collection – he is no longer the dominant figure. If any poet can be said to be in the position once held by Longfellow, it would most certainly be his contemporary, Walt Whitman. Consider, too, the fate of another American poet, John Greenleaf Whittier. Once considered by his countrymen to be second only to Longfellow, such was Whittier's popularity that after his death in 1892 – six months after that of Whitman – several states declared holidays to be celebrated in his honour. The status of Whittier has long since been diminished. He is represented here by only two poems, 'The Barefoot Boy' and 'Laus Deo', the latter a joyous celebration of the end of slavery.

Verse itself is not immune to the effects of time. Perhaps a measure of a poem's popularity is the frequency with which it diverges from its original state: errors have been made and carried forward at the hands of typesetters, ardent admirers have copied out incorrectly, or simply mis-quoted, and the verse changes subtly. While the poems included in this volume have largely been kept in their original form, some reflect a small degree of 'tweaking', often intended to enhance the read for the contemporary audience.

Other poets appear as if rescued by time. Emily Dickinson, who lived to see only seven of her poems in print, all published anonymously, today stands as one of the greatest and best-loved of American poets. Looking back from this vantage point of nearly two centuries, it seems incredible that at the time of his death John Keats was not considered to be a poet of note. Returning to more recent times, we find that admiration of Bliss Carman, once considered the unofficial poet laureate of Canada, has declined, while the appreciation of his contemporary Archibald Lampman continues to grow.

In considering Lampman's work – verse that is often cutting and critical, we realize that poetry need not be beautiful or sentimental to be loved. Indeed, some of the poems included, particularly those written during times of war, such as Wilfred Owen's 'Dulce Et Decorum Est' and W. S. S. Lyon's 'I Tracked A Dead Man Down A Trench', are by turns horrific, terrible and uncanny. Of course, this is expected of war poetry; and yet others managed to capture beauty and peace amid conflict. There is perhaps no greater example of this than Rupert Brooke's 'The Soldier', the opening lines of which continue to echo:

> If I should die, think only this of me:
> > That there's some corner of a foreign field
> That is for ever England.

In verse, much of what is loved becomes so through familiarity. Whitman's 'O Captain! My Captain!', written after the assassination of Abraham Lincoln, was once considered a minor work. However, during these last two decades the poem has risen in the public conscious, beginning with Leonard Cohen's homage 'The Captain', then continuing through its use in popular films such as *Dead Poets Society*. The most interesting revival might be 'Cradle Song', a three-centuries old poem by Elizabethan dramatist Thomas Dekker, which found use, with minor adaptation, in the Beatles' 'Golden Slumbers':

> Golden slumbers kiss your eyes,
> Smiles awake you when you rise;
> Sleep, pretty wantons, do not cry,
> And I will sing a lullaby,

A collection of classic, best-loved poems stands apart from all other anthologies in that there is no concern for the influential, the significant, the representative or even the best. And yet, because of this disregard, and because of the focus on what it is that touches the reader, it might be argued that the simple designation 'best loved' provides the truest reflection of current attitudes toward English-language verse.

John Boyes

# Family

AND

# Home

# A Cradle Song

Sweet dreams, form a shade
O'er my lovely infant's head!
Sweet dreams of pleasant streams
By happy, silent, moony beams!

Sweet Sleep, with soft down
Weave thy brows an infant crown!
Sweet Sleep, angel mild,
Hover o'er my happy child!

Sweet smiles, in the night
Hover over my delight!
Sweet smiles, mother's smiles,
All the livelong night beguiles.

Sweet moans, dovelike sighs,
Chase not slumber from thy eyes!
Sweet moans, sweeter smiles,
All the dovelike moans beguiles.

Sleep, sleep, happy child!
All creation slept and smiled.
Sleep, sleep, happy sleep,
While o'er thee thy mother weep.

Sweet babe, in thy face
Holy image I can trace;
Sweet babe, once like thee
Thy Maker lay, and wept for me:

Wept for me, for thee, for all,
When He was an infant small.
Thou His image ever see,
Heavenly face that smiles on thee!

Smiles on thee, on me, on all,
Who became an infant small;
Infant smiles are His own smiles;
Heaven and earth to peace beguiles.

WILLIAM BLAKE

℘ • ℛ

## *Mother And Babe*

I see the sleeping babe, nestling the breast of its mother;
The sleeping mother and babe — hush'd, I study them long and
long.

WALT WHITMAN

℘ • ℛ

## *Cradle Song*

Golden slumbers kiss your eyes,
Smiles awake you when you rise;
Sleep, pretty wantons, do not cry,
And I will sing a lullaby,
Rock them, rock them, lullaby.

Care is heavy, therefore sleep you,
You are care, and care must keep you;
Sleep, pretty wantons, do not cry,
And I will sing a lullaby,
Rock them, rock them, lullaby.

THOMAS DEKKER

## *A Child's Laughter*

All the bells of heaven may ring,
All the birds of heaven may sing,
All the wells on earth may spring,
All the winds on earth may bring
All sweet sounds together;
Sweeter far than all things heard,
Hand of harper, tone of bird,
Sound of woods at sundawn stirred,

Welling water's winsome word,
Wind in warm wan weather,

One thing yet there is, that none
Hearing ere its chime be done
Knows not well the sweetest one
Heard of man beneath the sun,
Hoped in heaven hereafter;
Soft and strong and loud and light,
Very sound of very light
Heard from morning's rosiest height,
When the soul of all delight
Fills a child's clear laughter.

Golden bells of welcome rolled
Never forth such notes, nor told
Hours so blithe in tones so bold,
As the radiant mouth of gold
Here that rings forth heaven.
If the golden-crested wren
Were a nightingale — why, then,
Something seen and heard of men
Might be half as sweet as when
Laughs a child of seven.

ALGERNON CHARLES SWINBURNE

$\mathcal{S} \cdot \mathcal{B}$

## A Question

Why is it, God, that mothers' hearts are made
So very deep and wide?
How does it help the world that we should hold
Such swelling floods of pain till we are old,
Because when we were young one grave was laid —
One baby died?

CHARLOTTE PERKINS GILMAN

*❦ • ❦*

## Sweet And Low

Sweet and low, sweet and low,
Wind of the western sea,
Low, low, breathe and blow,
Wind of the western sea!
Over the rolling waters go,
Come from the dying moon, and blow,
Blow him again to me;
While my little one, while my pretty one, sleeps.

Sleep and rest, sleep and rest,
Father will come to thee soon;
Rest, rest, on mother's breast,
Father will come to thee soon;

Father will come to his babe in the nest,
Silver sails all out of the west,
Under the silver moon:
Sleep, my little one, sleep, my pretty one, sleep.

ALFRED, LORD TENNYSON

## The Children's Hour

Between the dark and the daylight,
When the night is beginning to lower,
Comes a pause in the day's occupations,
That is known as the Children's Hour.

I hear in the chamber above me
The patter of little feet,
The sound of a door that is opened,
And voices soft and sweet.

From my study I see in the lamplight,
Descending the broad hall stair,
Grave Alice, and laughing Allegra,
And Edith with golden hair.

A whisper, and then a silence:
    Yet I know by their merry eyes
They are plotting and planning together
    To take me by surprise.

A sudden rush from the stairway,
    A sudden raid from the hall!
By three doors left unguarded
    They enter my castle wall!

They climb up into my turret
    O'er the arms and back of my chair;
If I try to escape, they surround me;
    They seem to be everywhere.

They almost devour me with kisses,
    Their arms about me entwine,
Till I think of the Bishop of Bingen
    In his Mouse-Tower on the Rhine!

Do you think, O blue-eyed banditti,
    Because you have scaled the wall,
Such an old mustache as I am
    Is not a match for you all!

I have you fast in my fortress,
    And will not let you depart,
But put you down into the dungeon
    In the round-tower of my heart.

And there will I keep you forever,
    Yes, forever and a day,
Till the walls shall crumble to ruin,
    And moulder in dust away.

HENRY WADSWORTH LONGFELLOW

☙ • ❧

## My Early Home

Here sparrows build upon the trees,
    And stock-dove hides her nest:
The leaves are winnowed by the breeze
    Into a calmer rest;
The black-cap's song was very sweet;
    That used the rose to kiss;
It made the paradise complete:
    My early home was this.

The redbreast from the sweetbrier bush
    Dropt down to pick the worm;
On the horse-chestnut sang the thrush,
    O'er the house where I was born.
The moonlight, like a shower of pearls,
    Fell o'er this 'bower of bliss',
And on the bench sat boys and girls;
    My early home was this.

The old house stooped just like a cave,
    Thatched o'er with mosses green;
Winter around the walls would rave,
    But all was calm within;
The trees are here all green again,
    Here bees the flowers still kiss,
But flowers and trees seemed sweeter then;
    My early home was this.

JOHN CLARE

## *To Flush, My Dog*

Yet, my pretty sportive friend,
Little is't to such an end
That I praise thy rareness!
Other dogs may be thy peers
Haply in these drooping ears,
And this glossy fairness.

But of thee it shall be said,
This dog watched beside a bed
Day and night unweary —
Watched within a curtained room,
Where no sunbeam brake the gloom
Round the sick and dreary.

Roses, gathered for a vase,
In that chamber died apace,
Beam and breeze resigning.
This dog only, waited on,
Knowing that when light is gone
Love remains for shining.

Other dogs in thymy dew
Tracked the hares, and followed through
Sunny moor or meadow.
This dog only, crept and crept
Next a languid cheek that slept,
Sharing in the shadow.

Other dogs of loyal cheer
Bounded at the whistle clear,
Up the woodside hieing.
This dog only, watched in reach
Of a faintly uttered speech,
Or a louder sighing.

And if one or two quick tears
Dropped upon his glossy ears,
Or a sigh came double —
Up he sprang in eager haste,
Fawning, fondling, breathing fast,
In a tender trouble.

And this dog was satisfied
If a pale thin hand would glide
Down his dewlaps sloping —
Which he pushed his nose within,
After platforming his chin
On the palm left open.

ELIZABETH BARRETT BROWNING

$\mathscr{E} \cdot \mathscr{B}$

## *Milk For The Cat*

When the tea is brought at five o'clock,
And all the neat curtains are drawn with care,
The little black cat with bright green eyes
Is suddenly purring there.

At first she pretends, having nothing to do,
She has come in merely to blink by the grate,
But, though tea may be late or the milk may be sour,
She is never late.

And presently her agate eyes
Take a soft large milky haze,
And her independent casual glance
Becomes a stiff, hard gaze.

Then she stamps her claws or lifts her ears,
Or twists her tail and begins to stir,
Till suddenly all her lithe body becomes
One breathing, trembling purr.

The children eat and wriggle and laugh;
The two old ladies stroke their silk:
But the cat is grown small and thin with desire,
Transformed to a creeping lust for milk.

The white saucer like some full moon descends
At last from the clouds of the table above;
She sighs and dreams and thrills and glows,
Transfigured with love.

She nestles over the shining rim,
Buries her chin in the creamy sea;
Her tail hangs loose; each drowsy paw
Is doubled under each bending knee.

A long, dim ecstasy holds her life;
Her world is an infinite shapeless white,
Till her tongue has curled the last holy drop,
Then she sinks back into the night,

Draws and dips her body to heap
Her sleepy nerves in the great arm-chair,
Lies defeated and buried deep
Three or four hours unconscious there.

HAROLD MONRO

# A Visit From St. Nicholas

'Twas the night before Christmas, when all through the house
Not a creature was stirring, not even a mouse;
The stockings were hung by the chimney with care,
In hopes that St. Nicholas soon would be there;
The children were nestled all snug in their beds,
While visions of sugar-plums danced in their heads;
And mamma in her 'kerchief, and I in my cap,
Had just settled our brains for a long winter's nap,
When out on the lawn there arose such a clatter,
I sprang from the bed to see what was the matter.
Away to the window I flew like a flash,
Tore open the shutters and threw up the sash.
The moon on the breast of the new-fallen snow
Gave the lustre of mid-day to objects below,
When, what to my wondering eyes should appear,
But a miniature sleigh, and eight tiny reindeer,
With a little old driver, so lively and quick,
I knew in a moment it must be St. Nick.
More rapid than eagles his coursers they came,
And he whistled, and shouted, and called them by name;
'Now, Dasher! now, Dancer! now, Prancer and Vixen!
On, Comet! on, Cupid! on, Donder and Blitzen!
To the top of the porch! to the top of the wall!
Now dash away! dash away! dash away all!'

As dry leaves that before the wild hurricane fly,
When they meet with an obstacle, mount to the sky;
So up to the house-top the coursers they flew,
With the sleigh full of Toys, and St. Nicholas too.
And then, in a twinkling, I heard on the roof
The prancing and pawing of each little hoof.
As I drew in my head, and was turning around,
Down the chimney St. Nicholas came with a bound.
He was dressed all in fur, from his head to his foot,
And his clothes were all tarnished with ashes and soot;
A bundle of Toys he had flung on his back,
And he looked like a peddler just opening his pack.
His eyes — how they twinkled! his dimples how merry!
His cheeks were like roses, his nose like a cherry!
His droll little mouth was drawn up like a bow
And the beard of his chin was as white as the snow;
The stump of a pipe he held tight in his teeth,
And the smoke it encircled his head like a wreath;
He had a broad face and a little round belly,
That shook when he laughed, like a bowlful of jelly.
He was chubby and plump, a right jolly old elf,
And I laughed when I saw him, in spite of myself;
A wink of his eye and a twist of his head,
Soon gave me to know I had nothing to dread;

He spoke not a word, but went straight to his work,
And filled all the stockings; then turned with a jerk,
And laying his finger aside of his nose,
And giving a nod, up the chimney he rose;
He sprang to his sleigh, to his team gave a whistle,
And away they all flew like the down of a thistle,
But I heard him exclaim, ere he drove out of sight,
'Happy Christmas to all, and to all a good-night.'

CLEMENT C. MOORE

*ℰ · ℛ*

## *Mother To Child*

How best can I serve thee, my child! My child!
Flesh of my flesh and dear heart of my heart!
Once thou wast within me — I held thee — I fed thee —
By the force of my loving and longing I led thee —
Now we are apart!

I may blind thee with kisses and crush with embracing,
Thy warm mouth in my neck and our arms interlacing;
But here in my body my soul lives alone,
And thou answerest me from a house of thine own —
The house which I builded!

17

Which we builded together, thy father and I;
In which thou must live, O my darling, and die!
Not one stone can I alter, one atom relay —
Not to save or defend thee or help thee to stay —
        That gift is completed!

How best can I serve thee? O child, if they knew
How my heart aches with loving! How deep and how true,
How brave and enduring, how patient, how strong,
How longing for good and how fearful of wrong,
        Is the love of thy mother!

Could I crown thee with riches! Surround, overflow thee
With fame and with power till the whole world should know
    thee;
With wisdom and genius to hold the world still,
To bring laughter and tears, joy and pain, at thy will,
        Still — thou mightst not be happy!

Such have lived — and in sorrow. The greater the mind
The wider and deeper the grief it can find.
The richer, the gladder, the more thou canst feel
The keen stings that a lifetime is sure to reveal.
        O my child! Must thou suffer?

Is there no way my life can save thine from a pain?
Is the love of a mother no possible gain?
No labor of Hercules — search for the Grail —
No way for this wonderful love to avail?
  God in Heaven — O teach me!

My prayer has been answered. The pain thou must bear
Is the pain of the world's life which thy life must share,
Thou art one with the world — though I love thee the best;
And to save thee from pain I must save all the rest —
  Well — with God's help I'll do it.

Thou art one with the rest. I must love thee in them.
Thou wilt sin with the rest; and thy mother must stem
The world's sin. Thou wilt weep, and thy mother must dry
The tears of the world lest her darling should cry.
  I will do it — God helping!

And I stand not alone. I will gather a band
Of all loving mothers from land unto land.
Our children are part of the world! Do ye hear?
They are one with the world — we must hold them all dear!
  Love all for the child's sake!

For the sake of my child I must hasten to save
All the children on earth from the jail and the grave.
For so, and so only, I lighten the share
Of the pain of the world that my darling must bear —
    Even so, and so only!

CHARLOTTE PERKINS GILMAN

*ℰ • ℬ*

## *It Is A Beauteous Evening*

It is a beauteous evening, calm and free,
The holy time is quiet as a nun
Breathless with adoration; the broad sun
Is sinking down in its tranquillity;
The gentleness of heaven broods o'er the sea:
Listen! the mighty Being is awake,
And doth with his eternal motion make
A sound like thunder — everlastingly.
Dear Child! dear Girl! that walkest with me here,
If thou appear untouched by solemn thought,
Thy nature is not therefore less divine:
Thou liest in Abraham's bosom all the year,
And worship'st at the Temple's inner shrine,
God being with thee when we know it not.

WILLIAM WORDSWORTH

*ℰ • ℬ*

## Mother o' Mine

If I were hanged on the highest hill,
*Mother o' mine, O mother o' mine!*
I know whose love would follow me still,
*Mother o' mine, O mother o' mine!*

If I were drowned in the deepest sea,
*Mother o' mine, O mother o' mine!*
I know whose tears would come down to me,
*Mother o' mine, O mother o' mine!*

If I were damned of body and soul,
I know whose prayers would make me whole,
*Mother o' mine, O mother o' mine!*

RUDYARD KIPLING

℘ • ℘

## My Grandmother's Love Letters

There are no stars to-night
But those of memory.
Yet how much room for memory there is
In the loose girdle of soft rain.

There is even room enough
For the letters of my mother's mother,
Elizabeth,

That have been pressed so long
Into a corner of the roof
That they are brown and soft,
And liable to melt as snow.

Over the greatness of such space
Steps must be gentle.
It is all hung by an invisible white hair.
It trembles as birch limbs webbing the air.

And I ask myself:

'Are your fingers long enough to play
Old keys that are but echoes:
Is the silence strong enough
To carry back the music to its source
And back to you again
As though to her?'

Yet I would lead my grandmother by the hand
Through much of what she would not understand;
And so I stumble. And the rain continues on the roof
With such a sound of gently pitying laughter.

HART CRANE

$\mathcal{I} \cdot \mathcal{B}$

## *The First Snow-Fall*

The snow had begun in the gloaming,
And busily all the night
Had been heaping field and highway
With a silence deep and white.

Every pine and fir and hemlock
Wore ermine too dear for an earl,
And the poorest twig on the elm-tree
Was ridged inch deep with pearl.

From sheds new-roofed with Carrara
Came Chanticleer's muffled crow,
The stiff rails softened to swan's-down,
And still fluttered down the snow.

I stood and watched by the window
The noiseless work of the sky,
And the sudden flurries of snow-birds,
Like brown leaves whirling by.

I thought of a mound in sweet Auburn
Where a little headstone stood;
How the flakes were folding it gently,
As did robins the babes in the wood.

Up spoke our own little Mabel,
Saying, 'Father, who makes it snow?'
And I told of the good All-father
Who cares for us here below.

Again I looked at the snowfall,
And thought of the leaden sky
That arched o'er our first great sorrow,
When that mound was heaped so high.

I remembered the gradual patience
That fell from that cloud like snow,
Flake by flake, healing and hiding
The scar of our deep-plunged woe.

And again to the child I whispered,
'The snow that husheth all,
Darling, the merciful Father
Alone can make it fall!'

Then, with eyes that saw not, I kissed her;
And she, kissing back, could not know
That my kiss was given to her sister,
Folded close under deepening snow.

JAMES RUSSELL LOWELL

&  ·  &

## To My Mother

Because I feel that, in the Heavens above,
    The angels, whispering to one another,
Can find, among their burning terms of love,
    None so devotional as that of 'Mother,'
Therefore by that dear name I long have called you —
    You who are more than mother unto me,
And fill my heart of hearts, where Death installed you
    In setting my Virginia's spirit free.
My mother- my own mother, who died early,
    Was but the mother of myself; but you
Are mother to the one I loved so dearly,
    And thus are dearer than the mother I knew
By that infinity with which my wife
    Was dearer to my soul than its soul-life.

EDGAR ALLAN POE

ℰ • ℬ

## Marriage

The die is cast, come weal, come woe,
Two lives are joined together,
For better or for worse, the link
Which naught but death can sever.

The die is cast, come grief, come joy,

Come richer, or come poorer,

If love but binds the mystic tie,

Blest is the bridal hour.

MARY WESTON FORDHAM

ℰ • ℬ

## *On His Deceased Wife*

Methought I saw my late espoused Saint

Brought to me like Alcestis from the grave,

Who Jove's great Son to her glad Husband gave,

Rescu'd from death by force though pale and faint.

Mine as whom washt from spot of child-bed taint

Purification in the old Law did save,

And such as yet once more I trust to have

Full sight of her in Heav'n without restraint,

Came vested all in white, pure as her mind:

Her face was veil'd, yet to my fancied sight

Love, sweetness, goodness in her person shin'd

So clear, as in no face with more delight.

But O as to embrace me she enclin'd

I wak'd, she fled, and day brought back my night.

JOHN MILTON

ℰ • ℬ

# A Tragedy

Among his books he sits all day
To think and read and write;
He does not smell the new-mown hay,
The roses red and white.

I walk among them all alone,
His silly, stupid wife;
The world seems tasteless, dead and done —
An empty thing is life.

At night his window casts a square
Of light upon the lawn;
I sometimes walk and watch it there
Until the chill of dawn.

I have no brain to understand
The books he loves to read;
I only have a heart and hand
He does not seem to need.

He calls me 'Child' — lays on my hair
Thin fingers, cold and mild;
Oh! God of Love, who answers prayer,
I wish I were a child!

And no one sees and no one knows
(He least would know or see),
That ere Love gathers next year's rose
Death will have gathered me.

EDITH NESBIT

$\mathcal{E} \cdot \mathcal{B}$

## *She Was A Phantom Of Delight*

She was a Phantom of delight
When first she gleamed upon my sight;
A lovely Apparition, sent
To be a moment's ornament;
Her eyes as stars of Twilight fair;
Like Twilight's, too, her dusky hair;
But all things else about her drawn
From May-time and the cheerful Dawn;
A dancing Shape, an Image gay,
To haunt, to startle, and way-lay.

I saw her upon nearer view,
A Spirit, yet a Woman too!
Her household motions light and free,

And steps of virgin-liberty;
A countenance in which did meet
Sweet records, promises as sweet;
A Creature not too bright or good
For human nature's daily food;
For transient sorrows, simple wiles,
Praise, blame, love, kisses, tears, and smiles.

And now I see with eye serene
The very pulse of the machine;
A Being breathing thoughtful breath,
A Traveller between life and death;
The reason firm, the temperate will,
Endurance, foresight, strength, and skill;
A perfect Woman, nobly planned,
To warn, to comfort, and command;
And yet a Spirit still, and bright
With something of angelic light.

WILLIAM WORDSWORTH

$\mathscr{G} \cdot \mathscr{R}$

# The Voice

Woman much missed, how you call to me, call to me,
Saying that now you are not as you were
When you had changed from the one who was all to me,
But as at first, when our day was fair.

Can it be you that I hear? Let me view you, then,
Standing as when I drew near to the town
Where you would wait for me: yes, as I knew you then,
Even to the original air-blue gown!

Or is it only the breeze, in its listlessness
Travelling across the wet mead to me here,
You being ever dissolved to wan wistlessness,
Heard no more again far or near?

Thus I; faltering forward,
Leaves around me falling,
Wind oozing thin through the thorn from norward,
And the woman calling.

THOMAS HARDY

## *To My Dear and Loving Husband*

If ever two were one, then surely we.
If ever man were lov'd by wife, then thee.
If ever wife was happy in a man,
Compare with me, ye women, if you can.
I prize thy love more than whole Mines of gold
Or all the riches that the East doth hold.
My love is such that Rivers cannot quench,
Nor aught but love from thee give recompense.
Thy love is such I can no way repay.
The heavens reward thee manifold, I pray.
Then while we live, in love let's so persever
That when we live no more, we may live ever.

ANNE BRADSTREET

## *The Widower*

For a season there must be pain —
For a little, little space
I shall lose the sight of her face,
Take back the old life again
While She is at rest in her place.

For a season this pain must endure,
For a little, little while
I shall sigh more often than smile
Till time shall work me a cure,
And the pitiful days beguile.

For that season we must be apart,
For a little length of years,
Till my life's last hour nears,
And, above the beat of my heart,
I hear Her voice in my ears.

But I shall not understand —
Being set on some later love,
Shall not know her for whom I strove,
Till she reach me forth her hand,
Saying, 'Who but I have the right?'
And out of a troubled night
Shall draw me safe to the land.

RUDYARD KIPLING

# An Epitaph Upon Husband and Wife

To these whom death again did wed

This grave's the second marriage-bed.

For though the hand of Fate could force

'Twixt soul and body a divorce,

It could not sunder man and wife,

Because they both lived but one life.

Peace, good reader, do not weep;

Peace, the lovers are asleep.

They, sweet turtles, folded lie

In the last knot that love could tie.

And though they lie as they were dead,

Their pillow stone, their sheets of lead,

(Pillow hard, and sheets not warm)

Love made the bed; they'll take no harm.

Let them sleep, let them sleep on,

Till the stormy night be gone,

And the eternal morrow dawn;

Then the curtains will be drawn,

And they wake into a light

Whose day shall never die in night.

RICHARD CRASHAW

*ℰ • ℛ*

# *Winter Evening*

Now stir the fire, and close the shutters fast,
Let fall the curtains, wheel the sofa round,
And, while the bubbling and loud-hissing urn
Throws up a steamy column, and the cups,
That cheer but not inebriate, wait on each,
So let us welcome peaceful ev'ning in...

Oh winter, ruler of th' inverted year...
I love thee, all unlovely as thou seem'st,
And dreaded as thou art! Thou hold'st the sun
A pris'ner in the yet undawning east,
Short'ning his journey between morn and noon,
And hurrying him, impatient of his stay,
Down to the rosy west; but kindly still
Compensating his loss with added hours
Of social converse and instructive ease,
And gath'ring, at short notice, in one group
The family dispers'd, and fixing thought,
Not less dispers'd by day-light and its cares.
I crown thee king of intimate delights,
Fire-side enjoyments, home-born happiness,
And all the comforts that the lowly roof
Of undisturb'd retirement, and the hours
Of long uninterrupted ev'ning, know.

WILLIAM COWPER

℘ • ℛ

 **Love**

AND

 **Romance**

# Loving In Truth, And Fain In Verse My Love To Show

Loving in truth, and fain in verse my love to show,

That She, dear She, might take some pleasure of my pain,

Pleasure might cause her read, reading might make her know,

Knowledge might pity win, and pity grace obtain,

I sought fit words to paint the blackest face of woe,

Studying inventions fine, her wits to entertain,

Oft turning others' leaves, to see if thence would flow

Some fresh and fruitful showers upon my sunburnt brain.

But words came halting forth, wanting Invention's stay;

Invention, Nature's child, fled step-dame Study's blows;

And others' feet still seemed but strangers in my way.

Thus, great with child to speak, and helpless in my throes,

Biting my truant pen, beating myself for spite:

'Fool!' said my Muse to me, 'Look in thy heart, and write!'

SIR PHILIP SIDNEY

$\mathcal{S} \cdot \mathcal{B}$

# How Do I Love Thee? Let Me Count The Ways

How do I love thee? Let me count the ways.
I love thee to the depth and breadth and height
My soul can reach, when feeling out of sight
For the ends of Being and ideal Grace.
I love thee to the level of everyday's
Most quiet need, by sun and candlelight.
I love thee freely, as men strive for Right;
I love thee purely, as they turn from Praise.
I love thee with the passion put to use
In my old griefs, and with my childhood's faith.
I love thee with a love I seemed to lose
With my lost saints, — I love thee with the breath,
Smiles, tears, of all my life! — and, if God choose,
I shall but love thee better after death.

ELIZABETH BARRETT BROWNING

*E • B*

## *The Garden Of Love*

I went to the Garden of Love,
And saw what I never had seen;
A Chapel was built in the midst,
Where I used to play on the green.

And the gates of this Chapel were shut,
And 'Thou shalt not' writ over the door;
So I turned to the Garden of Love
That so many sweet flowers bore.

And I saw it was filled with graves,
And tombstones where flowers should be;
And priests in black gowns were walking their rounds,
And binding with briars my joys and desires.

WILLIAM BLAKE

*ᴏ • ᴃ*

# *My Luve's Like A Red, Red Rose*

O my Luve's like a red, red rose,
That's newly sprung in June:
O my Luve's like the melodie,
That's sweetly played in tune.

As fair art thou, my bonnie lass,
So deep in luve am I;
And I will luve thee still, my dear,
Till a' the seas gang dry.

Till a' the seas gang dry, my dear,
And the rocks melt wi' the sun;
I will luve thee still, my dear,
While the sands o' life shall run.

And fare-thee-weel, my only Luve!
And fare-thee-weel, a while!
And I will come again, my Luve,
Tho' 'twere ten thousand mile!

ROBERT BURNS

# *Go, Lovely Rose*

Go, lovely rose!
Tell her that wastes her time and me,
That now she knows,
When I resemble her to thee,
How sweet and fair she seems to be.

Tell her that's young,
And shuns to have her graces spied,
That hadst thou sprung
In deserts where no men abide,
Thou must have uncommended died.

Small is the worth
Of beauty from the light retired;
Bid her come forth,
Suffer herself to be desired,
And not blush so to be admired.

Then die! that she
The common fate of all things rare
May read in thee;
How small a part of time they share
That are so wondrous sweet and fair.

EDMUND WALLER

# *Cherry-Ripe*

There is a garden in her face
　　Where roses and white lilies grow;
A heavenly paradise is that place,
　　Wherein all pleasant fruits do flow:
　　　　There cherries grow which none may buy
　　　　Till 'Cherry-ripe' themselves do cry.

Those cherries fairly do enclose
　　Of orient pearl a double row,
Which when her lovely laughter shows,
　　They look like rose-buds fill'd with snow;
　　　　Yet them nor peer nor prince can buy
　　　　Till 'Cherry-ripe' themselves do cry.

Her eyes like angels watch them still;
　　Her brows like bended bows do stand,
Threat'ning with piercing frowns to kill
　　All that attempt with eye or hand
　　　　Those sacred cherries to come nigh,
　　　　Till 'Cherry-ripe' themselves do cry.

THOMAS CAMPION

## She Walks In Beauty

She walks in beauty, like the night
Of cloudless climes and starry skies;
And all that's best of dark and bright
Meet in her aspect and her eyes:
Thus mellowed to that tender light
Which heaven to gaudy day denies.

One shade the more, one ray the less,
Had half impaired the nameless grace
Which waves in every raven tress,
Or softly lightens o'er her face;
Where thoughts serenely sweet express
How pure, how dear their dwelling-place.

And on that cheek, and o'er that brow,
So soft, so calm, yet eloquent,
The smiles that win, the tints that glow,
But tell of days in goodness spent,
A mind at peace with all below,
A heart whose love is innocent!

GEORGE GORDON, LORD BYRON

℘ • ℬ

## *Love's Philosophy*

The Fountains mingle with the river
    And the rivers with the ocean,
The winds of heaven mix for ever
    With a sweet emotion;
Nothing in the world is single,
    All things by a law divine
In one another's being mingle —
    Why not I with thine?

See the mountains kiss high heaven
    And the waves clasp one another;
No sister-flower would be forgiven
    If it disdain'd its brother:
And the sunlight clasps the earth,
And the moonbeams kiss the sea —
What are all these kissings worth,
    If thou kiss not me?

PERCY BYSSHE SHELLEY

# *One Day I Wrote Her Name Upon The Strand*

One day I wrote her name upon the strand,

But came the waves and washed it away:

Again I wrote it with a second hand,

But came the tide, and made my pains his prey.

Vain man, said she, that dost in vain assay

A mortal thing so to immortalize!

For I myself shall like to this decay,

And eke my name be wiped out likewise.

Not so quoth I, let baser things devise

To die in dust, but you shall live by fame:

My verse your virtues rare shall eternize,

And in the heavens write your glorious name;

Where, whenas death shall all the world subdue,

Our love shall live, and later life renew.

EDMUND SPENSER

# The Good-Morrow

I wonder, by my troth, what thou and I
Did, till we loved? Were we not weaned till then?
But sucked on country pleasures, childishly?
Or snorted we in the seven sleepers' den?
'Twas so; but this, all pleasures fancies be.
If ever any beauty I did see,
Which I desired, and got, 'twas but a dream of thee.

And now good-morrow to our waking souls,
Which watch not one another out of fear;
For love, all love of other sights controls,
And makes one little room an everywhere.
Let sea-discoverers to new worlds have gone,
Let maps to other, worlds on worlds have shown,
Let us possess one world, each hath one, and is one.

My face in thine eye, thine in mine appears,
And true plain hearts do in the faces rest;
Where can we find two better hemispheres
Without sharp North, without declining West?
Whatever dies was not mixed equally;
If our two loves be one, or thou and I
Love so alike that none do slacken, none can die.

JOHN DONNE

## *The Clod And The Pebble*

'Love seeketh not itself to please,
      Nor for itself hath any care,
But for another gives its ease,
      And builds a heaven in hell's despair.'

So sung a little clod of clay,
      Trodden with the cattle's feet,
But a pebble of the brook
      Warbled out these metres meet:

'Love seeketh only Self to please,
      To bind another to its delight,
Joys in another's loss of ease,
      And builds a hell in heaven's despite.'

WILLIAM BLAKE

## *The Sun Rising*

Busy old fool, unruly Sun,
Why dost thou thus,
Through windows, and through curtains, call on us?
Must to thy motions lovers' seasons run?
Saucy pedantic wretch, go chide
Late school-boys and sour prentices,
Go tell court-huntsmen that the king will ride,
Call country ants to harvest offices;
Love, all alike, no season knows nor clime,
Nor hours, days, months, which are the rags of time.

Thy beams so reverend, and strong
Why shouldst thou think?
I could eclipse and cloud them with a wink,
But that I would not lose her sight so long.
If her eyes have not blinded thine,
Look, and to-morrow late tell me,
Whether both th' Indias of spice and mine
Be where thou left'st them, or lie here with me.
Ask for those kings whom thou saw'st yesterday,
And thou shalt hear, 'All here in one bed lay.'

She's all states, and all princes, I;
Nothing else is;
Princes do but play us; compared to this,
All honour's mimic, all wealth alchemy.
Thou, Sun, art half as happy as we,
In that the world's contracted thus;
Thine age asks ease, and since thy duties be
To warm the world, that's done in warming us.
Shine here to us, and thou art everywhere;
This bed thy center is, these walls thy sphere.

JOHN DONNE

*♂ • ♀*

## *You Smiled, You Spoke And I Believed'*

You smiled, you spoke and I believed,
By every word and smile – deceived.
Another man would hope no more;
Nor hope I – what I hoped before.
But let not this last wish be vain;
Deceive, deceive me once again!

WALTER SAVAGE LANDOR

*♂ • ♀*

## *The Definition Of Love*

My Love is of a birth as rare
      As 'tis, for object, strange and high;
It was begotten by Despair,
      Upon Impossibility.

Magnanimous Despair alone
      Could show me so divine a thing,
Where feeble hope could ne'er have flown,
      But vainly flapped its tinsel wing.

And yet I quickly might arrive
      Where my extended soul is fixed;
But Fate does iron wedges drive,
      And always crowds itself betwixt.

For Fate with jealous eye does see
      Two perfect loves, nor lets them close;
Their union would her ruin be,
      And her tyrannic power depose.

And therefore her decrees of steel
      Us as the distant poles have placed,
(Though Love's whole world on us doth wheel),
      Not by themselves to be embraced,

Unless the giddy heaven fall,
      And earth some new convulsion tear.
And, us to join, the world should all
      Be cramp'd into a planisphere.

As lines, so Love's oblique, may well
      Themselves in every angle greet:
But ours, so truly parallel,
      Though infinite, can never meet.

Therefore the Love which us doth bind,
      But Fate so enviously debars,
Is the conjunction of the mind,
      And opposition of the stars.

ANDREW MARVELL

## *To Celia*

Drink to me only with thine eyes,
　　And I will pledge with mine;
Or leave a kiss but in the cup
　　And I'll not look for wine.
The thirst that from the soul doth rise
　　Doth ask a drink divine;
But might I of Jove's nectar sup,
　　I would not change for thine.

I sent thee late a rosy wreath,
　　Not so much honouring thee
As giving it a hope that there
　　It could not wither'd be;
But thou thereon didst only breathe,
　　And sent'st it back to me;
Since when it grows, and smells, I swear,
　　Not of itself but thee!

BEN JONSON

*B • B*

## Severed Selves

Two separate divided silences,
Which, brought together, would find loving voice;
Two glances which together would rejoice
In love, now lost like stars beyond dark trees;
Two hands apart whose touch alone gives ease;
Two bosoms which, heart-shrined with mutual flame,
Would, meeting in one clasp, be made the same;
Two souls, the shores wave-mocked of sundering seas: —
Such are we now. Ah! may our hope forecast
Indeed one hour again, when on this stream
Of darkened love once more the light shall gleam? —
An hour how slow to come, how quickly past, —
Which blooms and fades, and only leaves at last,
Faint as shed flowers, the attenuated dream.

DANTE GABRIEL ROSSETTI

∂ • ℬ

## Love's Secret

Never seek to tell thy love,
　　Love that never told can be;
For the gentle wind doth move
　　Silently, invisibly.

I told my love, I told my love,
    I told her all my heart,
Trembling, cold, in ghastly fears.
    Ah! she did depart!

Soon after she was gone from me,
    A traveller came by,
Silently, invisibly:
    He took her with a sigh.

WILLIAM BLAKE

*❦ • ❦*

## *To My Inconstant Mistress*

When thou, poor excommunicate
From all the joys of love, shalt see
The full reward and glorious fate
Which my strong faith shall purchase me,
Then curse thine own inconstancy.

A fairer hand than thine shall cure
That heart which thy false oaths did wound;
And to my soul a soul more pure
Than thine shall by Love's hand be bound,
And both with equal glory crowned.

Then shalt thou weep, entreat, complain
To Love, as I did once to thee;
When all thy tears shall be as vain
As mine were then, for thou shalt be
Damned for thy false apostasy.

THOMAS CAREW

*ʃ • ℬ*

## *The Appeal*

And wilt thou leave me thus!
Say nay, say nay, for shame!
— To save thee from the blame
Of all my grief and grame.
And wilt thou leave me thus?
Say nay! say nay!

And wilt thou leave me thus,
That hath loved thee so long
In wealth and woe among:
And is thy heart so strong
As for to leave me thus?
Say nay! say nay!

And wilt thou leave me thus,
That hath given thee my heart
Never for to depart
Neither for pain nor smart:
And wilt thou leave me thus?
    Say nay! say nay!

And wilt thou leave me thus,
And have no more pitye
Of him that loveth thee?
Alas, thy cruelty!
And wilt thou leave me thus?
    Say nay! say nay!

SIR THOMAS WYATT

## *His Lady's Cruelty*

With how sad steps, O moon, thou climb'st the skies!
How silently, and with how wan a face!
What! may it be that even in heavenly place
That busy archer his sharp arrows tries?
Sure, if that long-with-love-acquainted eyes
Can judge of love, thou feel'st a lover's case:
I read it in thy looks; thy languish'd grace
To me, that feel the like, thy state descries.

Then, even of fellowship, O moon, tell me,
Is constant love deem'd there but want of wit?
Are beauties there as proud as here they be?
Do they above love to be loved, and yet
      Those lovers scorn whom that love doth possess?
      Do they call 'virtue' there — ungratefulness?

SIR PHILIP SIDNEY

*❦ • ❧*

## *Carrier Letter*

My hands have not touched water since your hands, —
   No; — nor my lips freed laughter since 'farewell'.
     And with the day, distance again expands
     Between us, voiceless as an uncoiled shell.

Yet, — much follows, much endures... Trust birds alone:
     A dove's wings clung about my heart last night
      With surging gentleness; and the blue stone
     Set in the tryst-ring has but worn more bright.

HART CRANE

*❦ • ❧*

## *Let Me Not To The Marriage Of True Minds*

Let me not to the marriage of true minds
Admit impediments. Love is not love
Which alters when it alteration finds,
Or bends with the remover to remove:
O no! it is an ever-fixèd mark
That looks on tempests and is never shaken;
It is the star to every wandering bark,
Whose worth's unknown, although his height be taken.
Love's not Time's fool, though rosy lips and cheeks
Within his bending sickle's compass come:
Love alters not with his brief hours and weeks,
But bears it out even to the edge of doom.

    If this be error and upon me proved,
    I never writ, nor no man ever loved.

WILLIAM SHAKESPEARE

## *To His Coy Mistress*

Had we but world enough, and time,
This coyness, lady, were no crime.
We would sit down and think which way
To walk, and pass our long love's day;
Thou by the Indian Ganges' side
Shouldst rubies find; I by the tide

Of Humber would complain. I would
Love you ten years before the Flood;
And you should, if you please, refuse
Till the conversion of the Jews.
My vegetable love should grow
Vaster than empires, and more slow.
An hundred years should go to praise
Thine eyes, and on thy forehead gaze;
Two hundred to adore each breast,
But thirty thousand to the rest;
An age at least to every part,
And the last age should show your heart.
For, lady, you deserve this state,
Nor would I love at lower rate.

   But at my back I always hear
Time's winged chariot hurrying near;
And yonder all before us lie
Deserts of vast eternity.
Thy beauty shall no more be found,
Nor, in thy marble vault, shall sound
My echoing song; then worms shall try
That long preserv'd virginity,
And your quaint honour turn to dust,
And into ashes all my lust.
The grave's a fine and private place,
But none I think do there embrace.

Now therefore, while the youthful hue
Sits on thy skin like morning dew,
And while thy willing soul transpires
At every pore with instant fires,
Now let us sport us while we may;
And now, like am'rous birds of prey,
Rather at once our time devour,
Than languish in his slow-chapp'd power.
Let us roll all our strength, and all
Our sweetness, up into one ball;
And tear our pleasures with rough strife
Thorough the iron gates of life.
Thus, though we cannot make our sun
Stand still, yet we will make him run.

ANDREW MARVELL

*ℰ • ℬ*

## Silent Noon

Your hands lie open in the long fresh grass, —
The finger-points look through like rosy blooms:
Your eyes smile peace. The pasture gleams and glooms
'Neath billowing skies that scatter and amass.
All round our nest, far as the eye can pass,
Are golden kingcup-fields with silver edge
Where the cow-parsley skirts the hawthorn-hedge.
'Tis visible silence, still as the hour-glass.

Deep in the sun-searched growths the dragon-fly
Hangs like a blue thread loosened from the sky: —
So this wing'd hour is dropt to us from above.
Oh! clasp we to our hearts, for deathless dower,
This close-companioned inarticulate hour
When twofold silence was the song of love.

DANTE GABRIEL ROSSETTI

## *At The Mid Hour Of Night*

At the mid hour of night, when stars are weeping, I fly
To the lone vale we lov'd, when life shone warm in thine eye;
And I think oft, if spirits can steal from the regions of air,
To revisit past scenes of delight, thou wilt come to me there,
And tell me our love is remember'd, ev'n in the sky.

Then I sing the wild song, 'twas once such rapture to hear
When our voices commingling, breath'd like one on the ear;
And, as echo far off through the vale my sad orison rolls,
I think, oh my love! 'tis thy voice from the kingdom of souls
Faintly answering still the notes that once were so dear.

THOMAS MOORE

## The First Day

I wish I could remember the first day,
First hour, first moment of your meeting me,
If bright or dim the season, it might be
Summer or winter for aught I can say;
So unrecorded did it slip away,
So blind was I to see and to foresee,
So dull to mark the budding of my tree
That would not blossom, yet, for many a May.
If only I could recollect it. such
A day of days! I let it come and go
As traceless as a thaw of bygone snow;
It seemed to mean so little, meant so much;
If only now I could recall that touch,
First touch of hand in hand — Did one, but know!

CHRISTINA GEORGINA ROSSETTI

$\mathcal{A} \cdot \mathcal{B}$

## Bright Star, Would I Were Steadfast As Thou Art

Bright star, would I were steadfast as thou art —
Not in lone splendour hung aloft the night
And watching, with eternal lids apart,
Like nature's patient, sleepless Eremite,

The moving waters at their priestlike task
    Of pure ablution round earth's human shores,
Or gazing on the new soft-fallen mask
    Of snow upon the mountains and the moors —
No — yet still steadfast, still unchangeable,
    Pillow'd upon my fair love's ripening breast,
To feel for ever its soft fall and swell,
    Awake for ever in a sweet unrest,
Still, still to hear her tender-taken breath,
    And so live ever — or else swoon to death.

JOHN KEATS

*❧ · ❧*

## Shall I Compare Thee To A Summer's Day?

Shall I compare thee to a summer's day?
    Thou art more lovely and more temperate:
Rough winds do shake the darling buds of May,
    And summer's lease hath all too short a date:
Sometime too hot the eye of heaven shines,
    And often is his gold complexion dimm'd;
And every fair from fair sometime declines,
    By chance, or nature's changing course, untrimm'd;

But thy eternal summer shall not fade,
    Nor lose possession of that fair thou owest;
Nor shall Death brag thou wander'st in his shade,
    When in eternal lines to time thou growest;
So long as men can breathe, or eyes can see,
    So long lives this, and this gives life to thee.

WILLIAM SHAKESPEARE

## *False Though She Be*

False though she be to me and love,
    I'll ne'er pursue revenge;
For still the charmer I approve,
    Though I deplore her change.

In hours of bliss we oft have met:
    They could not always last;
And though the present I regret,
    I'm grateful for the past.

WILLIAM CONGREVE

## *My Mistress' Eyes Are Nothing Like The Sun*

My mistress' eyes are nothing like the sun;

    Coral is far more red than her lips' red;

If snow be white, why then her breasts are dun;

    If hairs be wires, black wires grow on her head.


I have seen roses damask'd, red and white,

    But no such roses see I in her cheeks;

And in some perfumes is there more delight

    Than in the breath that from my mistress reeks.


I love to hear her speak, yet well I know

    That music hath a far more pleasing sound;

I grant I never saw a goddess go;

    My mistress, when she walks, treads on the ground.

And yet, by heaven, I think my love as rare

    As any she belied with false compare.

WILLIAM SHAKESPEARE

                        *♡ • ♡*

## *Without Her*

What of her glass without her? The blank grey
There where the pool is blind of the moon's face.
Her dress without her? The tossed empty space
Of cloud-rack when the moon has passed away.
Her paths without her? Day's appointed sway
Usurped by desolate night. Her pillowed place
Without her? Tears, ah me! For love's good grace,
And cold forgetfulness of night or day.

What of the heart without her? Nay, poor heart,
Of thee what word remains ere speech be still?
A wayfarer by barren ways and chill,
Steep ways and weary, without her thou art,
Where the long cloud, the long wood's counterpart,
Sheds doubled darkness up the labouring hill.

DANTE GABRIEL ROSSETTI

*D · R*

# *Song*

Go and catch a falling star,
Get with child a mandrake root,
Tell me where all past years are,
Or who cleft the devil's foot,
Teach me to hear mermaids singing,
Or to keep off envy's stinging,
    And find
    What wind
Serves to advance an honest mind.

If thou be'st born to strange sights,
Things invisible to see,
Ride ten thousand days and nights,
Till age snow white hairs on thee,
Thou, when thou return'st, wilt tell me,
All strange wonders that befell thee,
    And swear,
    No where
Lives a woman true and fair.

If thou find'st one, let me know,
Such a pilgrimage were sweet;
Yet do not, I would not go,
Though at next door we might meet,

Though she were true, when you met her,
And last, till you write your letter,
    Yet she
    Will be
False, ere I come, to two, or three.

JOHN DONNE

## Ruth

She stood breast-high amid the corn,
Clasp'd by the golden light of morn,
    Like the sweetheart of the sun,
Who many a glowing kiss had won.

On her cheek an autumn flush,
Deeply ripen'd; — such a blush
    In the midst of brown was born,
Like red poppies grown with corn.

Round her eyes her tresses fell,
Which were blackest none could tell,
    But long lashes veil'd a light,
That had else been all too bright.

And her hat, with shady brim,
Made her tressy forehead dim;
Thus she stood amid the stooks,
Praising God with sweetest looks:?

Sure, I said, Heav'n did not mean,
Where I reap thou shouldst but glean,
Lay thy sheaf adown and come,
Share my harvest and my home.

THOMAS HOOD

♂ · ♀

## Now Sleeps The Crimson Petal

Now sleeps the crimson petal, now the white;
Nor waves the cypress in the palace walk;
Nor winks the gold fin in the porphyry font:
The fire-fly wakens: waken thou with me.

Now droops the milkwhite peacock like a ghost,
And like a ghost she glimmers on to me.

Now lies the Earth all Danaë to the stars,
And all thy heart lies open unto me.

Now slides the silent meteor on, and leaves
A shining furrow, as thy thoughts in me.

Now folds the lily all her sweetness up,
And slips into the bosom of the lake:
So fold thyself, my dearest, thou, and slip
Into my bosom and be lost in me.

ALFRED, LORD TENNYSON

## *Farewell, Ungrateful Traitor!*

Farewell, ungrateful traitor!
Farewell, my perjur'd swain!
Let never injur'd woman
Believe a man again.
The pleasure of possessing
Surpasses all expressing,
But 'tis too short a blessing,
And love too long a pain.

'Tis easy to deceive us
In pity of your pain,

But when we love, you leave us
To rail at you in vain.
Before we have descried it,
There is no joy beside it,
But she that once has tried it
Will never love again.

The passion you pretended
Was only to obtain,
But once the charm is ended,
The charmer you disdain.
Your love by ours we measure
Till we have lost our treasure,
But dying is a pleasure
When living is a pain.

JOHN DRYDEN

# *A Broken Appointment*

You did not come,
And marching Time drew on, and wore me numb.
Yet less for loss of your dear presence there
Than that I thus found lacking in your make
That high compassion which can overbear
Reluctance for pure loving kindness' sake
Grieved I, when, as the hope-hour stroked its sum,
You did not come.

You love not me,
And love alone can lend you loyalty;
— I know and knew it. But, unto the store
Of human deeds divine in all but name,
Was it not worth a little hour or more
To add yet this: Once you, a woman, came
To soothe a time-torn man; even though it be
You love not me?

THOMAS HARDY

$\mathscr{C} \cdot \mathscr{R}$

## *Elizabeth Of Bohemia*

You meaner beauties of the night,
  That poorly satisfy our eyes
More by your number than your light,
  You common people of the skies;
  What are you when the sun shall rise?

You curious chanters of the wood,
  That warble forth Dame Nature's lays,
Thinking your voices understood
  By your weak accents; what's your praise
  When Philomel her voice shall raise?

You violets that first appear,
  By your pure purple mantles known
Like the proud virgins of the year,
  As if the spring were all your own;
  What are you when the rose is blown?

So, when my mistress shall be seen
  In form and beauty of her mind,
By virtue first, then choice, a Queen,
  Tell me, if she were not design'd
  Th' eclipse and glory of her kind?

SIR HENRY WOTTON

# *To Mary*

Mary! I want a lyre with other strings,
Such aid from Heaven as some have feign'd they drew,
An eloquence scarce given to mortals, new
And undebased by praise of meaner things;
That ere through age or woe I shed my wings,
I may record thy worth with honour due,
In verse as musical as thou art true,
And that immortalizes whom it sings:
But thou hast little need. There is a Book
By seraphs writ with beams of heavenly light,
On which the eyes of God not rarely look,
A chronicle of actions just and bright —
   There all thy deeds, my faithful Mary, shine;
   And since thou own'st that praise, I spare thee mine.

WILLIAM COWPER

*♂ • ♀*

# *Renouncement*

I must not think of thee; and, tired yet strong,
   I shun the love that lurks in all delight —
The love of thee — and in the blue heaven's height,
   And in the dearest passage of a song.

Oh, just beyond the sweetest thoughts that throng
This breast, the thought of thee waits hidden yet bright;
But it must never, never come in sight;
I must stop short of thee the whole day long.
But when sleep comes to close each difficult day,
When night gives pause to the long watch I keep,
And all my bonds I needs must loose apart,
Must doff my will as raiment laid away, —
With the first dream that comes with the first sleep
I run, I run, I am gather'd to thy heart.

ALICE MEYNELL

* • *

## Meeting At Night

The grey sea and the long black land;
And the yellow half-moon large and low;
And the startled little waves that leap
In fiery ringlets from their sleep,
As I gain the cove with pushing prow,
And quench its speed i' the slushy sand.

Then a mile of warm sea-scented beach;
Three fields to cross till a farm appears;
A tap at the pane, the quick sharp scratch
And blue spurt of a lighted match,
And a voice less loud, thro' its joys and fears,
Than the two hearts beating each to each!

ROBERT BROWNING

*ℰ · ℬ*

## *When We Two Parted*

When we two parted
In silence and tears,
Half broken-hearted
To sever for years,
Pale grew thy cheek and cold,
Colder thy kiss;
Truly that hour foretold
Sorrow to this.

The dew of the morning
Sunk chill on my brow
It felt like the warning
Of what I feel now.

Thy vows are all broken,
And light is thy fame:
I hear thy name spoken,
And share in its shame.

They name thee before me,
A knell to mine ear;
A shudder comes o'er me
Why wert thou so dear?
They know not I knew thee,
Who knew thee too well:
Long, long shall I rue thee,
Too deeply to tell.

In secret we met,
In silence I grieve,
That thy heart could forget,
Thy spirit deceive.
If I should meet thee
After long years,
How should I greet thee?
With silence and tears.

GEORGE GORDON, LORD BYRON

* • B*

# *Echo*

Come to me in the silence of the night;
    Come in the speaking silence of a dream;
Come with soft rounded cheeks and eyes as bright
    As sunlight on a stream;
        Come back in tears,
O memory, hope, love of finished years.

O dream how sweet, too sweet, too bitter sweet,
    Whose wakening should have been in Paradise,
Where souls brimfull of love abide and meet;
    Where thirsting longing eyes
        Watch the slow door
That opening, letting in, lets out no more.

Yet come to me in dreams, that I may live
    My very life again tho' cold in death:
Come back to me in dreams, that I may give
    Pulse for pulse, breath for breath:
        Speak low, lean low,
As long ago, my love, how long ago.

CHRISTINA GEORGINA ROSSETTI

## *The Ecstasy*

Where, like a pillow on a bed,
    A pregnant bank swell'd up, to rest
The violet's reclining head,
    Sat we two, one another's best.

Our hands were firmly cemented
    With a fast balm, which thence did spring;
Our eye-beams twisted, and did thread
    Our eyes upon one double string.

So to intergraft our hands, as yet
    Was all the means to make us one ;
And pictures in our eyes to get
    Was all our propagation.

As, 'twixt two equal armies, Fate
    Suspends uncertain victory,
Our souls — which to advance their state,
    Were gone out — hung 'twixt her and me.

And whilst our souls negotiate there,
    We like sepulchral statues lay;
All day, the same our postures were,
    And we said nothing, all the day.

If any, so by love refined,
        That he soul's language understood,
And by good love were grown all mind,
        Within convenient distance stood,

He — though he knew not which soul spake,
        Because both meant, both spake the same —
Might thence a new concoction take,
        And part far purer than he came.

This ecstasy doth unperplex
        (We said) and tell us what we love;
We see by this, it was not sex;
        We see, we saw not, what did move:

But as all several souls contain
        Mixture of things they know not what,
Love these mix'd souls doth mix again,
        And makes both one, each this, and that.

A single violet transplant,
        The strength, the colour, and the size —
All which before was poor and scant —
        Redoubles still, and multiplies.

When love with one another so
      Interanimates two souls,
That abler soul, which thence doth flow,
      Defects of loneliness controls.

We then, who are this new soul, know,
      Of what we are composed, and made,
For th' atomies of which we grow
      Are souls, whom no change can invade.

But, O alas! so long, so far,
      Our bodies why do we forbear?
They are ours, though not we; we are
      Th' intelligences, they the spheres.

We owe them thanks, because they thus
      Did us, to us, at first convey,
Yielded their forces, sense, to us,
      Nor are dross to us, but allay.

On man heaven's influence works not so,
      But that it first imprints the air;
So soul into the soul may flow,
      Though it to body first repair.

As our blood labours to beget
      Spirits, as like souls as it can;
Because such fingers need to knit
      That subtle knot, which makes us man;

So must pure lovers' souls descend
      To affections, and to faculties,
Which sense may reach and apprehend,
      Else a great prince in prison lies.

To our bodies turn we then, that so
      Weak men on love reveal'd may look ;
Love's mysteries in souls do grow,
      But yet the body is his book.

And if some lover, such as we,
      Have heard this dialogue of one,
Let him still mark us, he shall see
      Small change when we're to bodies gone.

JOHN DONNE

## *To His Mistress Going To Bed*

Come madam, come, all rest my powers defy;
Until I labour, I in labour lie.
The foe ofttimes, having the foe in sight,
Is tired with standing, though he never fight.
Off with that girdle, like heaven's zone glittering,
But a far fairer world encompassing.
Unpin that spangled breast-plate, which you wear,
That th' eyes of busy fools may be stopp'd there.
Unlace yourself, for that harmonious chime
Tells me from you that now it is bed-time.
Off with that happy busk, which I envy,
That still can be, and still can stand so nigh.
Your gown going off such beauteous state reveals,
As when from flowery meads th' hill's shadow steals.
Off with your wiry coronet, and show
The hairy diadem which on you doth grow.
Off with your hose and shoes; then softly tread
In this love's hallow'd temple, this soft bed.
In such white robes heaven's angels used to be
Revealed to men; thou, angel, bring'st with thee
A heaven-like Mahomet's paradise; and though
Ill spirits walk in white, we easily know
By this these angels from an evil sprite;
Those set our hairs, but these our flesh upright.

Licence my roving hands, and let them go
Before, behind, between, above, below.
O, my America, my Newfoundland,
My kingdom, safest when with one man mann'd,
My mine of precious stones, my empery;
How blest am I in this discovering thee!
To enter in these bonds, is to be free;
Then, where my hand is set, my seal shall be.

Full nakedness ! All joys are due to thee;
As souls unbodied, bodies unclothed must be
To taste whole joys. Gems which you women use
Are like Atlanta's ball cast in men's views;
That, when a fool's eye lighteth on a gem,
His earthly soul may covert theirs, not them:
Like pictures, or like books' gay coverings made
For laymen, are all women thus array'd.
Themselves are mystic books, which only we
— Whom their imputed grace will dignify —
Must see reveal'd. Then, since that I may know,
As liberally as to thy midwife show
Thyself; cast all, yea, this white linen hence;
There is no penance much less innocence:
To teach thee, I am naked first; why then,
What needst thou have more covering than a man?

JOHN DONNE

## *To Mary*

I sleep with thee, and wake with thee,
And yet thou art not there;
I fill my arms with thoughts of thee,
And press the common air,
Thy eyes are gazing upon mine,
When thou art out of sight;
My lips are always touching thine,
At morning, noon, and night.

I think and speak of other things
To keep my mind at rest;
But still to thee my memory clings
Like love in woman's breast.
I hide it from the world's wide eye,
And think and speak contrary;
But soft the wind comes from the sky,
And whispers tales of Mary.

The night wind whispers in my ear,
The moon shines in my face;
A burden still of chilling fear
I find in every place.

The breeze is whispering in the bush,
And the dews fall from the tree,
All sighing on, and will not hush,
Some pleasant tales of thee.

JOHN CLARE

# The Apparition

When by thy scorne, O murdresse, I am dead,
And that thou thinkst thee free
From all solicitation from mee,
Then shall my ghost come to thy bed,
And thee, fain'd vestall, in worse armes shall see;
Then thy sicke taper will begin to winke,
And he, whose thou art then, being tyr'd before,
Will, if thou stirre, or pinch to wake him, thinke
        Thou call'st for more,
And in false sleepe will from thee shrinke,
And then poore Aspen wretch, neglected thou
Bath'd in a cold quicksilver sweat wilt lye
        A veryer ghost than I;
What I will say, I will not tell thee now,

Lest that preserve thee; and since my love is spent,

I'had rather thou shouldst painfully repent,

Than by my threatenings rest still innocent.


JOHN DONNE

☙ • ❧


## *Strange Fits of Passion Have I Known*

Strange fits of passion have I known:

And I will dare to tell,

But in the Lover's ear alone,

What once to me befell.


When she I loved looked every day

Fresh as a rose in June,

I to her cottage bent my way,

Beneath an evening moon.


Upon the moon I fixed my eye,

All over the wide lea;

With quickening pace my horse drew nigh

Those paths so dear to me.

And now we reached the orchard-plot;
And, as we climbed the hill,
The sinking moon to Lucy's cot
Came near, and nearer still.

In one of those sweet dreams I slept,
Kind Nature's gentlest boon!
And all the while my eyes I kept
On the descending moon.

My horse moved on; hoof after hoof
He raised, and never stopped:
When down behind the cottage roof,
At once, the bright moon dropped.

What fond and wayward thoughts will slide
Into a Lover's head!
'O mercy!' to myself I cried,
'If Lucy should be dead!'

WILLIAM WORDSWORTH

## *Longing*

Come to me in my dreams, and then
By day I shall be well again!
For then the night will more than pay
The hopeless longing of the day.

Come, as thou cam'st a thousand times,
A messenger from radiant climes,
And smile on thy new world, and be
As kind to others as to me!

Or, as thou never cam'st in sooth,
Come now, and let me dream it truth,
And part my hair, and kiss my brow,
And say, *My love! why sufferest thou*?

Come to me in my dreams, and then
By day I shall be well again!
For then the night will more than pay
The hopeless longing of the day.

MATTHEW ARNOLD

*ℰ • ℬ*

## *Sudden Light*

I have been here before,
But when or how I cannot tell:
I know the grass beyond the door,
The sweet keen smell,
The sighing sound, the lights around the shore.

You have been mine before, —
How long ago I may not know:
But just when at that swallow's soar
Your neck turned so,
Some veil did fall, — I knew it all of yore.

Has this been thus before?
And shall not thus time's eddying flight
Still with our lives our love restore
In death's despite,
And day and night yield one delight once more?

DANTE GABRIEL ROSSETTI

## *Love Is Enough*

Love is enough: though the World be a-waning,
And the woods have no voice but the voice of complaining,
    Though the sky be too dark for dim eyes to discover
The gold-cups and daisies fair blooming thereunder,
Though the hills be held shadows, and the sea a dark wonder,
    And this day draw a veil over all deeds pass'd over,
Yet their hands shall not tremble, their feet shall not falter;
The void shall not weary, the fear shall not alter
    These lips and these eyes of the loved and the lover.

WILLIAM MORRIS

# Youth

AND

# Age

## *Looking Forward*

When I am grown to man's estate
I shall be very proud and great,
And tell the other girls and boys
Not to meddle with my toys.

ROBERT LOUIS STEVENSON

♔ • ♕

## *Infant Sorrow*

My mother groaned, my father wept,
Into the dangerous world I leapt;
Helpless, naked, piping loud,
Like a fiend hid in a cloud.

Struggling in my father's hands,
Striving against my swaddling bands,
Bound and weary, I thought best
To sulk upon my mother's breast.

WILLIAM BLAKE

♔ • ♕

## *The Child Is Father To The Man*

'The child is father to the man.'
How can he be? The words are wild.
Suck any sense from that who can:
'The child is father to the man.'
No; what the poet did write ran,
'The man is father to the child.'
'The child is father to the man!'
How *can* he be? The words are wild.

GERARD MANLEY HOPKINS

## *Answer To A Child's Question*

Do you ask what the birds say? The sparrow, the dove,
The linnet and thrush say, 'I love and I love!'
In the winter they're silent — the wind is so strong;
What it says, I don't know, but it sings a loud song.
But green leaves, and blossoms, and sunny warm weather,
And singing, and loving — all come back together.
But the lark is so brimful of gladness and love,
The green fields below him, the blue sky above,
That he sings, and he sings; and for ever sings he —
'I love my Love, and my Love loves me!'

SAMUEL TAYLOR COLERIDGE

## The Old Man's Comforts

You are old, Father William, the young man cried,
  The few locks which are left you are grey;
You are hale, Father William, a hearty old man,
  Now tell me the reason, I pray.

In the days of my youth, Father William replied,
  I remember'd that youth would fly fast,
And abused not my health and my vigour at first,
  That I never might need them at last.

You are old, Father William, the young man cried,
  And pleasures with youth pass away;
And yet you lament not the days that are gone,
  Now tell me the reason, I pray.

In the days of my youth, Father William replied,
  I remember'd that youth could not last;
I thought of the future, whatever I did,
  That I never might grieve for the past.

You are old, Father William, the young man cried,
  And life must be hastening away;
You are cheerful, and love to converse upon death,
  Now tell me the reason, I pray.

I am cheerful, young man, Father William replied,
  Let the cause thy attention engage;
In the days of my youth I remember'd my God!
  And He hath not forgotten my age.

ROBERT SOUTHEY

*G · B*

## *You Are Old, Father William*

'You are old, Father William,' the young man said,
  'And your hair has become very white;
And yet you incessantly stand on your head —
  Do you think, at your age, it is right?'

'In my youth,' Father William replied to his son,
  'I feared it might injure the brain;
But, now that I'm perfectly sure I have none,
  Why, I do it again and again.'

'You are old,' said the youth, 'as I mentioned before,
  And have grown most uncommonly fat;
Yet you turned a back-somersault in at the door —
  Pray what is the reason of that?'

'In my youth,' said the sage, as he shook his grey locks,
    'I kept all my limbs very supple
By the use of this ointment — one shilling the box —
Allow me to sell you a couple?'

'You are old,' said the youth, 'and your jaws are too weak
    For anything tougher than suet;
Yet you finished the goose, with the bones and the beak —
    Pray, how did you manage to do it?'

'In my youth,' said his father, 'I took to the law,
    And argued each case with my wife;
And the muscular strength, which it gave to my jaw,
    Has lasted the rest of my life.'

'You are old,' said the youth, 'one would hardly suppose
    That your eye was as steady as ever;
Yet you balanced an eel on the end of your nose —
    What made you so awfully clever?'

'I have answered three questions, and that is enough,'
    Said his father; 'don't give yourself airs!
Do you think I can listen all day to such stuff?
    Be off, or I'll kick you downstairs!'

LEWIS CARROLL

## The Barefoot Boy

Blessings on thee, little man,
Barefoot boy, with cheek of tan!
With thy turned-up pantaloons,
And thy merry whistled tunes;
With thy red lip, redder still
Kissed by strawberries on the hill;
With the sunshine on thy face,
Through thy torn brim's jaunty grace;
From my heart I give thee joy, —
I was once a barefoot boy!
Prince thou art, — the grown-up man
Only is republican.
Let the million-dollared ride!
Barefoot, trudging at his side,
Thou hast more than he can buy
In the reach of ear and eye, —
Outward sunshine, inward joy:
Blessings on thee, barefoot boy!

Oh for boyhood's painless play,
Sleep that wakes in laughing day,
Health that mocks the doctor's rules,
Knowledge never learned of schools,

Of the wild bee's morning chase,
Of the wild-flower's time and place,
Flight of fowl and habitude
Of the tenants of the wood;
How the tortoise bears his shell,
How the woodchuck digs his cell,
And the ground-mole sinks his well;
How the robin feeds her young,
How the oriole's nest is hung;
Where the whitest lilies blow,
Where the freshest berries grow,
Where the ground-nut trails its vine,
Where the wood-grape's clusters shine;
Of the black wasp's cunning way,
Mason of his walls of clay,
And the architectural plans
Of gray hornet artisans!
For, eschewing books and tasks,
Nature answers all he asks;
Hand in hand with her he walks,
Face to face with her he talks,
Part and parcel of her joy, —
Blessings on the barefoot boy!

Oh for boyhood's time of June,
Crowding years in one brief moon,
When all things I heard or saw,
Me, their master, waited for.
I was rich in flowers and trees,
Humming-birds and honey-bees;
For my sport the squirrel played,
Plied the snouted mole his spade;
For my taste the blackberry cone
Purpled over hedge and stone;
Laughed the brook for my delight
Through the day and through the night,
Whispering at the garden wall,
Talked with me from fall to fall;
Mine the sand-rimmed pickerel pond,
Mine the walnut slopes beyond,
Mine, on bending orchard trees,
Apples of Hesperides!
Still as my horizon grew,
Larger grew my riches too;
All the world I saw or knew
Seemed a complex Chinese toy,
Fashioned for a barefoot boy!

Oh for festal dainties spread,
Like my bowl of milk and bread;
Pewter spoon and bowl of wood,
On the door-stone, gray and rude!
O'er me, like a regal tent,
Cloudy-ribbed, the sunset bent,
Purple-curtained, fringed with gold,
Looped in many a wind-swung fold;
While for music came the play
Of the pied frogs' orchestra;
And, to light the noisy choir,
Lit the fly his lamp of fire.
I was monarch: pomp and joy
Waited on the barefoot boy!

Cheerily, then, my little man,
Live and laugh, as boyhood can!
Though the flinty slopes be hard,
Stubble-speared the new-mown sward,
Every morn shall lead thee through
Fresh baptisms of the dew;
Every evening from thy feet
Shall the cool wind kiss the heat:
All too soon these feet must hide
In the prison cells of pride,

Lose the freedom of the sod,
Like a colt's for work be shod,
Made to tread the mills of toil,
Up and down in ceaseless moil:
Happy if their track be found
Never on forbidden ground;
Happy if they sink not in
Quick and treacherous sands of sin.
Ah! that thou couldst know thy joy,
Ere it passes, barefoot boy!

JOHN GREENLEAF WHITTIER

## Boy Remembers The Field

What if the sun comes out
And the new furrows do not look smeared?

This is April, and the sumach candles
Have guttered long ago.
The crows in the twisted apple limbs
Are as moveless and dark.

Drops on the wires, cold cheeks,
The mist, the long snorts, silence…
The horses will steam when the sun comes;
Crows, go, shrieking.

Another bird now; sweet…
Pitiful life, useless,
Innocently creeping
On a useless planet
Again.

If any voice called, I would hear?
It has been the same before.
Soil glistens, the furrow rolls, sleet shifts, brightens.

RAYMOND KNISTER

*T • B*

## Nurse's Song

When the voices of children are heard on the green
And whisp'rings are in the dale:
The days of my youth rise fresh in my mind,
My face turns green and pale.

Then come home, my children, the sun is gone down
And the dews of night arise
Your spring and your day are wasted in play
And your winter and night in disguise.

WILLIAM BLAKE

𝒟 • ℬ

## *Annabel Lee*

It was many and many a year ago,
In a kingdom by the sea,
That a maiden there lived whom you may know
By the name of Annabel Lee;
And this maiden she lived with no other thought
Than to love and be loved by me.

She was a child and I was a child,
In this kingdom by the sea:
But we loved with a love that was more than love —
I and my Annabel Lee;
With a love that the winged seraphs of heaven
Coveted her and me.

And this was the reason that, long ago,
In this kingdom by the sea,
A wind blew out of a cloud, by night
Chilling my Annabel Lee;
So that her high-born kinsmen came
And bore her away from me,
To shut her up in a sepulchre
In this kingdom by the sea.

The angels, not half so happy in heaven,
Went envying her and me —
Yes! that was the reason (as all men know,
In this kingdom by the sea)
That the wind came out of the cloud one night,
Chilling and killing my Annabel Lee.

But our love it was stronger by far than the love
Of those who were older than we —
Of many far wiser than we —
And neither the angels in heaven above,
Nor the demons down under the sea,
Can ever dissever my soul from the soul
Of the beautiful Annabel Lee;

For the moon never beams without bringing me dreams
Of the beautiful Annabel Lee;
And the stars never rise but I see the bright eyes
Of the beautiful Annabel Lee;
And so, all the night-tide, I lie down by the side
Of my darling — my darling — my life and my bride,
In her sepulchre there by the sea —
In her tomb by the sounding sea.

EDGAR ALLAN POE

## First Love

I ne'er was struck before that hour
With love so sudden and so sweet.
Her face it bloomed like a sweet flower
And stole my heart away complete.
My face turned pale, a deadly pale
My legs refused to walk away,
And when she looked what could I ail
My life and all seemed turned to clay.

And then my blood rushed to my face
And took my eyesight quite away,
The trees and bushes round the place
Seemed midnight at noonday.
I could not see a single thing
Words from my eyes did start;
They spoke as chords do from the string
And blood burnt round my heart.

Are flowers the winter's choice
Is love's bed always snow?
She seemed to hear my silent voice
Not love's appeals to know.
I never saw so sweet a face
As that I stood before,
My heart has left its dwelling place
And can return no more.

JOHN CLARE

## Spring Night

The park is filled with night and fog,
     The veils are drawn about the world,
The drowsy lights along the paths
     Are dim and pearled.

Gold and gleaming the empty streets,
     Gold and gleaming the misty lake,
The mirrored lights like sunken swords,
     Glimmer and shake.

Oh, is it not enough to be
Here with this beauty over me?
My throat should ache with praise, and I
Should kneel in joy beneath the sky.
O beauty, are you not enough?
Why am I crying after love,
With youth, a singing voice, and eyes
To take earth's wonder with surprise?
Why have I put off my pride,
Why am I unsatisfied, —
I, for whom the pensive night
Binds her cloudy hair with light, —
I, for whom all beauty burns

Like incense in a million urns?
O beauty, are you not enough?
Why am I crying after love?

SARA TEASDALE

*ଅ • ଅ*

## *A Little Girl Lost*

Children of the future age,
Reading this indignant page,
Know that in a former time
Love, sweet love, was thought a crime.

In the age of gold,
Free from winter's cold,
Youth and maiden bright,
To the holy light,
Naked in the sunny beams delight.

Once a youthful pair,
Filled with softest care,
Met in garden bright
Where the holy light
Had just removed the curtains of the night.

There, in rising day,
On the grass they play;
Parents were afar,
Strangers came not near,
And the maiden soon forgot her fear.

Tired with kisses sweet,
They agree to meet
When the silent sleep
Waves o'er heaven's deep,
And the weary tired wanderers weep.

To her father white
Came the maiden bright;
But his loving look,
Like the holy book
All her tender limbs with terror shook.

'Ona, pale and weak,
To thy father speak!
Oh, the trembling fear!
Oh, the dismal care
That shakes the blossoms of my hoary hair!'

WILLIAM BLAKE

# *When I Was One-And-Twenty*

When I was one-and-twenty
     I heard a wise man say,
'Give crowns and pounds and guineas
     But not your heart away;
Give pearls away and rubies
     But keep your fancy free.'
But I was one-and-twenty,
     No use to talk to me.

When I was one-and-twenty
     I heard him say again,
'The heart out of the bosom
     Was never given in vain;
'Tis paid with sighs a-plenty
     And sold for endless rue.'
And I am two-and-twenty,
     And oh, 'tis true, 'tis true.

A. E. HOUSMAN

# Believe Me, If All Those Endearing Young Charms

Believe me, if all those endearing young charms,
    Which I gaze on so fondly to-day,
Were to change by to-morrow, and fleet in my arms,
    Like fairy-gifts fading away,
Thou wouldst still be adored, as this moment thou art,
    Let thy loveliness fade as it will,
And around the dear ruin each wish of my heart
    Would entwine itself verdantly still.

It is not while beauty and youth are thine own,
    And thy cheeks unprofaned by a tear,
That the fervor and faith of a soul may be known,
    To which time will but make thee more dear!
No, the heart that has truly loved never forgets,
    But as truly loves on to the close,
As the sunflower turns to her god when he sets
    The same look which she turned when he rose!

THOMAS MOORE

## *My Lost Youth*

Often I think of the beautiful town
     That is seated by the sea;
Often in thought go up and down
     The pleasant streets of that dear old town,
And my youth comes back to me.
     And a verse of a Lapland song
Is haunting my memory still:
     'A boy's will is the wind's will,
And the thoughts of youth are long, long thoughts.'

I can see the shadowy lines of its trees,
     And catch, in sudden gleams,
The sheen of the far-surrounding seas,
     And islands that were the Hesperides
Of all my boyish dreams.
     And the burden of that old song,
It murmurs and whispers still:
     'A boy's will is the wind's will,
And the thoughts of youth are long, long thoughts.'

I remember the black wharves and the slips,
     And the sea-tides tossing free;
And Spanish sailors with bearded lips,
     And the beauty and mystery of the ships,
And the magic of the sea.

And the voice of that wayward song
Is singing and saying still:
    'A boy's will is the wind's will,
And the thoughts of youth are long, long thoughts.'


I remember the bulwarks by the shore,
    And the fort upon the hill;
The sunrise gun with its hollow roar,
    The drum-beat repeated o'er and o'er,
And the bugle wild and shrill.
    And the music of that old song
Throbs in my memory still:
    'A boy's will is the wind's will,
And the thoughts of youth are long, long thoughts.'


I remember the sea-fight far away,
    How it thunder'd o'er the tide!
And the dead sea-captains, as they lay
    In their graves o'erlooking the tranquil bay
Where they in battle died.
    And the sound of that mournful song
Goes through me with a thrill:
    'A boy's will is the wind's will,
And the thoughts of youth are long, long thoughts.'

I can see the breezy dome of groves,
  The shadows of Deering's woods;
And the friendships old and the early loves
  Come back with a Sabbath sound, as of doves
In quiet neighbourhoods.
  And the verse of that sweet old song,
It flutters and murmurs still:
  'A boy's will is the wind's will,
And the thoughts of youth are long, long thoughts.'

I remember the gleams and glooms that dart
  Across the schoolboy's brain;
The song and the silence in the heart,
  That in part are prophecies, and in part
Are longings wild and vain.
  And the voice of that fitful song
 Sings on, and is never still:
  'A boy's will is the wind's will,
 And the thoughts of youth are long, long thoughts.'

There are things of which I may not speak;
  There are dreams that cannot die;
There are thoughts that make the strong heart weak,
  And bring a pallor into the cheek,
And a mist before the eye.

And the words of that fatal song
Come over me like a chill:
    'A boy's will is the wind's will,
And the thoughts of youth are long, long thoughts.'

Strange to me now are the forms I meet
    When I visit the dear old town;
But the native air is pure and sweet,
    And the trees that o'ershadow each well-known street,
As they balance up and down,
    Are singing the beautiful song,
Are sighing and whispering still:
    'A boy's will is the wind's will,
And the thoughts of youth are long, long thoughts.'

And Deering's woods are fresh and fair,
    And with joy that is almost pain
My heart goes back to wander there,
    And among the dreams of the days that were
I find my lost youth again.
    And the strange and beautiful song,
The groves are repeating it still:
    'A boy's will is the wind's will,
And the thoughts of youth are long, long thoughts.'

HENRY WADSWORTH LONGFELLOW

* · *

# Youth And Age

Verse, a breeze 'mid blossoms straying,
Where Hope clung feeding, like a bee —
Both were mine! Life went a-maying
With Nature, Hope, and Poesy,
When I was young!

When I was young? — Ah, woeful When!
Ah! for the change 'twixt Now and Then!
This breathing house not built with hands,
This body that does me grievous wrong,
O'er aery cliffs and glittering sands
How lightly then it flashed along,
Like those trim skiffs, unknown of yore,
On winding lakes and rivers wide,
That ask no aid of sail or oar,
That fear no spite of wind or tide!
Nought cared this body for wind or weather
When Youth and I lived in't together.

Flowers are lovely; Love is flower-like;
Friendship is a sheltering tree;
O the joys! that came down shower-like,
Of Friendship, Love, and Liberty,
Ere I was old!

Ere I was old? Ah woeful Ere,
Which tells me, Youth's no longer here!
O Youth! for years so many and sweet
'Tis known that Thou and I were one,
I'll think it but a fond conceit —
It cannot be that Thou art gone!
Thy vesper-bell hath not yet tolled —
And thou wert aye a masker bold!
What strange disguise hast now put on,
To make believe that thou art gone?
I see these locks in silvery slips,
This drooping gait, this altered size:
But Springtide blossoms on thy lips,
And tears take sunshine from thine eyes:
Life is but Thought: so think I will
That Youth and I are housemates still.

Dew-drops are the gems of morning,
But the tears of mournful eve!
Where no hope is, life's a warning
That only serves to make us grieve
When we are old:

That only serves to make us grieve
With oft and tedious taking-leave,

Like some poor nigh-related guest
That may not rudely be dismist;
Yet hath out-stayed his welcome while,
And tells the jest without the smile.

SAMUEL TAYLOR COLERIDGE

             *𝒜 · ℬ*

## *Young And Old*

When all the world is young, lad,
And all the trees are green;
And every goose a swan, lad,
And every lass a queen;
Then hey for boot and horse, lad,
And round the world away:
Young blood must have its course, lad,
And every dog his day.

When all the world is old, lad,
And all the trees are brown;
And all the sport is stale, lad,
And all the wheels run down;
Creep home, and take your place there,

The spent and maimed among:
God grant you find one face there,
You loved when all was young.

CHARLES KINGSLEY

.*❦* .*❦*

## *The Old Familiar Faces*

I have had playmates, I have had companions,
In my days of childhood, in my joyful school-days;
All, all are gone, the old familiar faces.

I have been laughing, I have been carousing,
Drinking late, sitting late, with my bosom cronies;
All, all are gone, the old familiar faces.

I loved a Love once, fairest among women:
Closed are her doors on me, I must not see her —
All, all are gone, the old familiar faces.

I have a friend, a kinder friend hath no man:
Like an ingrate, I left my friend abruptly;
Left him to muse on the old familiar faces.

Ghost-like I paced round the haunts of my childhood,
Earth seem'd a desert I was bound to traverse,
Seeking to find the old familiar faces.

Friend of my bosom, thou more than a brother,
Why wert not thou born in my father's dwelling?
So might we talk of the old familiar faces.

How some they have died, and some they have left me,
And some are taken from me; all are departed;
All, all are gone, the old familiar faces.

CHARLES LAMB

# A Song Of A Young Lady To Her Ancient Lover

Ancient Person, for whom I
All the flattering youth defy,
Long be it ere thou grow old,
Aching, shaking, crazy cold;
But still continue as thou art,
Ancient Person of my heart.
On thy withered lips and dry,

Which like barren furrows lie,
Brooding kisses I will pour,
Shall thy youthful heat restore,
Such kind show'rs in autumn fall,
And a second spring recall;
Nor from thee will ever part,
Ancient Person of my heart.

Thy nobler parts, which but to name
In our sex would be counted shame,
By age's frozen grasp possest,
From their ice shall be released,
And, soothed by my reviving hand,
In former warmth and vigour stand.
All a lover's wish can reach,
For thy joy my love shall teach;
And for thy pleasure shall improve
All that art can add to love.
Yet still I love thee without art,
Ancient Person of my heart.

JOHN WILMOT, EARL OF ROCHESTER

## *The Old Man Dreams*

Oh for one hour of youthful joy!
Give back my twentieth spring!
I'd rather laugh, a bright-haired boy,
Than reign, a gray-beard king.

Off with the spoils of wrinkled age!
Away with Learning's crown!
Tear out life's Wisdom-written page,
And dash its trophies down!

One moment let my life-blood stream
From boyhood's fount of flame!
Give me one giddy, reeling dream
Of life all love and fame!

.....

My listening angel heard the prayer,
And, calmly smiling, said,
'If I but touch thy silvered hair
Thy hasty wish hath sped.

'But is there nothing in thy track,
To bid thee fondly stay,
While the swift seasons hurry back
To find the wished-for day?'

'Ah, truest soul of womankind!
Without thee what were life?
One bliss I cannot leave behind:
I'll take — my — precious — wife!'

The angel took a sapphire pen
And wrote in rainbow dew,
*The man would be a boy again,*
*And be a husband too*!

'And is there nothing yet unsaid,
Before the change appears?
Remember, all their gifts have fled
With those dissolving years.'

'Why, yes;' for memory would recall
My fond paternal joys;
'I could not bear to leave them all —
I'll take — my — girl — and — boys.'

The smiling angel dropped his pen, —
'Why, this will never do;
The man would be a boy again,
And be a father too!'

.....

And so I laughed, — my laughter woke
The household with its noise, —
And wrote my dream, when morning broke,
To please the gray-haired boys.

OLIVER WENDELL HOLMES SR.

*❦ • ❦*

## *I Remember, I Remember*

I remember, I remember
The house where I was born,
The little window where the sun
Came peeping in at morn;
He never came a wink too soon
Nor brought too long a day;
But now, I often wish the night
Had borne my breath away.

I remember, I remember
The roses red and white,
The violets and the lily cups —
Those flowers made of light!

The lilacs where the robin built,
And where my brother set
The laburnum on his birthday, —
The tree is living yet!

I remember, I remember
Where I was used to swing,
And thought the air must rush as fresh
To swallows on the wing;
My spirit flew in feathers then
That is so heavy now,
And summer pools could hardly cool
The fever on my brow.

I remember, I remember
The fir-trees dark and high;
I used to think their slender tops
Were close against the sky:
It was a childish ignorance,
But now 'tis little joy
To know I'm farther off from Heaven
Than when I was a boy.

THOMAS HOOD

## *Youth And June*

I was your lover long ago, sweet June,

  Ere life grew hard; I am your lover still,

And follow gladly to the wondrous tune

  You pipe on golden reeds to vale and hill.

I am your lover still; to me you seem

  To hold the fragrance of the joys long dead,

The brightness and the beauty of the dream

  We dreamed in youth, to hold the tears we shed,

The laughter of our lips, the faith that lies

  Back in that season dear to every heart,

Life's springtime, when God's earth and God's blue skies

  Are, measured by our glance, not far apart.

JEAN BLEWETT

*∂ • ß*

## *Oft In The Stilly Night*

Oft in the stilly night,

  Ere Slumber's chain has bound me,

Fond Memory brings the light

  Of other days around me:

    The smiles, the tears

    Of boyhood's years,

The words of love then spoken;
The eyes that shone,
Now dimm'd and gone,
The cheerful hearts now broken!
Thus, in the stilly night,
Ere slumber's chain has bound me,
Sad Memory brings the light
Of other days around me.

When I remember all
The friends, so linked together,
I've seen around me fall
Like leaves in wintry weather;
I feel like one
Who treads alone
Some banquet-hall deserted,
Whose lights are fled,
Whose garlands dead,
And all but he departed!
Thus, in the stilly night,
Ere Slumber's chain has bound me,
Sad Memory brings the light
Of other days around me.

THOMAS MOORE

## *The Last Leaf*

I saw him once before,
As he passed by the door,
　And again
The pavement stones resound,
As he totters o'er the ground
　With his cane.

They say that in his prime,
Ere the pruning-knife of Time
　Cut him down,
Not a better man was found
By the Crier on his round
　Through the town.

But now he walks the streets,
And looks at all he meets
　Sad and wan,
And he shakes his feeble head,
That it seems as if he said,
　'They are gone.'

The mossy marbles rest
On the lips that he has prest
　In their bloom,

And the names he loved to hear
Have been carved for many a year
    On the tomb.

My grandmamma has said —
Poor old lady, she is dead
    Long ago —
That he had a Roman nose,
And his cheek was like a rose
    In the snow;

But now his nose is thin,
And it rests upon his chin
    Like a staff,
And a crook is in his back,
And a melancholy crack
    In his laugh.

I know it is a sin
For me to sit and grin
    At him here;
But the old three-cornered hat,
And the breeches, and all that,
    Are so queer!

And if I should live to be
The last leaf upon the tree
  In the spring,
Let them smile, as I do now,
At the old forsaken bough
  Where I cling.

OLIVER WENDELL HOLMES SR.

 *⁂* ·  *ℬ*

## *Nature*

As a fond mother, when the day is o'er,
Leads by the hand her little child to bed,
Half willing, half reluctant to be led,
And leave his broken playthings on the floor,
Still gazing at them through the open door,
Nor wholly reassured and comforted
By promises of others in their stead,
Which, though more splendid, may not please him more:

So Nature deals with us, and takes away
Our playthings one by one, and by the hand

Leads us to rest so gently, that we go

Scarce knowing if we wish to go or stay,

Being too full of sleep to understand

How far the unknown transcends the what we know.

HENRY WADSWORTH LONGFELLOW

ℰ · ℬ

# *A Superscription*

Look in my face; my name is Might-have-been;

I am also call'd No-more, Too-late, Farewell;

Unto thine ear I hold the dead-sea shell

Cast up thy Life's foam-fretted feet between;

Unto thine eyes the glass where that is seen


Which had Life's form and Love's, but by my spell

Is now a shaken shadow intolerable,

Of ultimate things unutter'd the frail screen.

Mark me, how still I am! But should there dart

One moment through thy soul the soft surprise


Of that wing'd Peace which lulls the breath of sighs, —

Then shalt thou see me smile, and turn apart

Thy visage to mine ambush at thy heart
Sleepless with cold commemorative eyes.

DANTE GABRIEL ROSSETTI

# Irreverence

AND

# Satire

## *To Nysus*

How shall we please this Age? If in a song
We put above six Lines, they count it long;
If we contract it to an epigram,
As deep the dwarfish poetry they damn;
If we write plays, few see above an act,
And those lewd masks, or noisy fops distract:
Let us write satire then, and at our ease
Vex th'ill-natured fools we cannot please.

SIR CHARLES SEDLEY

✿ • ✿

## *An Argument*

I've oft been told by learned friars,
That wishing and the crime are one,
And Heaven punishes desires
As much as if the deed were done.

If wishing damns us, you and I
Are damned to all our heart's content;
Come, then, at least we may enjoy
Some pleasure for our punishment!

THOMAS MOORE

✿ • ✿

# Decalogue

**Decalogue**, n. *A series of commandments, ten in number — just enough to permit an intelligent selection for observance, but not enough to embarrass the choice. Following is the revised edition of the Decalogue, calculated for this meridian.*

Thou shalt no God but me adore:
'Twere too expensive to have more.

No images nor idols make
For Roger Ingersoll to break.

Take not God's name in vain: select
A time when it will have effect.

Work not on Sabbath days at all,
But go to see the teams play ball.

Honor thy parents. That creates
For life insurance lower rates.

Kill not, abet not those who kill;
Thou shalt not pay thy butcher's bill.

Kiss not thy neighbor's wife, unless
Thine own thy neighbor doth caress.

Don't steal; thou'lt never thus compete
Successfully in business. Cheat.

Bear not false witness — that is low —
But 'hear 'tis rumored so and so.'

Covet thou naught that thou hast got
By hook or crook, or somehow, got.

AMBROSE BIERCE

$\mathcal{A} \cdot \mathcal{B}$

# *Let Us All Be Unhappy On Sunday*

We zealots, made up of stiff clay,
    The sour-looking children of sorrow,
While not over jolly to-day,
    Resolve to be wretched tomorrow.
We can't for a certainty tell
    What mirth may molest us on Monday;
But, at least, to begin the week well,
    Let us all be unhappy on Sunday.

What though a good precept we strain
    Till hateful and hurtful we make it!
While though, in thus pulling the rein,
    We may draw it so tight as to break it!
Abroad we forbid folks to roam,
    For fear they get social or frisky;
But of course they can sit still at home,
    And get dismally drunk upon whisky.

CHARLES, LORD NEAVES

## *The Little Vagabond*

Dear mother, dear mother, the church is cold,
But the alehouse is healthy, and pleasant, and warm;
    Besides I can tell where I am used well;
    Such usage in heaven will never do well.

But if at the church they would give us some ale,
    And a pleasant fire our souls to regale,
    We'd sing and we'd pray all the livelong day,
    Nor ever once wish from the church to stray.

Then the parson might preach, and drink, and sing,
    And we'd be as happy as birds in the spring;
And modest Dame Lurch, who is always at church,
Would not have bandy children, nor fasting, nor birch.

And God, like a father, rejoicing to see
His children as pleasant and happy as he,
Would have no more quarrel with the Devil or the barrel,
But kiss him, and give him both drink and apparel.

WILLIAM BLAKE

❧ • ☙

## Waste

I had written to Aunt Maud,
Who was on a trip abroad,
When I heard she'd died of cramp
Just too late to save the stamp.

HARRY GRAHAM

❧ • ☙

## On A Girdle

That which her slender waist confined
Shall now my joyful temples bind:
No monarch but would give his crown,
His arms might do what this has done.

It was my Heaven's extremest sphere,
The pale which held that lovely deer:
My joy, my grief, my hope, my love,
    Did all within this circle move!

A narrow compass! and yet there
Dwelt all that's good, and all that's fair:
Give me but what this ribband bound,
Take all the rest the Sun goes round.

EDMUND WALLER

𝒜 • ℬ

## *Song*

Pious Selinda goes to prayers,
    If I but ask a favour;
And yet the tender fool's in tears,
    When she believes I'll leave her.

Would I were free from this restraint,
    Or else had hopes to win her;
Would she would make of me a saint,
    Or I of her a sinner!

WILLIAM CONGREVE

𝒜 • ℬ

## *The Canonization*

For God's sake hold your tongue, and let me love,
  Or chide my palsy, or my gout;
  My five grey hairs, or ruin'd fortune flout;
With wealth your state, your mind with arts improve,
   Take you a course, get you a place,
   Observe his Honour, or his Grace;
Or the king's real, or his stamp'd face
  Contemplate; what you will, approve,
  So you will let me love.

Alas, alas, who's injured by my love?
  What merchant's ships have my sighs drowned?
  Who says my tears have overflowed his ground?
When did my colds a forward spring remove?
   When did the heats which my veins fill
   Add one more to the plaguy bill?
Soldiers find wars, and lawyers find out still
  Litigious men, which quarrels move,
  Though she and I do love.

Call us what you will, we are made such by love;
  Call her one, me another fly,
  We're tapers too, and at our own cost die,
And we in us find the eagle and the dove.
   The phœnix riddle hath more wit

By us; we two being one are it.
So, to one neutral thing both sexes fit.
We die and rise the same, and prove
Mysterious by this love.

We can die by it, if not live by love,
And if unfit for tomb or hearse
Our legend be, it will be fit for verse;
And if no piece of chronicle we prove,
We'll build in sonnets pretty rooms;
As well a well-wrought urn becomes
The greatest ashes, as half-acre tombs,
And by these hymns, all shall approve
Us canonized for love:

And thus invoke us, 'You, whom reverend love
Made one another's hermitage;
You, to whom love was peace, that now is rage;
Who did the whole world's soul contract, and drove
Into the glasses of your eyes;
(So made such mirrors, and such spies,
That they did all to you epitomize);
Countries, towns, courts beg from above
A pattern of your love.'

JOHN DONNE

*J • B*

## *A Poison Tree*

I was angry with my friend:
I told my wrath, my wrath did end.
I was angry with my foe:
I told it not, my wrath did grow.

And I watered it in fears
Night and morning with my tears,
And I sunned it with smiles
And with soft deceitful wiles.

And it grew both day and night,
Till it bore an apple bright,
And my foe beheld it shine,
And he knew that it was mine —

And into my garden stole
When the night had veiled the pole;
In the morning, glad, I see
My foe outstretched beneath the tree.

WILLIAM BLAKE

## A Little Lamb

Mary had a little lamb,
She ate it with mint sauce.
And everywhere that Mary went
The lamb went too, of course.

ANONYMOUS

℘ • ℛ

## The Latest Decalogue

Thou shalt have one God only; who
Would be at the expense of two?
No graven images may be
Worshipp'd, except the currency:
Swear not at all; for for thy curse
Thine enemy is none the worse:
At church on Sunday to attend
Will serve to keep the world thy friend:
Honour thy parents; that is, all
From whom advancement may befall:
Thou shalt not kill; but needst not strive
Officiously to keep alive:
Do not adultery commit;
Advantage rarely comes of it:

Thou shalt not steal; an empty feat,
When it's so lucrative to cheat:
Bear not false witness; let the lie
Have time on its own wings to fly:
Thou shalt not covert; but tradition
Approves all forms of competition.

The sum of all is, thou shalt love,
If any body, God above:
At any rate shall never labour
*More* than thyself to love thy neighbour.

ARTHUR HUGH CLOUGH

## The Righteous Man

The righteous man will rob none but the defenceless,
Whatsoever can reckon with him he will neither plunder nor
    kill;
He will steal an egg from a hen or a lamb from an ewe,
For his sheep and his hens cannot reckon with him hereafter —
They live not in any odour of defencefulness:
Therefore right is with the righteous man, and he taketh
    advantage righteously,
Praising God and plundering.

The righteous man will enslave his horse and his dog,

Making them serve him for their bare keep and for nothing
further,

Shooting them, selling them for vivisection when they can no
longer profit him,

Backbiting them and beating them if they fail to please him;

For his horse and his dog can bring no action for damages,

Wherefore, then, should he not enslave them, shoot them, sell
them for vivisection?

But the righteous man will not plunder the defenceful —

Not if he be alone and unarmed — for his conscience will
smite him;

He will not rob a she-bear of her cubs, nor an eagle of her
eaglets —

Unless he have a rifle to purge him from the fear of sin:

Then may he shoot rejoicing in innocency — from ambush or
a safe distance;

Or he will beguile them, lay poison for them, keep no faith
with them;

For what faith is there with that which cannot reckon here-
after,

Neither by itself, nor by another, nor by any residuum of ill
consequences?

Surely, where weakness is utter, honour ceaseth.

Nay, I will do what is right in the eyes of him who can harm
  me,
And not in those of him who cannot call me to account.
Therefore yield me up thy pretty wings, O humming-bird!
Sing for me in a prison, O lark!
Pay me thy rent, O widow! for it is mine.
Where there is reckoning there is sin,
And where there is no reckoning sin is not.

SAMUEL BUTLER

*S · B*

# The Laws Of God, The Laws Of Man

The laws of God, the laws of man
He may keep that will and can
Not I: Let God and man decree
Laws for themselves and not for me;
And if my ways are not as theirs
Let them mind their own affairs.
Their deeds I judge and much condemn
Yet when did I make laws for them?
Please yourselves, Say I, and they
Need only look the other way.

But no, they will not; they must still
Wrest their neighbor to their will,
And make me dance as they desire
With jail and gallows and hellfire.
And how am I to face the odds
Of man's bedevilment and God's?
I, a stranger and afraid
In a world I never made
They will be master, right or wrong;
Though, both are foolish, both are strong
And since, my soul, we cannot flee
To Saturn or to Mercury
Keep we must, if keep we can
These foreign laws of God and man.

A. E. HOUSMAN

*ℰ • ℬ*


## The Pulley

When God at first made man,
Having a glasse of blessings standing by,
'Let us,' said he, 'poure on him all we can;
Let the world's riches, which dispersèd lie,
    Contract into a span.'

So strength first made a way;
Then beautie flow'd, then wisdome, honour, pleasure;
When almost all was out, God made a stay,
Perceiving that, alone of all his treasure,
    Rest in the bottom lay.

'For if I should,' said he,
'Bestow this jewel also on my creature,
He would adore my gifts instead of me,
And rest in Nature, not the God of Nature;
    So both should losers be.

Yet let him keep the rest,
But keep them with repining restlessnesse;
Let him be rich and wearie, that at least,
If goodnesse leade him not, yet weariness
    May toss him to my breast.'

GEORGE HERBERT

⌀ • ⌀

# *Richard Cory*

Whenever Richard Cory went down town,
    We people on the pavement looked at him:
He was a gentleman from sole to crown,
    Clean favored, and imperially slim.

And he was always quietly arrayed,
  And he was always human when he talked;
But still he fluttered pulses when he said,
  'Good-morning,' and he glittered when he walked.

And he was rich — yes, richer than a king,
  And admirably schooled in every grace:
In fine, we thought that he was everything
  To make us wish that we were in his place.

So on we worked, and waited for the light,
  And went without the meat, and cursed the bread;
And Richard Cory, one calm summer night,
  Went home and put a bullet through his head.

EDWIN ARLINGTON ROBINSON

℘ · ℬ

# *To The Virgins, To Make Much Of Time*

Gather ye rosebuds while ye may,
  Old time is still a-flying:
And this same flower that smiles to-day
  To-morrow will be dying.

The glorious lamp of heaven, the sun,
    The higher he's a-getting,
The sooner will his race be run,
    And nearer he's to setting.

That age is best which is the first,
    When youth and blood are warmer;
But being spent, the worse, and worst
    Times still succeed the former.

Then be not coy, but use your time,
    And while ye may go marry:
For having lost but once your prime,
    You may for ever tarry.

ROBERT HERRICK

# Why So Pale And Wan, Fond Lover?

Why so pale and wan, fond lover?
        Prithee, why so pale?
Will, when looking well can't move her,
        Looking ill prevail?
        Prithee, why so pale?

Why so dull and mute, young sinner?
       Prithee, why so mute?
Will, when speaking well can't win her,
       Saying nothing do 't?
       Prithee, why so mute?

Quit, quit for shame! This will not move;
       This cannot take her.
If of herself she will not love,
       Nothing can make her:
       The devil take her!

SIR JOHN SUCKLING

ᴈ · ℬ

# Rich And Poor; Or Saint And Sinner

The poor man's sins are glaring;
In the face of ghostly warning
       He is caught in the fact
       Of an overt act —
Buying greens on Sunday morning.

The rich man's sins are hidden
In the pomp of wealth and station;
       And escape the sight
       Of the children of light,
Who are wise in their generation.

The rich man has a kitchen,
And cooks to dress his dinner;
  The poor who would roast
  To the baker's must post,
And thus becomes a sinner.

The rich man has a cellar,
And a ready butler by him;
  The poor man must steer
  For his pint of beer
Where the saint can't choose but spy him.

The rich man's painted windows
Hide the concerts of the quality;
  The poor can but share
  A cracked fiddle in the air,
Which offends all sound morality.

The rich man is invisible
In the crowd of his gay society;
  But the poor man's delight
  Is a sore in the sight,
And a stench in the nose of piety.

THOMAS LOVE PEACOCK

## *To A Millionaire*

The world in gloom and splendour passes by,
And thou in the midst of it with brows that gleam,
A creature of that old distorted dream
That makes the sound of life an evil cry.
Good men perform just deeds, and brave men die,
And win not honour such as gold can give,
While the vain multitudes plod on, and live,
And serve the curse that pins them down:  But I
Think only of the unnumbered broken hearts,
The hunger and the mortal strife for bread,
Old age and youth alike mistaught, misfed,
By want and rags and homelessness made vile,
The griefs and hates, and all the meaner parts
That balance thy one grim misgotten pile.

ARCHIBALD LAMPMAN

## *The Constant Lover*

Out upon it, I have loved
Three whole days together!
And am like to love three more,
If it prove fair weather.

Time shall moult away his wings
  Ere he shall discover
In the whole wide world again
  Such a constant lover.

But the spite on 't is, no praise
  Is due at all to me:
Love with me had made no stays,
  Had it any been but she.

Had it any been but she,
  And that very face,
There had been at least ere this
  A dozen dozen in her place.

SIR JOHN SUCKLING

## The Sorrows Of Werther

Werther had a love for Charlotte
  Such as words could never utter;
Would you know how first he met her?
  She was cutting bread and butter.

Charlotte was a married lady,
  And a moral man was Werther,
And for all the wealth of Indies,
  Would do nothing for to hurt her.

So he sigh'd and pined and ogled,
  And his passion boiled and bubbled,
Till he blew his silly brains out,
  And no more by it was troubled.

Charlotte, having seen his body
  Borne before her on a shutter,
Like a well-conducted person,
  Went on cutting bread and butter.

WILLIAM MAKEPEACE THACKERAY
    * · *

# *The Despairing Lover*

Distracted with care,
For Phyllis the fair;
Since nothing could move her,
Poor Damon, her lover,
Resolves in despair

No longer to languish,
Nor bear so much anguish;
But, mad with his love,
To a precipice goes;
Where a leap from above
Would soon finish his woes.
When in rage he came there,
Beholding how steep
The sides did appear,
And the bottom how deep;
His torments projecting,
And sadly reflecting,
That a lover forsaken
A new love may get;
But a neck, when once broken,
Can never be set:
And that he could die
Whenever he would;
But that he could live
But as long as he could;
How grievous soever
The torment might grow,
He scorn'd to endeavour
To finish it so.
But bold, unconcern'd

At the thoughts of the pain,
He calmly returned
To his cottage again.

WILLIAM WALSH

## On A Certain Lady At Court

I know the thing that's most uncommon;
(Envy, be silent, and attend!);
I know a reasonable woman,
Handsome and witty, yet a friend.
Not warped by passion, awed by rumour,
Not grave through pride, or gay through folly,
An equal mixture of good humour,
And sensible soft melancholy.
'Has she no faults then (Envy says), Sir?'
Yes, she has one, I must aver:
When all the World conspires to praise her,
The woman's deaf, and does not hear.

ALEXANDER POPE

## *On A Painted Woman*

To youths, who hurry thus away,
How silly your desire is
At such an early hour to pay
Your compliments to Iris.

Stop, prithee, stop, ye hasty beaux,
No longer urge this race on;
Though Iris has put on her clothes,
She has not put her face on.

PERCY BYSSHE SHELLEY

*❦ • ❦*


## *Impromptu On Charles II*

God bless our good and gracious King,
Whose promise none relies on;
Who never said a foolish thing,
Nor ever did a wise one.

JOHN WILMOT, EARL OF ROCHESTER

*❦ • ❦*

## The Georges

George the First was always reckoned
Vile, but viler George the Second;
And what mortal ever heard
Any good of George the Third?
When from earth the Fourth descended
(God be praised!) the Georges ended!

WALTER SAVAGE LANDOR

## When A Man
## Hath No Freedom

When a man hath no freedom to fight for at home,
Let him combat for that of his neighbours;
Let him think of the glories of Greece and of Rome,
And get knock'd on the head for his labours.
To do good to mankind is the chivalrous plan,
And, is always as nobly requited;
Then battle for freedom wherever you can,
And, if not shot or hang'd, you'll get knighted.

GEORGE GORDON, LORD BYRON

## The Politician

Carven in leathern mask or brazen face,
    Were I time's sculptor, I would set this man.
    Retreating from the truth, his hawk-eyes scan
The platforms of all public thought for place.
There wriggling with insinuating grace,
    He takes poor hope and effort by the hand,
    And flatters with half-truths and accents bland,
Till even zeal and earnest love grow base.

Knowing no right, save power's grim right-of-way;
    No nobleness, save life's ignoble praise;
No future, save this sordid day to day;
    He is the curse of these material days:
Juggling with mighty wrongs and mightier lies,
This worshipper of Dagon and his flies!

WILFRED CAMPBELL

𝒟 • ℬ

## The Modern Politician

What manner of soul is his to whom high truth
    Is but the plaything of a feverish hour,

A dangling ladder to the ghost of power!
Gone are the grandeurs of the world's iron youth,
When kings were mighty, being made by swords.
Now comes the transit age, the age of brass,
When clowns into the vacant empires pass,
Blinding the multitude with specious words.
To them faith, kinship, truth and verity,
Man's sacred rights and very holiest thing,
Are but the counters at a desperate play,
Flippant and reckless what the end may be,
So that they glitter, each his little day,
The little mimic of a vanished king.

ARCHIBALD LAMPMAN

$\mathcal{A} \cdot \mathcal{B}$

# *Epitaph*

The angler rose, he took his rod,
He kneeled and made his prayers to God.
The living God sat overhead:
The angler tripped, the eels were fed.

ROBERT LOUIS STEVENSON

$\mathcal{A} \cdot \mathcal{B}$

# *We Live In A Rickety House*

We live in a rickety house,
      In a dirty dismal street,
Where the naked hide from day,
      And thieves and drunkards meet.

And pious folks with their tracts,
      When our dens they enter in,
They point to our shirtless backs,
      As the fruits of beer and gin.

And they quote us texts to prove
      That our hearts are hard as stone,
And they feed us with the fact
      That the fault is all our own.

It will be long ere the poor
      Will learn their grog to shun
While it's raiment, food and fire,
      And religion all in one.

I wonder some pious folks
      Can look us straight in the face,
For our ignorance and crime
      Are the Church's shame and disgrace.

We live in a rickety house,
In a dirty dismal street,
Where the naked hide from day,
And thieves and drunkards meet.

ALEXANDER McLACHLAN

☙ • ❧

# *The City Of The End Of Things*

Beside the pounding cataracts
Of midnight streams unknown to us
'Tis builded in the leafless tracts
And valleys huge of Tartarus.
Lurid and lofty and vast it seems;
It hath no rounded name that rings,
But I have heard it called in dreams
The City of the End of Things.

Its roofs and iron towers have grown
None knoweth how high within the night,
But in its murky streets far down
A flaming terrible and bright
Shakes all the stalking shadows there,
Across the walls, across the floors,
And shifts upon the upper air

From out a thousand furnace doors;
And all the while an awful sound
Keeps roaring on continually,
And crashes in the ceaseless round
Of a gigantic harmony.
Through its grim depths re-echoing
And all its weary height of walls,
With measured roar and iron ring,
The inhuman music lifts and falls.
Where no thing rests and no man is,
And only fire and night hold sway;
The beat, the thunder and the hiss
Cease not, and change not, night nor day.
And moving at unheard commands,
The abysses and vast fires between,
Flit figures that with clanking hands
Obey a hideous routine;
They are not flesh, they are not bone,
They see not with the human eye,
And from their iron lips is blown
A dreadful and monotonous cry;
And whoso of our mortal race
Should find that city unaware,
Lean Death would smite him face to face,
And blanch him with its venomed air:

Or caught by the terrific spell,
Each thread of memory snapt and cut,
His soul would shrivel and its shell
Go rattling like an empty nut.

It was not always so, but once,
In days that no man thinks upon,
Fair voices echoed from its stones,
The light above it leaped and shone:
Once there were multitudes of men,
That built that city in their pride,
Until its might was made, and then
They withered age by age and died.
But now of that prodigious race,
Three only in an iron tower,
Set like carved idols face to face,
Remain the masters of its power;
And at the city gate a fourth,
Gigantic and with dreadful eyes,
Sits looking toward the lightless north,
Beyond the reach of memories;
Fast rooted to the lurid floor,
A bulk that never moves a jot,
In his pale body dwells no more,
Or mind or soul, — an idiot!
But some time in the end those three

Shall perish and their hands be still,
And with the master's touch shall flee
Their incommunicable skill.
A stillness absolute as death
Along the slacking wheels shall lie,
And, flagging at a single breath,
The fires shall moulder out and die.
The roar shall vanish at its height,
And over that tremendous town
The silence of eternal night
Shall gather close and settle down.
All its grim grandeur, tower and hall,
Shall be abandoned utterly,
And into rust and dust shall fall
From century to century;
Nor ever living thing shall grow,
Nor trunk of tree, nor blade of grass;
No drop shall fall, no wind shall blow,
Nor sound of any foot shall pass:
Alone of its accursèd state,
One thing the hand of Time shall spare,
For the grim Idiot at the gate
Is deathless and eternal there.

ARCHIBALD LAMPMAN

𝒟 • ℬ

## Sally In Our Alley

Of all the Girls that are so smart
    There's none like pretty SALLY,
She is the Darling of my Heart,
    And she lives in our Alley.
There is no Lady in the Land
    Is half so sweet as SALLY,
She is the Darling of my Heart,
    And she lives in our Alley.

Her Father he makes Cabbage-nets,
    And through the Streets does cry 'em;
Her Mother she sells Laces long,
    To such as please to buy 'em:
But sure such Folks could ne'er beget
    So sweet a Girl as SALLY!
She is the Darling of my Heart,
    And she lives in our Alley.

When she is by I leave my Work,
    (I love her so sincerely)
My Master comes like any Turk,
    And bangs me most severely;
But, let him bang his Belly full,
    I'll bear it all for SALLY;
She is the Darling of my Heart,
    And she lives in our Alley.

Of all the Days that's in the Week,
    I dearly love but one Day,
And that's the Day that comes betwixt
    A Saturday and Monday;
For then I'm drest, all in my best,
    To walk abroad with SALLY;
She is the Darling of my Heart,
    And she lives in our Alley.

My Master carries me to Church,
    And often am I blamed,
Because I leave him in the lurch,
    As soon as Text is named:
I leave the Church in Sermon time,
    And slink away to SALLY;
She is the Darling of my Heart,
    And she lives in our Alley.

When Christmas comes about again,
    O then I shall have Money;
I'll hoard it up, and Box and all
    I'll give it to my Honey:
And, would it were ten thousand Pounds,
    I'd give it all to SALLY;
She is the Darling of my Heart,
    And she lives in our Alley.

My Master and the Neighbours all,
  Make game of me and SALLY;
And (but for her) I'd better be
  A Slave and row a Galley:
But when my seven long Years are out,
  O then I'll marry SALLY!
O then we'll wed and then we'll bed,
  But not in our Alley.

HENRY CAREY

*S • B*

## Terence, This Is Stupid Stuff

'Terence, this is stupid stuff!
You eat your victuals fast enough;
There can't be much amiss, 'tis clear,
To see the rate you drink your beer.
But oh, good Lord, the verse you make,
It gives a chap the belly-ache!
The cow, the old cow, she is dead;
It sleeps well, the horned head...
We poor lads, 'tis our turn now
To hear such tunes as killed the cow!

Pretty friendship 'tis to rhyme
Your friends to death before their time
Moping melancholy mad!
Come, pipe a tune to dance to, lad!'

Why, if 'tis dancing you would be,
There's brisker pipes than poetry.
Say, for what were hop-yards meant,
Or why was Burton built on Trent?
Oh many a peer of England brews
Livelier liquor than the Muse,
And malt does more than Milton can
To justify God's ways to man.
Ale, man, ale's the stuff to drink
For fellows whom it hurts to think:
Look into the pewter pot
To see the world as the world's not.
And faith, 'tis pleasant till 'tis past:
The mischief is that 'twill not last.
Oh I have been to Ludlow fair
And left my necktie God knows where,
And carried half way home, or near,
Pints and quarts of Ludlow beer:
Then the world seemed none so bad,
And I myself a sterling lad;

And down in lovely muck I've lain,
Happy till I woke again.
Then I saw the morning sky:
Heigho, the tale was all a lie;
The world, it was the old world yet,
I was I, my things were wet,
And nothing now remained to do
But begin the game anew.

Therefore, since the world has still
Much good, but much less good than ill,
And while the sun and moon endure
Luck's a chance, but trouble's sure,
I'd face it as a wise man would,
And train for ill and not for good.
'Tis true, the stuff I bring for sale
Is not so brisk a brew as ale:
Out of a stem that scored the hand
I wrung it in a weary land.
But take it: if the smack is sour,
The better for the embittered hour;
It should do good to heart and head
When your soul is in my soul's stead;
And I will friend you, if I may,
In the dark and cloudy day.

There was a king reigned in the East:
There, when kings will sit to feast,
They get their fill before they think
With poisoned meat and poisoned drink.
He gathered all the springs to birth
From the many-venomed earth;
First a little, thence to more,
He sampled all her killing store;
And easy, smiling, seasoned sound,
Sate the king when healths went round.
They put arsenic in his meat
And stared aghast to watch him eat;
They poured strychnine in his cup
And shook to see him drink it up:
They shook, they stared as white's their shirt:
Them it was their poison hurt.
— I tell the tale that I heard told.
Mithridates, he died old.

A. E. HOUSMAN

$\mathcal{O} \cdot \mathcal{B}$

# A Satirical Elegy

His Grace! impossible! what, dead!
Of old age, too, and in his bed!
And could that Mighty Warrior fall?
And so inglorious, after all!
Well, since he's gone, no matter how,
The last loud trump must wake him now:
And, trust me, as the noise grows stronger,
He'd wish to sleep a little longer.
And could he be indeed so old
As by the newspapers we're told?
Threescore, I think, is pretty high;
'Twas time in conscience he should die.
This world he cumber'd long enough;
He burnt his candle to the snuff;
And that's the reason, some folks think,
He left behind so great a stink.
Behold his funeral appears,
Nor widows' sighs, nor orphans' tears,
Wont at such times each heart to pierce,
Attend the progress of his hearse.
But what of that, his friends may say,
He had those honours in his day.

True to his profit and his pride,
He made them weep before he died.

    Come hither, all ye empty things!
Ye bubbles rais'd by breath of Kings!
Who float upon the tide of state,
Come hither, and behold your fate!
Let pride be taught by this rebuke,
How very mean a thing's a duke;
From all his ill-got honours flung,
Turn'd to that dirt from whence he sprung.

JONATHAN SWIFT

    * · *

## Dr Johnson

Here lies poor Johnson. Reader! have a care:
Tread lightly, lest you rouse a sleeping bear:
  Religious, moral, generous and humane,
  He was, but self-conceited, rude and vain:
    Ill-bred and overbearing in dispute,
  A scholar, and a Christian, yet a brute.
Would you know all his wisdom and his folly,
His actions, sayings, mirth, and melancholy,

Boswell and Thrale, retailers of his wit,
Will tell you how he wrote, and talked, and spit.

SOAME JENYNS

℘ • ℘

## *Bardolph Redivivus*

When Plato in his cradle slept, the bees
      Swarmed at his lips, for so the legend goes;
But, fickle creatures, coy and hard to please,
      They sure mistook, and settled on your nose!
Mayhap it is your wife who love to teaze,

And on your patient knob incessant blows
Doth strike for her own sweet amusement's sake.
      Perchance it cometh of the drams you take,
This subtle, fiery redness-who can tell?
      Ay, who can tell, great nasal organ bright!
What vintages and distillations dwell
      Pent in those caverns awful in our sight?
Dark with the morn, but, in the darkness, light,
      A purple cloud by day, a flame by night!

CHARLES MAIR

℘ • ℘

## *The Lover Showeth How He Is Forsaken Of Such As He Sometime Enjoyed*

They flee from me, that sometime did me seek,
　　With naked foot stalking in my chamber.
Once have I seen them gentle, tame, and meek,
　　That now are wild, and do not once remember
That sometime they have put themselves in danger
　　To take bread at my hand; and now they range,
　　　　Busily seeking in continual change.

Thank'd be fortune, it hath been otherwise
　　Twenty times better; but once, in special,
　　　　In thin array, after a pleasant guise,
When her loose gown from her shoulders did fall,
And she me caught in her arms long and small,
　　And therewithall so sweetly did me kiss,
And softly said, 'Dear heart, how like you this?'

It was no dream, for I lay broad waking:
But all is turn'd now, through my gentleness,
　　Into a bitter fashion of forsaking;
And I have leave to go, of her goodness;

And she also to use new fangleness.
But since that I unkindly so am served,
I fain would know what she hath deserved.

SIR THOMAS WYATT

## Upon Julia's Clothes

Whenas in silks my Julia goes,
Then, then, methinks, how sweetly flows
The liquefaction of her clothes!

Next, when I cast mine eyes and see
That brave vibration each way free,
O how that glittering taketh me!

ROBERT HERRICK

## Woman

When lovely woman stoops to folly,
And finds too late that men betray,
What charm can soothe her melancholy?
What art can wash her tears away?

The only art her guilt to cover,
  To hide her shame from ev'ry eye,
To give repentance to her lover,
  And wring his bosom is — to die.

OLIVER GOLDSMITH

*℘ • ℘*

## *Somebody*

Somebody being a nobody,
Thinking to look like a somebody,
Said that he thought me a nobody:
Good little somebody-nobody,
Had you not known me a somebody,
Would you have called me a nobody?

ALFRED, LORD TENNYSON

*℘ • ℘*

## *The Workman's Song*

Come all ye weary sons of toil,
  And listen to my song,
We've eat oppression's bitter bread,
  And eat it far too long.

Oh poverty's a dreadful thing,
  Her bite is always keen,
Oppression's foot is always shod,
  And greed is always mean.

The great, the greasy multitude,
  Should neither think nor feel,
They've but to lick the hand that holds
  Their noses to the wheel.

ALEXANDER McLACHLAN

$\mathcal{O} \cdot \mathcal{B}$

## *Some Can Gaze And Not Be Sick*

Some can gaze and not be sick,
But I could never learn the trick.
There's this to say for blood and breath,
They give a man a taste for death.

A. E. HOUSMAN

$\mathcal{O} \cdot \mathcal{B}$

# The Hyænas

After the burial-parties leave
    And the baffled kites have fled;
The wise hyænas come out at eve
    To take account of our dead.

How he died and why he died
    Troubles them not a whit.
They snout the bushes and stones aside
    And dig till they come to it.

They are only resolute they shall eat
    That they and their mates may thrive,
And they know that the dead are safer meat
    Than the weakest thing alive.

(For a goat may butt, and a worm may sting,
    And a child will sometimes stand;
But a poor dead soldier of the King
    Can never lift a hand.)

They whoop and halloo and scatter the dirt
    Until their tushes white
Take good hold of the Army shirt,
    And tug the corpse to light,

And the pitiful face is shown again
  For an instant ere they close;
But it is not discovered to living men —
  Only to God and to those

Who, being soulless, are free from shame,
  Whatever meat they may find.
Nor do they defile the dead man's name —
  That is reserved for his kind.

RUDYARD KIPLING

$\mathcal{D} \cdot \mathcal{B}$

## *The Ruined Maid*

'O 'Melia, my dear, this does everything crown!
Who could have supposed I should meet you in Town?
And whence such fair garments, such prosperi-ty?' —
'O didn't you know I'd been ruined?' said she.

— 'You left us in tatters, without shoes or socks,
Tired of digging potatoes, and spudding up docks;
And now you've gay bracelets and bright feathers three!' —
'Yes: that's how we dress when we're ruined,' said she.

— 'At home in the barton you said 'thee' and 'thou',
And 'thik oon', and 'theäs oon', and 't'other'; but now
Your talking quite fits 'ee for high compa-ny!' —
'Some polish is gained with one's ruin,' said she.

— 'Your hands were like paws then, your face blue and bleak
But now I'm bewitched by your delicate cheek,
And your little gloves fit as on any la-dy!' —
'We never do work when we're ruined,' said she.

— 'You used to call home-life a hag-ridden dream,
And you'd sigh, and you'd sock; but at present you seem
To know not of megrims or melancho-ly!' —
'True. One's pretty lively when ruined,' said she.

— 'I wish I had feathers, a fine sweeping gown,
And a delicate face, and could strut about Town!' —
'My dear — a raw country girl, such as you be,
Cannot quite expect that. You ain't ruined,' said she.

THOMAS HARDY

*𝒯 • ℬ*

# 'Twas Ever Thus

*(In imitation of Thomas Moore)*

I never reared a young gazelle,
(Because, you see, I never tried);
But had it known and loved me well,
No doubt the creature would have died.
My rich and aged Uncle John
Has known me long and loves me well,
But still persists in living on —
I would he were a young gazelle.

I never loved a tree or flower;
But, if I had, I beg to say
The blight, the wind, the sun, or shower
Would soon have withered it away.
I've dearly loved my Uncle John,
From childhood to the present hour,
And yet he will go living on —
I would he were a tree or flower!

HENRY SAMBROOKE LEIGH

*ℰ • ℬ*

## *Infant Innocence*

The Grizzly Bear is huge and wild;
He has devoured the infant child.
The infant child is not aware
It has been eaten by the bear.

A. E. HOUSMAN

## *In Memoriam*

Willie had a purple monkey climbing on a yellow stick,
And when he had sucked the paint all off it made him deadly
    sick;
And in his latest hours he clasped that monkey in his hand,
And bade good-bye to earth and went into a better land.

Oh no more he'll shoot his sister with his little wooden gun;
And no more he'll twist the pussy's tail and make her yowl,
    for fun.
The pussy's tail now stands out straight; the gun is laid aside;
The monkey doesn't jump around since little Willie died.

MAX ADELER

## *Nonsense*

Good reader, if you e'er have seen,
When Phoebus hastens to his pillow,
The mermaids, with their tresses green,
Dancing upon the western billow;
If you have seen, at twilight dim,
When the lone spirit's vesper-hymn
Floats wild along the winding shore,
If you have seen, through mist of eve,
The fairy train their ringlets weave,
Glancing along the spangled green; -
If you have seen all this and more,
God bless me! what a deal you've seen!

THOMAS MOORE

⊘ • ℬ

## *Finis*

I strove with none, for none was worth my strife.
Nature I loved and, next to Nature, Art:
I warm'd both hands before the fire of life;
It sinks, and I am ready to depart.

WALTER SAVAGE LANDOR

# Travel

AND

# Place

## *From A Railway Carriage*

Faster than fairies, faster than witches,
Bridges and houses, hedges and ditches;
And charging along like troops in a battle
All through the meadows the horses and cattle:
All of the sights of the hill and the plain
Fly as thick as driving rain;
And ever again, in the wink of an eye,
Painted stations whistle by.

Here is a child who clambers and scrambles,
All by himself and gathering brambles;
Here is a tramp who stands and gazes;
And there is the green for stringing the daisies!
Here is a cart run away in the road
Lumping along with man and load;
And here is a mill, and there is a river:
Each a glimpse and gone for ever!

ROBERT LOUIS STEVENSON

*𝒟 • ℛ*

# *London*

I wander through each chartered street,
    Near where the chartered Thames does flow,
And mark in every face I meet,
    Marks of weakness, marks of woe.

In every cry of every man,
    In every infant's cry of fear,
In every voice, in every ban,
    The mind-forged manacles I hear:

How the chimney-sweeper's cry
    Every blackening church appalls,
And the hapless soldier's sigh
    Runs in blood down palace walls.

But most, through midnight streets I hear
    How the youthful harlot's curse
Blasts the new-born infant's tear,
    And blights with plagues the marriage hearse.

WILLIAM BLAKE

# *Composed Upon Westminster Bridge*

### Sept. 3, 1802

Earth has not anything to show more fair:
Dull would he be of soul who could pass by
A sight so touching in its majesty:
This City now doth like a garment wear
The beauty of the morning; silent, bare,
Ships, towers, domes, theatres, and temples lie
Open unto the fields, and to the sky;
All bright and glittering in the smokeless air.
Never did sun more beautifully steep
In his first splendour, valley, rock, or hill;
Ne'er saw I, never felt, a calm so deep!
The river glideth at his own sweet will:
Dear God! the very houses seem asleep;
And all that mighty heart is lying still!

WILLIAM WORDSWORTH

## *Exile*

I chose the place where I would rest
When death should come to claim me,
With the red-rose roots to wrap my breast
And a quiet stone to name me.

But I am laid on a northern steep
With the roaring tides below me,
And only the frosts to bind my sleep,
And only the winds to know me.

MARJORIE PICKTHALL

♘ • ♗

## *Symphony In Yellow*

An omnibus across the bridge
Crawls like a yellow butterfly,
And, here and there a passer-by
Shows like a little restless midge.

Big barges full of yellow hay
Are moored against the shadowy wharf,
And, like a yellow silken scarf,
The thick fog hangs along the quay.

The yellow leaves begin to fade
And flutter from the Temple elms,
And at my feet the pale green Thames
Lies like a rod of rippled jade.

OSCAR WILDE

*❦ · ❦*

## *The Way Through The Woods*

They shut the road through the woods
Seventy years ago.
Weather and rain have undone it again,
And now you would never know
There was once a road through the woods
Before they planted the trees.
It is underneath the coppice and heath,
And the thin anemones.
Only the keeper sees
That, where the ring-dove broods,
And the badgers roll at ease,
There was once a road through the woods.

Yet, if you enter the woods
Of a summer evening late,
When the night-air cools on the trout-ringed pools

Where the otter whistles his mate,
(They fear not men in the woods,
Because they see so few);
You will hear the beat of a horse's feet,
And the swish of a skirt in the dew,
Steadily cantering through
The misty solitudes,
As though they perfectly knew
The old lost road through the woods...
But there is no road through the woods.

RUDYARD KIPLING

ℰ • ℬ

## *Wenlock Edge*

On Wenlock Edge the wood's in trouble;
His forest fleece the Wrekin heaves;
The gale, it plies the saplings double,
And thick on Severn snow the leaves.

'Twould blow like this through holt and hanger
When Uricon the city stood;
'Tis the old wind in the old anger,
But then it threshed another wood.

Then, 'twas before my time, the Roman
At yonder heaving hill would stare:
The blood that warms an English yeoman,
The thoughts that hurt him, they were there.

There, like the wind through woods in riot,
Through him the gale of life blew high;
The tree of man was never quiet:
Then 'twas the Roman, now 'tis I.

The gale, it plies the saplings double,
It blows so hard, 'twill soon be gone:
Today the Roman and his trouble
Are ashes under Uricon.

A. E. HOUSMAN

*ℰ • ℬ*

## *Dover Beach*

The sea is calm to-night.
The tide is full, the moon lies fair
Upon the straits; on the French coast the light
Gleams and is gone; the cliffs of England stand;
Glimmering and vast, out in the tranquil bay.
Come to the window, sweet is the night-air!

Only, from the long line of spray
Where the sea meets the moon-blanched land,
Listen! you hear the grating roar
Of pebbles which the waves draw back, and fling,
At their return, up the high strand,
Begin, and cease, and then again begin,
With tremulous cadence slow, and bring
The eternal note of sadness in.

Sophocles long ago
Heard it in the Aegaean, and it brought
Into his mind the turbid ebb and flow
Of human misery; we
Find also in the sound a thought,
Hearing it by this distant northern sea.

The Sea of Faith
Was once, too, at the full, and round earth's shore
Lay like the folds of a bright girdle furled.
But now I only hear
Its melancholy, long, withdrawing roar,
Retreating, to the breath
Of the night-wind, down the vast edges drear
And naked shingles of the world.

Ah, love, let us be true
To one another! for the world, which seems
To lie before us like a land of dreams,
So various, so beautiful, so new,
Hath really neither joy, nor love, nor light,
Nor certitude, nor peace, nor help for pain;
And we are here as on a darkling plain
Swept with confused alarms of struggle and flight,
Where ignorant armies clash by night.

MATTHEW ARNOLD

𝒟 • ℬ

## Home Thoughts, From Abroad

Oh, to be in England
Now that April's there,
And whoever wakes in England
Sees, some morning, unaware,
That the lowest boughs and the brushwood sheaf
Round the elm-tree bole are in tiny leaf,
While the chaffinch sings on the orchard bough
In England — now!

And after April, when May follows,
And the whitethroat builds, and all the swallows!
Hark, where my blossom'd pear-tree in the hedge
Leans to the field and scatters on the clover
Blossoms and dewdrops — at the bent spray's edge —
That's the wise thrush; he sings each song twice over,
Lest you should think he never could recapture
The first fine careless rapture!
And though the fields look rough with hoary dew,
All will be gay when noontide wakes anew
The buttercups, the little children's dower
— Far brighter than this gaudy melon-flower!

ROBERT BROWNING

*ℐ • ℬ*

## *My Heart's In The Highlands*

My heart's in the Highlands, my heart is not here;
My heart's in the Highlands a-chasing the deer;
A-chasing the wild deer, and following the roe,
My heart's in the Highlands wherever I go.

Farewell to the Highlands, farewell to the North,
The birthplace of Valour, the country of Worth;
Wherever I wander, wherever I rove,
The hills of the Highlands for ever I love.

Farewell to the mountains high covered with snow;
Farewell to the straths and green valleys below;
Farewell to the forests and wild-hanging woods;
Farewell to the torrents and loud-pouring floods.

My heart's in the Highlands, my heart is not here;
My heart's in the Highlands a-chasing the deer;
A-chasing the wild deer, and following the roe,
My heart's in the Highlands wherever I go.

ROBERT BURNS

## *A Niagara Landscape*

Heavy with haze that merges and melts free
Into the measureless depth on either hand,
The full day rests upon the luminous land
In one long noon of golden reverie.
Now hath the harvest come and gone with glee.
The shaven fields stretch smooth and clean away,
Purple and green, and yellow, and soft grey,

Chequered with orchards. Farther still I see
Towns and dim villages, whose roof-tops fill
    The distant mist, yet scarcely catch the view.
Thorold set sultry on its plateau'd hill,
    And far to westward, where yon pointed towers
Rise faint and ruddy from the vaporous blue,
    Saint Catharines, city of the host of flowers.

ARCHIBALD LAMPMAN

## A Canadian Boat Song

Faintly as tolls the evening chime
Our voices keep tune and our oars keep time.
Soon as the woods on shore look dim,
We'll sing at St. Anne's our parting hymn.
Row, brothers, row, the stream runs fast,
The rapids are near and the daylight's past.

Why should we yet our sail unfurl?
There is not a breath the blue wave to curl.
But when the wind blows off the shore,
Oh! sweetly we'll rest our weary oar.
Blow, breezes, blow, the stream runs fast,
The rapids are near and the daylight's past.

Utawas' tide! this trembling moon
Shall see us float over thy surges soon.
Saint of this green isle! hear our prayers,
Oh, grant us cool heavens and favouring airs.
Blow, breezes, blow, the stream runs fast,
The rapids are near and the daylight's past.

THOMAS MOORE

## A Psalm Of Montreal

Stowed away in a Montreal lumber room
The Discobolus standeth and turneth his face to the wall;
Dusty, cobweb-covered, maimed and set at naught,
Beauty crieth in an attic and no man regardeth:

O God! O Montreal!

Beautiful by night and day, beautiful in summer and winter,
Whole or maimed, always and alike beautiful
He preacheth gospel of grace to the skin of owls
And to one who seasoneth the skins of Canadian owls:

O God! O Montreal!

When I saw him I was wroth and I said, 'O Discobolus!
Beautiful Discobolus, a Prince both among gods and men!
What doest thou here, how camest thou hither, Discobolus,
Preaching gospel in vain to the skins of owls?'

O God! O Montreal!

And I turned to the man of skins and said unto him, 'O thou
    man of skins,
Wherefore hast thou done thus to shame the beauty of the
    Discobolus?'
But the Lord had hardened the heart of the man of skins
And he answered, 'My brother-in-law is haberdasher to Mr.
    Spurgeon.'

O God! O Montreal!

'The Discobolus is put here because he is vulgar
He has neither vest nor pants with which to cover his limbs;
I, Sir, am a person of most respectable connections
My brother-in-law is haberdasher to Mr. Spurgeon.'

O God! O Montreal!

Then I said, 'O brother-in-law to Mr. Spurgeon's haberdasher,
Who seasonest also the skins of Canadian owls,
Thou callest trousers 'pants', whereas I call them 'trousers'
Therefore thou art in hell-fire and may the Lord pity thee!'

O God! O Montreal!

'Preferrest thou the gospel of Montreal to the gospel of Hellas,
  The gospel of thy connection with Mr. Spurgeon's haber-
  dashery to the gospel of Discobolus?'
Yet none the less blasphemed he beauty saying, 'The
  Discobolus hath no gospel,
But my brother-in-law is haberdasher to Mr. Spurgeon.'
                                                O God! O Montreal!

SAMUEL BUTLER

*ℰ • ℬ*

# *Home Thoughts, From The Sea*

Nobly, nobly, Cape Saint Vincent to the Northwest died
  away;
Sunset ran, one glorious blood-red, reeking into Cadiz Bay;
Bluish 'mid the burning water, full in face Trafalgar lay;
In the dimmest Northeast distance dawned Gibraltar  grand
  and gray;
'Here and here did England help me: how can I help
  England?' — say,
Whoso turns as I, this evening, turn to God to praise and pray,
While Jove's planet rises yonder, silent over Africa.

ROBERT BROWNING

*ℰ • ℬ*

# *Adlestrop*

Yes. I remember Adlestrop —
The name, because one afternoon
Of heat the express-train drew up there
Unwontedly. It was late June.

The steam hissed. Someone cleared his throat
No one left and no one came
On the bare platform. What I saw
Was Adlestrop — only the name

And willows, willow-herb, and grass,
And meadowsweet, and haycocks dry,
No whit less still and lonely fair
Than the high cloudlets in the sky.

And for that minute a blackbird sang
Close by, and round him, mistier,
Farther and farther, all the birds
Of Oxfordshire and Gloucestershire.

EDWARD THOMAS

*E • B*

## *North Labrador*

A land of leaning ice
Hugged by plaster-grey arches of sky,
Flings itself silently
Into eternity.

'Has no one come here to win you,
Or left you with the faintest blush
Upon your glittering breasts?
Have you no memories, O Darkly Bright?'

Cold-hushed, there is only the shifting of moments
That journey toward no Spring —
No birth, no death, no time nor sun
In answer.

HART CRANE

*∂ • β*

## *Midnight On The Great Western*

In the third-class seat sat the journeying boy,
And the roof-lamp's oily flame
Played down on his listless form and face,
Bewrapt past knowing to what he was going,
Or whence he came.

In the band of his hat the journeying boy
Had a ticket stuck; and a string
Around his neck bore the key of his box,
That twinkled gleams of the lamp's sad beams
Like a living thing.

What past can be yours, O journeying boy
Towards a world unknown,
Who calmly, as if incurious quite
On all at stake, can undertake
This plunge alone?

Knows your soul a sphere, O journeying boy,
Our rude realms far above,
Whence with spacious vision you mark and mete
This region of sin that you find you in,
But are not of?

THOMAS HARDY

## *On A Rhine Steamer*

Republic of the West
    Enlightened, free, sublime,
Unquestionably best
    Production of our time,

The telephone is thine,
    And thine the Pullman car,
The caucus, the divine
    Intense electric star.

To thee we likewise owe
    The venerable names
Of Edgar Allan Poe,
    And Mr. Henry James.

In short it's due to thee,
    Thou kind of Western star,
That we have come to be
    Precisely what we are.

But every now and then,
    It cannot be denied,
You breed a kind of men
    Who are not dignified,

Or courteous or refined,
　　Benevolent or wise,
Or gifted with a mind
　　Beyond the common size,

Or notable for tact,
　　Agreeable to me,
Or anything, in fact,
　　That people ought to be.

J. K. STEPHEN

*❧ • ❧*

## *The Banks o' Doon*

Ye flowery banks o' bonnie Doon,
　　How can ye blume sae fair!
How can ye chant, ye little birds,
　　And I sae fu' o' care!

Thou'll break my heart, thou bonnie bird,
　　That sings upon the bough;
Thou minds me o' the happy days
　　When my fause luve was true.

Thou'll break my heart, thou bonnie bird,
    That sings beside thy mate;
For sae I sat, and sae I sang,
    And wist na o' my fate.

Aft hae I roved by bonnie Doon,
    To see the woodbine twine;
And ilka bird sang o' its luve,
    And sae did I o' mine.

Wi' lightsome heart I pu'd a rose
    Frae off its thorny tree;
And my fause luver staw the rose,
    But left the thorn wi' me.

ROBERT BURNS

*R · B*

## Sweet Afton

Flow gently, sweet Afton, among thy green braes,
Flow gently, I'll sing thee a song in thy praise;
My Mary's asleep by the murmuring stream,
Flow gently, sweet Afton, disturb not her dream.

Thou stock-dove whose echo resounds thro' the glen,
Ye wild whistling blackbirds in yon thorny den,
Thou green-crested lapwing, thy screaming forbear,
I charge you, disturb not my slumbering fair.

How lofty, sweet Afton, thy neighbouring hills,
Far marked with the courses of clear, winding rills;
There daily I wander, as noon rises high,
My flocks and my Mary's sweet cot in my eye.

How pleasant thy banks and green valleys below,
Where wild in the woodlands the primroses blow;
There oft, as mild ev'ning weeps over the lea,
The sweet-scented birk shades my Mary and me.

Thy crystal stream, Afton, how lovely it glides,
And winds by the cot where my Mary resides;
How wanton thy waters her snowy feet lave,
As, gathering sweet flowerets, she stems thy clear wave.

Flow gently, sweet Afton, among thy green braes,
Flow gently, sweet river, the theme of my lays;
My Mary's asleep by thy murmuring stream,
Flow gently, sweet Afton, disturb not her dream.

ROBERT BURNS

*S · B*

## *In Rotten Row*

In Rotten Row a cigarette
I sat and smoked, with no regret
For all the tumult that had been.
The distances were still and green,
And streaked with shadows cool and wet.

Two sweethearts on a bench were set,
Two birds among the boughs were met;
So love and song were heard and seen
In Rotten Row.

A horse or two there was to fret
The soundless sand; but work and debt,
Fair flowers and falling leaves between,
While clocks are chiming clear and keen,
A man may very well forget
In Rotten Row.

WILLIAM ERNEST HENLEY

## *Facing West From California's Shores*

Facing west, from California's shores,

Inquiring, tireless, seeking what is yet unfound,

I, a child, very old, over waves, towards the house of mater-
nity, the land of migrations, look afar,

Look off the shores of my Western Sea — the circle almost circled;

For, starting westward from Hindustan, from the vales of
Kashmere,

From Asia — from the north — from the God, the sage, and
the hero,

From the south — from the flowery peninsulas, and the spice
islands;

Long having wander'd since — round the earth having wander'd,

Now I face home again — very pleas'd and joyous;

(But where is what I started for, so long ago?

And why is it yet unfound?)

WALT WHITMAN

$\mathscr{O} \cdot \mathscr{B}$

## *To Brooklyn Bridge*

How many dawns, chill from his rippling rest

The seagull's wings shall dip and pivot him,

Shedding white rings of tumult, building high

Over the chained bay waters Liberty —

Then, with inviolate curve, forsake our eyes
As apparitional as sails that cross
Some page of figures to be filed away;
— Till elevators drop us from our day . . .

I think of cinemas, panoramic sleights
With multitudes bent toward some flashing scene
Never disclosed, but hastened to again,
Foretold to other eyes on the same screen;

And Thee, across the harbor, silver-paced
As though the sun took step of thee, yet left
Some motion ever unspent in thy stride, —
Implicitly thy freedom staying thee!

Out of some subway scuttle, cell or loft
A bedlamite speeds to thy parapets,
Tilting there momently, shrill shirt ballooning,
A jest falls from the speechless caravan.

Down Wall, from girder into street noon leaks,
A rip-tooth of the sky's acetylene;
All afternoon the cloud-flown derricks turn . . .
Thy cables breathe the North Atlantic still.

And obscure as that heaven of the Jews,
Thy guerdon . . . Accolade thou dost bestow
Of anonymity time cannot raise:
Vibrant reprieve and pardon thou dost show.

O harp and altar, of the fury fused,
(How could mere toil align thy choiring strings!)
Terrific threshold of the prophet's pledge,
Prayer of pariah, and the lover's cry, —

Again the traffic lights that skim thy swift
Unfractioned idiom, immaculate sigh of stars,
Beading thy path — condense eternity:
And we have seen night lifted in thine arms.

Under thy shadow by the piers I waited;
Only in darkness is thy shadow clear.
The City's fiery parcels all undone,
Already snow submerges an iron year . . .

O Sleepless as the river under thee,
Vaulting the sea, the prairies' dreaming sod,
Unto us lowliest sometime sweep, descend
And of the curveship lend a myth to God.

HART CRANE

☙ • ❧

# Once I Pass'd Through A Populous City

Once I pass'd through a populous city imprinting my brain
    for future use with its shows, architecture, customs,
    traditions,
Yet now of all that city I remember only a woman I casually
    met there who detain'd me for love of me,
Day by day and night by night we were together — all else
    has long been forgotten by me,
I remember I say only that woman who passionately clung to me
Again we wander, we love, we separate again,
Again she holds me by the hand, I must not go,
I see her close beside me with silent lips sad and tremulous.

WALT WHITMAN

# I Travelled Among Unknown Men

I travelled among unknown men,
    In lands beyond the sea;
Nor, England! did I know till then
    What love I bore to thee.

'Tis past, that melancholy dream!
    Nor will I quit thy shore
A second time; for still I seem
    To love thee more and more.

Among thy mountains did I feel
    The joy of my desire;
And she I cherished turned her wheel
    Beside an English fire.

Thy mornings showed, thy nights concealed,
    The bowers where Lucy played;
And thine too is the last green field
    That Lucy's eyes surveyed.

WILLIAM WORDSWORTH

# I Knew By The Smoke That So Gracefully Curled

I KNEW by the smoke that so gracefully curled
    Above the green elms, that a cottage was near,
And I said, 'If there's peace to be found in the world,
    A heart that is humble might hope for it here!'

It was noon, and on flowers that languished around
    In silence reposed the voluptuous bee;
Every leaf was at rest, and I heard not a sound
    But the woodpecker tapping the hollow beech tree.

And 'Here in this lone little wood,' I exclaimed,
    'With a maid who was lovely to soul and to eye,
Who would blush when I praised her, and weep if I
      blamed,
    How blest could I live, and how calm could I die!

'By the shade of yon sumach, whose red beity dips
    In the gush of the fountain, how sweet to recline,
And to know that I sighed upon innocent lips,
    Which had never been sighed on by any but mine!'

THOMAS MOORE

❧ • ☙

# Reflection

AND

# Comment

## *Daffodils*

I wander'd lonely as a cloud
That floats on high o'er vales and hills,
When all at once I saw a crowd,
A host of golden daffodils,
Beside the lake, beneath the trees,
Fluttering and dancing in the breeze.

Continuous as the stars that shine
And twinkle on the milky way,
They stretched in never-ending line
Along the margin of a bay:
Ten thousand saw I at a glance,
Tossing their heads in sprightly dance.

The waves beside them danced, but they
Out-did the sparkling waves in glee:
A poet could not but be gay
In such a jocund company!
I gazed — and gazed — but little thought
What wealth the show to me had brought:

For oft, when on my couch I lie
In vacant or in pensive mood,

They flash upon that inward eye
Which is the bliss of solitude;
And then my heart with pleasure fills,
And dances with the daffodils.

WILLIAM WORDSWORTH

* • *

## *Alone*

From childhood's hour I have not been
As others were; I have not seen
As others saw; I could not bring
My passions from a common spring.
From the same source I have not taken
My sorrow; I could not awaken
My heart to joy at the same tone;
And all I loved, I loved alone.
Then — in my childhood, in the dawn
Of a most stormy life — was drawn
From every depth of good and ill
The mystery which binds me still:
From the torrent, or the fountain,
From the red cliff of the mountain,

From the sun that round me rolled

In its autumn tint of gold,

From the lightning in the sky

As it passed me flying by,

From the thunder and the storm,

And the cloud that took the form

(When the rest of Heaven was blue)

Of a demon in my view.


EDGAR ALLAN POE

𝒮 · ℬ


## The World Is Too Much With Us

The world is too much with us; late and soon,

Getting and spending, we lay waste our powers:

Little we see in Nature that is ours;

We have given our hearts away, a sordid boon!

The Sea that bares her bosom to the moon;

The winds that will be howling at all hours,

And are up-gathered now like sleeping flowers;

For this, for everything, we are out of tune;

It moves us not. — Great God! I'd rather be

A Pagan suckled in a creed outworn;

So might I, standing on this pleasant lea,
Have glimpses that would make me less forlorn;
Have sight of Proteus rising from the sea;
Or hear old Triton blow his wreathed horn.

WILLIAM WORDSWORTH

## The Night Has A Thousand Eyes

The night has a thousand eyes,
And the day but one;
Yet the light of the bright world dies
With the dying sun.

The mind has a thousand eyes,
And the heart but one;
Yet the light of a whole life dies
When love is done.

FRANCIS WILLIAM BOURDILLON

## *To Helen*

Helen, thy beauty is to me
Like those Nicean barks of yore
That gently, o'er a perfumed sea,
The weary, way-worn wanderer bore
To his own native shore.

On desperate seas long wont to roam,
Thy hyacinth hair, thy classic face,
Thy Naiad airs have brought me home
To the glory that was Greece,
To the grandeur that was Rome.

Lo, in yon brilliant window niche
How statue-like I see thee stand,
The agate lamp within thy hand,
Ah! Psyche, from the regions which
Are Holy Land!

EDGAR ALLAN POE

# *I Sit And Look Out*

I sit and look out upon all the sorrows of the world, and
    upon all oppression and shame,

I hear secret convulsive sobs from young men at anguish
    with themselves, remorseful after deeds done;

I see in low life the mother misused by her children, dying,
    neglected, gaunt, desperate;

I see the wife misused by her husband, I see the treacherous
    seducer of young women,

I mark the ranklings of jealousy and unrequited love
    attempted to be hid, I see these sights on the earth,

I see the workings of battle, pestilence, tyranny, I see martyrs
    and prisoners,

I observe a famine at sea, I observe the sailors casting lots
    who shall be kill'd to preserve the lives of the rest;

I observe the slights and degradations cast by arrogant
    persons upon laborers, the poor, and upon negroes, and the
    like;

All these — all the meanness and agony without end, I
    sitting, look out upon,

See, hear, and am silent.

WALT WHITMAN

&#x222E; &middot; &#x212C;

# *We Wear The Mask*

We wear the mask that grins and lies,
It hides our cheeks and shades our eyes, —
This debt we pay to human guile;
With torn and bleeding hearts we smile,
And mouth with myriad subtleties.

Why should the world be overwise,
In counting all our tears and sighs?
Nay, let them only see us, while
We wear the mask.

We smile, but, O great Christ, our cries
To thee from tortured souls arise.
We sing, but oh the clay is vile
Beneath our feet, and long the mile;
But let the world dream otherwise,
We wear the mask!

PAUL LAURENCE DUNBAR

# How Like A Winter Hath My Absence Been

How like a winter hath my absence been
From Thee, the pleasure of the fleeting year!
What freezings have I felt; what dark days seen,
What old December's bareness everywhere!
And yet this time removed was summer's time:
The teeming autumn big with rich increase,
Bearing the wanton burden of the prime
Like widow'd wombs after their lords' decease;
Yet this abundant issue seem'd to me
But hope of orphans, and unfather'd fruit;
For summer and his pleasures wait on thee,
And, thou away, the very birds are mute;
Or if they sing, 'tis with so dull a cheer,
That leaves look pale, dreading the winter's near.

WILLIAM SHAKESPEARE

ℰ • ℬ

# Sympathy

I know what the caged bird feels, alas!
When the sun is bright on the upland slopes;
When the wind stirs soft through the springing grass,
And the river flows like a stream of glass;
When the first bird sings and the first bud opes,
And the faint perfume from its chalice steals—
I know what the caged bird feels!

I know why the caged bird beats his wing
Till its blood is red on the cruel bars;
For he must fly back to his perch and cling
When he fain would be on the bough a-swing;
And a pain still throbs in the old, old scars
And they pulse again with a keener sting—
I know why he beats his wing!

I know why the caged bird sings, ah me,
When his wing is bruised and his bosom sore, —
When he beats his bars and he would be free;
It is not a carol of joy or glee,
But a prayer that he sends from his heart's deep core,
But a plea, that upward to Heaven he flings—
I know why the caged bird sings!

PAUL LAURENCE DUNBAR

## *The Owl*

Downhill I came, hungry, and yet not starved;
Cold, yet had heat within me that was proof
Against the North wind; tired, yet so that rest
Had seemed the sweetest thing under a roof.

Then at the inn I had food, fire, and rest,
Knowing how hungry, cold, and tired was I.
All of the night was quite barred out except
An owl's cry, a most melancholy cry

Shaken out long and clear upon the hill,
No merry note, nor cause of merriment,
But one telling me plain what I escaped
And others could not, that night, as in I went.

And salted was my food, and my repose,
Salted and sobered, too, by the bird's voice
Speaking for all who lay under the stars,
Soldiers and poor, unable to rejoice.

EDWARD THOMAS

℘ · ℬ

## *Worn Out*

You bid me hold my peace
And dry my fruitless tears,
Forgetting that I bear
A pain beyond my years.

You say that I should smile
And drive the gloom away;
I would, but sun and smiles
Have left my life's dark day.

All time seems cold and void,
And naught but tears remain;
Life's music beats for me
A melancholy strain.

I used at first to hope,
But hope is past and gone;
And now without a ray
My cheerless life drags on.

Like to an ash-stained hearth
When all its fires are spent;
Like to an autumn wood
By storm winds rudely shent,

So sadly goes my heart,
Unclothed of hope and peace;
It asks not joy again,
But only seeks release.

PAUL LAURENCE DUNBAR

꙳ • ꙳

# Requiem

Under the wide and starry sky,
Dig the grave and let me lie.
Glad did I live and gladly die,
And I laid me down with a will.

This be the verse you grave for me:
*Here he lies where he longed to be;*
*Home is the sailor, home from sea,*
*And the hunter home from the hill.*

ROBERT LOUIS STEVENSON

꙳ • ꙳

## *My Life Closed Twice*

My life closed twice before its close;
It yet remains to see
If Immortality unveil
A third event to me,

So huge, so hopeless to conceive,
As these that twice befell.
Parting is all we know of heaven,
And all we need of hell.

EMILY DICKINSON

## *Sympathy*

There should be no despair for you
While nightly stars are burning;
While evening pours its silent dew,
And sunshine gilds the morning.
There should be no despair — though tears
May flow down like a river:
Are not the best beloved of years
Around your heart for ever?

They weep, you weep, it must be so;
  Winds sigh as you are sighing,
And winter sheds its grief in snow
  Where Autumn's leaves are lying:
Yet, these revive, and from their fate
  Your fate cannot be parted:
Then, journey on, if not elate,
  Still, *never* broken-hearted!

EMILY BRONTË

&#x2767;

# *To An Athlete Dying Young*

The time you won your town the race
We chaired you through the market-place;
  Man and boy stood cheering by,
And home we brought you shoulder-high.

To-day, the road all runners come,
Shoulder-high we bring you home,
  And set you at your threshold down,
Townsman of a stiller town.

Smart lad, to slip betimes away
From fields where glory does not stay

And early though the laurel grows
It withers quicker than the rose.

Eyes the shady night has shut
Cannot see the record cut,
And silence sounds no worse than cheers
After earth has stopped the ears:

Now you will not swell the rout
Of lads that wore their honours out,
Runners whom renown outran
And the name died before the man.

So set, before its echoes fade,
The fleet foot on the sill of shade,
And hold to the low lintel up
The still-defended challenge-cup.

And round that early-laurelled head
Will flock to gaze the strengthless dead,
And find unwithered on its curls
The garland briefer than a girl's.

A. E. HOUSMAN

$\mathcal{E} \cdot \mathcal{B}$

## Eros

The sense of the world is short, —
Long and various the report, —
  To love and be beloved;
Men and gods have not outlearned it,
And, how oft soe'er they've turned it,
  'Tis not to be improved.

RALPH WALDO EMERSON

*꙰ • ꙰*

## I Said, This Misery Must End

I Said, This misery must end:
  Shall I, that am a man and know
that sky and wind are yet my friend,
  sit huddled under any blow?
so speaking left the dismal room
  and stept into the mother-night
all fill'd with sacred quickening gloom
where the few stars burn'd low and bright,
  and darkling on my darkling hill
heard thro' the beaches' sullen boom
  heroic note of living will
rung trumpet-clear against the fight;

so stood and heard, and rais'd my eyes
erect, that they might drink of space,
and took the night upon my face,
till time and trouble fell away
and all my soul sprang up to feel
as one among the stars that reel
in rhyme on their rejoicing way,
breaking the elder dark, nor stay
but speed beyond each trammelling gyre,
till time and sorrow fall away
and night be wither'd up, and fire
consume the sickness of desire.

CHRISTOPHER BRENNAN

*C • B*

## *Greater Love*

Red lips are not so red
As the stained stones kissed by the English dead.
Kindness of wooed and wooer
Seems shame to their love pure.
O Love, your eyes lose lure
When I behold eyes blinded in my stead!

Your slender attitude
Trembles not exquisite like limbs knife-skewed,
Rolling and rolling there
Where God seems not to care;
Till the fierce love they bear
Cramps them in death's extreme decrepitude.

Your voice sings not so soft,-
Though even as wind murmuring through raftered loft, —
Your dear voice is not dear,
Gentle, and evening clear,
As theirs whom none now hear,
Now earth has stopped their piteous mouths that coughed.

Heart, you were never hot
Nor large, nor full like hearts made great with shot;
And though your hand be pale,
Paler are all which trail
Your cross through flame and hail:
Weep, you may weep, for you may touch them not.

WILFRED OWEN

𝒪 • ℬ

## *The Day Is Done*

The day is done, and the darkness
Falls from the wings of Night,
As a feather is wafted downward
From an eagle in his flight.

I see the lights of the village
Gleam through the rain and the mist,
And a feeling of sadness comes o'er me
That my soul cannot resist:

A feeling of sadness and longing,
That is not akin to pain,
And resembles sorrow only
As the mist resembles the rain.

Come, read to me some poem,
Some simple and heartfelt lay,
That shall soothe this restless feeling,
And banish the thoughts of day.

Not from the grand old masters,
Not from the bards sublime,
Whose distant footsteps echo
Through the corridors of Time.

For, like strains of martial music,
Their mighty thoughts suggest
Life's endless toil and endeavor;
And to-night I long for rest.

Read from some humbler poet,
Whose songs gushed from his heart,
As showers from the clouds of summer,
Or tears from the eyelids start;

Who, through long days of labor,
And nights devoid of ease,
Still heard in his soul the music
Of wonderful melodies.

Such songs have power to quiet
The restless pulse of care,
And come like the benediction
That follows after prayer.

Then read from the treasured volume
The poem of thy choice,
And lend to the rhyme of the poet
The beauty of thy voice.

And the night shall be filled with music,
And the cares, that infest the day,
Shall fold their tents, like the Arabs,
And as silently steal away.

HENRY WADSWORTH LONGFELLOW

𝒯 · ℬ

## *The Rose*

The Rose was given to man for this:
He, sudden seeing it in later years,
Should swift remember Love's first lingering kiss
And Grief's last lingering tears;

Or, being blind, should feel its yearning soul
Knit all its piercing perfume round his own,
Till he should see on memory's ample scroll
All roses he had known;

Or, being hard, perchance his finger-tips
Careless might touch the satin of its cup,
And he should feel a dead babe's budding lips
To his lips lifted up;

Or, being deaf and smitten with its star,
　　Should, on a sudden, almost hear a lark
Rush singing up — the nightingale afar
　　Sing thro' the dew-bright dark;

Or, sorrow-lost in paths that round and round
　　Circle old graves, its keen and vital breath
Should call to him within the yew's bleak bound
　　Of Life, and not of Death.

ISABELLA VALANCY CRAWFORD

*Ɛ* • *Ɓ*

## *Rest*

O Earth, lie heavily upon her eyes;
Seal her sweet eyes weary of watching, Earth;
Lie close around her; leave no room for mirth
With its harsh laughter, nor for sound of sighs.
She hath no questions, she hath no replies,
Hushed in and curtained with a blessèd dearth
Of all that irked her from the hour of birth;
With stillness that is almost Paradise.
Darkness more clear than noonday holdeth her,
Silence more musical than any song;

Even her very heart has ceased to stir:
Until the morning of Eternity
Her rest shall not begin nor end, but be;
And when she wakes she will not think it long.

CHRISTINA GEORGINA ROSSETTI

$\mathcal{C}\cdot\mathcal{B}$

# The Rainy Day

The day is cold, and dark, and dreary;
It rains, and the wind is never weary;
The vine still clings to the mouldering wall,

But at every gust the dead leaves fall,
And the day is dark and dreary.

My life is cold, and dark, and dreary;
It rains, and the wind is never weary;
My thoughts still cling to the mouldering past,
But the hopes of youth fall thick in the blast,
And the days are dark and dreary.

Be still, sad heart, and cease repining;
Behind the clouds is the sun still shining;

Thy fate is the common fate of all,

Into each life some rain must fall,

    Some days must be dark and dreary.

      HENRY WADSWORTH LONGFELLOW

        *ℰ • ℬ*

## *Ode On A Grecian Urn*

Thou still unravish'd bride of quietness,

    Thou foster-child of silence and slow time,

Sylvan historian, who canst thus express

    A flowery tale more sweetly than our rhyme:

What leaf-fring'd legend haunts about thy shape

    Of deities or mortals, or of both,

      In Tempe or the dales of Arcady?

    What men or gods are these? What maidens loth?

What mad pursuit?  What struggle to escape?

    What pipes and timbrels? What wild ecstasy?

Heard melodies are sweet, but those unheard

    Are sweeter: therefore, ye soft pipes, play on;

Not to the sensual ear, but, more endear'd,

    Pipe to the spirit ditties of no tone:

Fair youth, beneath the trees, thou canst not leave
   Thy song, nor ever can those trees be bare;
     Bold lover, never, never canst thou kiss,
   Though winning near the goal — yet, do not grieve;
She cannot fade, though thou hast not thy bliss,
   For ever wilt thou love, and she be fair!

Ah, happy, happy boughs! that cannot shed
    Your leaves, nor ever bid the spring adieu;
And, happy melodist, unwearied,
    For ever piping songs for ever new;
More happy love! more happy, happy love!
    For ever warm and still to be enjoy'd,
     For ever panting, and for ever young;
  All breathing human passion far above,
That leaves a heart high-sorrowful and cloy'd,
   A burning forehead, and a parching tongue.

Who are these coming to the sacrifice?
    To what green altar, O mysterious priest,
Lead'st thou that heifer lowing at the skies,
    And all her silken flanks with garlands drest?
What little town by river or sea shore,
    Or mountain-built with peaceful citadel,
     Is emptied of this folk, this pious morn?

And, little town, thy streets for evermore
Will silent be; and not a soul to tell
    Why thou art desolate, can e'er return.

O Attic shape! Fair attitude! with brede
    Of marble men and maidens overwrought,
With forest branches and the trodden weed;
    Thou, silent form, dost tease us out of thought
As doth eternity: Cold Pastoral!
    When old age shall this generation waste,
        Thou shalt remain, in midst of other woe
    Than ours, a friend to man, to whom thou say'st,
'Beauty is truth, truth beauty.' — that is all
    Ye know on earth, and all ye need to know.

JOHN KEATS

## So We'll Go No More A-Roving

So we'll go no more a-roving
    So late into the night,
Though the heart be still as loving,
    And the moon be still as bright.

For the sword outwears its sheath,
>And the soul outwears the breast,
And the heart must pause to breathe,
>And love itself have rest.

Though the night was made for loving,
>And the day returns too soon,
Yet we'll go no more a-roving
>By the light of the moon.

GEORGE GORDON, LORD BYRON

$\mathcal{G} \cdot \mathcal{B}$

## *My Heart Was Wandering In The Sands*

My heart was wandering in the sands,
a restless thing, a scorn apart;
Love set his fire in my hands,
I clasp'd the flame unto my heart.

Surely, I said, my heart shall turn
one fierce delight of pointed flame;
and in that holocaust shall burn
its old unrest and scorn and shame:
Surely my heart the heavens at last

shall storm with fiery orisons,
and know, enthroned in the vast,
the fervid peace of molten suns.

The flame that feeds upon my heart
fades or flares, by wild winds controll'd;
my heart still walks a thing apart,
my heart is restless as of old.

CHRISTOPHER BRENNAN

ℰ • ℬ

# *With Rue My Heart Is Laden*

With rue my heart is laden
    For golden friends I had,
For many a rose-lipt maiden
    And many a lightfoot lad.

By brooks too broad for leaping
    The lightfoot boys are laid;
The rose-lipt girls are sleeping
    In fields where roses fade.

A. E. HOUSMAN

ℰ • ℬ

# Ode On Melancholy

No, no! go not to Lethe, neither twist
      Wolf's-bane, tight-rooted, for its poisonous wine;
Nor suffer thy pale forehead to be kissed
      By nightshade, ruby grape of Proserpine;
Make not your rosary of yew-berries,
      Nor let the beetle nor the death-moth be
         Your mournful Psyche, nor the downy owl
A partner in your sorrow's mysteries;
      For shade to shade will come too drowsily,
         And drown the wakeful anguish of the soul.

But when the melancholy fit shall fall
      Sudden from heaven like a weeping cloud,
That fosters the droop-headed flowers all,
      And hides the green hill in an April shroud;
Then glut thy sorrow on a morning rose,
      Or on the rainbow of the salt sand-wave,
         Or on the wealth of globed peonies;
Or if thy mistress some rich anger shows,
      Emprison her soft hand, and let her rave,
         And feed deep, deep upon her peerless eyes.

She dwells with Beauty — Beauty that must die;
    And Joy, whose hand is ever at his lips
Bidding adieu; and aching Pleasure nigh,
    Turning to poison while the bee-mouth sips;
Ay, in the very temple of delight
    Veiled Melancholy has her sovran shrine,
      Though seen of none save him whose
                strenuous tongue
Can burst Joy's grape against his palate fine;
    His soul shall taste the sadness of her might,
      And be among her cloudy trophies hung.

JOHN KEATS

           * • *

## *No Worst, There Is None*

No worst, there is none. Pitched past pitch of grief,
More pangs will, schooled at forepangs, wilder wring.
    Comforter, where, where is your comforting?
    Mary, mother of us, where is your relief?
My cries heave, herds-long; huddle in a main, a chief
Woe, world-sorrow; on an age-old anvil wince and sing —

Then lull, then leave off. Fury had shrieked 'No ling-
  ering! Let me be fell: force I must be brief'.
O the mind, mind has mountains; cliffs of fall
Frightful, sheer, no-man-fathomed. Hold them cheap
May who ne'er hung there. Nor does long our small
Durance deal with that steep or deep. Here! creep,
Wretch, under a comfort serves in a whirlwind: all
Life death does end and each day dies with sleep.

GERARD MANLEY HOPKINS

$\mathcal{O} \cdot \mathcal{B}$

## *Epistle To A Young Friend*

I lang hae thought, my youthfu' friend,
    A something to have sent you,
Tho' it should serve nae ither end
    Than just a kind memento:
But how the subject-theme may gang,
    Let time and change determine;
Perhaps it may turn out a sang:
    Perhaps turn out a sermon.

Ye'll try the world soon my lad;
And, Andrew dear, believe me,
Ye'll find mankind an unco squad,
And muckle they may grieve ye.
For care and trouble set your thought,
Ev'n when your end's attained;
And a' your views may come to nought,
Where ev'ry nerve is strained.

I'll no say, men are villains a';
The real, harden'd wicked,
What hae nae check but human law,
Are to a few restricked;
But, och! mankind are unco weak,
An' little to be trusted;
If self the wavering balance shake,
It's rarely right adjusted!

Yet they wha fa' in fortune's strife,
Their fate we should na censure;
For still, th'important end of life
They equally may answer;
A man may hae in honest heart,
Tho' poortith hourly stare him;
A man may tak a neibor's part,
Yet hae nae cash to spare him.

Aye free, aff-han', your story tell,
When wi' a bosom crony;
But still keep something to yoursel"
Ye scarcely tell to ony:
Conceal yoursel' as weel' ye can
Frae critical dissection;
But keek thro' ev'ry other man,
Wi' sharpen'd, sly inspection.

The sacred lowe o' well-plac'd love,
Luxuriantly indulge it;
But never tempt th' illicit rove,
Tho' naething should divulge it:
I waive the quantum o' the sin,
The hazard of concealing;
But, och! it hardens a' within,
And petrifies the feeling!

To catch dame Fortune's golden smile,
Assiduous wait upon her;
And gather gear by ev'ry wile
That's justified by honour;
Not for to hide it in a hedge,
Nor for a train attendant;
But for the glorious privilege
Of being independent.

The fear o' hell's a hangman's whip,
    To haud the wretch in order;
But where ye feel your honour grip,
    Let that aye be your border;
Its slightest touches, instant pause —
    Debar a' side-pretences;
And resolutely keep its laws,
    Uncaring consequences.

The great Creator to revere,
    Must sure become the creature;
But still the preaching cant forbear,
    And ev'n the rigid feature:
Yet ne'er with wits profane to range,
    Be complaisance extended;
An atheist-laugh's a poor exchange
    For Deity offended!

When ranting round in pleasure's ring,
    Religion may be blinded;
Or if she gie a random sting,
    It may be little minded;
But when on life we're tempest-driv'n —
    A conscience but a canker,
A correspondence fix'd wi' Heav'n,
    Is sure a noble anchor!

Adieu, dear, amiable youth!
Your heart can ne'er be wanting!
May prudence, fortitude, and truth,
Erect your brow undaunting!
In ploughman phrase, 'God send you speed,'
Still daily to grow wiser;
And may ye better reck the rede,
Than ever did th' adviser!

ROBERT BURNS

*&* · *&*

## *The Arrow And The Song*

I shot an arrow into the air,
It fell to earth, I knew not where;
For, so swiftly it flew, the sight
Could not follow it in its flight.

I breathed a song into the air,
It fell to earth, I knew not where;
For who has sight so keen and strong,
That it can follow the flight of song?

Long, long afterward, in an oak
I found the arrow, still unbroke;
And the song, from beginning to end,
I found again in the heart of a friend.

HENRY WADSWORTH LONGFELLOW

*Ɛ • Ɓ*

## *The Revelation*

An idle poet, here and there,
  Looks round him, but, for all the rest,
The world, unfathomably fair,
  Is duller than a witling's jest.
Love wakes men, once a lifetime each;
  They lift their heavy lids, and look;
And, lo, what one sweet page can teach,
  They read with joy, then shut the book.
And give some thanks, and some blaspheme,
  And most forget, but, either way,
That and the child's unheeded dream
  Is all the light of all their day.

COVENTRY PATMORE

*Ɛ • Ɓ*

## Music, When Soft Voices Die

Music, when soft voices die,
Vibrates in the memory;
Odours, when sweet violets sicken,
Live within the sense they quicken.

Rose leaves, when the rose is dead,
Are heap'd for the beloved's bed;
And so thy thoughts, when thou art gone,
Love itself shall slumber on.

PERCY BYSSHE SHELLEY

## Freedom And Love

How delicious is the winning
Of a kiss at love's beginning,
When two mutual hearts are sighing
For the knot there's no untying!

Yet remember, 'midst your wooing
Love has bliss, but Love has ruing;
Other smiles may make you fickle,
Tears for other charms may trickle.

Love he comes and Love he tarries
Just as fate or fancy carries;
Longest stays, when sorest chidden;
Laughs and flies, when press'd and bidden.

Bind the sea to slumber stilly,
Bind its odour to the lily,
Bind the aspen ne'er to quiver,
Then bind Love to last for ever.

Love's a fire that needs renewal
Of fresh beauty for its fuel;
Love's wing moults when caged and captured,
Only free, he soars enraptured.

Can you keep the bees from ranging,
Or the ringdove's neck from changing?
No! nor fetter'd Love from dying
In the knot there's no untying.

THOMAS CAMPBELL

## *The Torch Of Love*

The torch of love dispels the gloom
Of life, and animates the tomb;
But never let it idly flare
On gazers in the open air,
Nor turn it quite away from one
To whom it serves for moon and sun,
And who alike in night or day
Without it could not find his way.

WALTER SAVAGE LANDOR

## *Give All To Love*

Give all to love;
Obey thy heart;
Friends, kindred, days,
Estate, good-fame,
Plans, credit, and the Muse, —
Nothing refuse.

'Tis a brave master;
Let it have scope:

Follow it utterly,
Hope beyond hope:
High and more high
It dives into noon,
With wing unspent,
Untold intent;
But it is a God,
Knows its own path
And the outlets of the sky.

It was never for the mean;
It requireth courage stout.
Souls above doubt,
Valor unbending,
It will reward, —
They shall return
More than they were,
And ever ascending.

Leave all for love;
Yet, hear me, yet,
One word more thy heart behoved,
One pulse more of firm endeavor, —
Keep thee to-day,
To-morrow, forever,

Free as an Arab
Of thy beloved.

Cling with life to the maid;
But when the surprise,
First vague shadow of surmise
Flits across her bosom young,
Of a joy apart from thee,
Free be she, fancy-free;
Nor thou detain her vesture's hem,
Nor the palest rose she flung
From her summer diadem.

Though thou loved her as thyself,
As a self of purer clay,
Though her parting dims the day,
Stealing grace from all alive;
Heartily know,
When half-gods go,
The gods arrive.

RALPH WALDO EMERSON

## *Misgivings*

When ocean-clouds over inland hills
        Sweep storming in late autumn brown,
  And horror the sodden valley fills,
        And the spire falls crashing in the town,
    I muse upon my country's ills —
    The tempest burning from the waste of Time
On the world's fairest hope linked with man's foulest crime.

    Nature's dark side is heeded now —
        (Ah! optimist-cheer disheartened flown) —
    A child may read the moody brow
        Of yon black mountain lone.
    With shouts the torrents down the gorges go,
    And storms are formed behind the storms we feel:
The hemlock shakes in the rafter, the oak in the driving keel.

HERMAN MELVILLE

❦ · ❦

## *Break, Break, Break*

Break, break, break,
On thy cold grey stones, O Sea!
And I would that my tongue could utter
The thoughts that arise in me.

O, well for the fisherman's boy,
That he shouts with his sister at play!
O, well for the sailor lad,
That he sings in his boat on the bay!

And the stately ships go on
To their haven under the hill;
But O for the touch of a vanished hand,
And the sound of a voice that is still!

Break, break, break,
At the foot of thy crags, O Sea!
But the tender grace of a day that is dead
Will never come back to me.

ALFRED, LORD TENNYSON

            *ℐ • ℬ*

## *Vitae Summa Brevis Spem Nos Vetat Incohare Longam*

They are not long, the weeping and the laughter,
Love and desire and hate:
I think they have no portion in us after
We pass the gate.

They are not long, the days of wine and roses:
 Out of a misty dream
Our path emerges for a while, then closes
 Within a dream.

ERNEST DOWSON

🖉 • ℬ

## Self-Pity

I never saw a wild thing
sorry for itself.
A small bird will drop frozen dead from a bough
without ever having felt sorry for itself.

D. H. LAWRENCE

🖉 • ℬ

## The Solitary Reaper

Behold her, single in the field,
 Yon solitary Highland Lass!
Reaping and singing by herself;
 Stop here, or gently pass!
Alone she cuts and binds the grain,
And sings a melancholy strain;

O listen! for the Vale profound
Is overflowing with the sound.

No Nightingale did ever chaunt
More welcome notes to weary bands
Of travellers in some shady haunt,
Among Arabian sands:
A voice so thrilling ne'er was heard
In spring-time from the Cuckoo-bird,
Breaking the silence of the seas
Among the farthest Hebrides.

Will no one tell me what she sings? —
Perhaps the plaintive numbers flow
For old, unhappy, far-off things,
And battles long ago:
Or is it some more humble lay,
Familiar matter of to-day?
Some natural sorrow, loss, or pain,
That has been, and may be again?

Whate'er the theme, the Maiden sang
As if her song could have no ending;
I saw her singing at her work,
And o'er the sickle bending; —

listened, motionless and still;
And, as I mounted up the hill,
The music in my heart I bore,
Long after it was heard no more.

WILLIAM WORDSWORTH

♂ • ♀

# The Poet

He sang of life, serenely sweet,
　　With, now and then, a deeper note.
　　From some high peak, nigh yet remote,
He voiced the world's absorbing beat.

He sang of love when earth was young,
　　And Love, itself, was in his lays.
　　But, ah, the world, it turned to praise
A jingle in a broken tongue.

PAUL LAURENCE DUNBAR

♂ • ♀

## *We Outgrow Love, Like Other Things*

We outgrow love, like other things
And put it in the drawer
Till it an antique fashion shows
Like costumes grandsires wore.

EMILY DICKINSON

ℐ · ℛ

## *Ode On Solitude*

Happy the man, whose wish and care
A few paternal acres bound,
Content to breathe his native air,
In his own ground.

Whose herds with milk, whose fields with bread,
Whose flocks supply him with attire,
Whose trees in summer yield him shade,
In winter fire.

Bless'd who can unconcern'dly find
Hours, days, and years slide soft away,
In health of body, peace of mind,
Quiet by day,

Sound sleep by night; study and ease
    Together mix'd; sweet recreation,
And innocence, which most does please,
    With meditation.

Thus let me live, unseen, unknown;
    Thus unlamented let me die;
Steal from the world, and not a stone
    Tell where I lye.

ALEXANDER POPE

*Thanatopsis*

To him who in the love of nature holds
Communion with her visible forms, she speaks
A various language; for his gayer hours
She has a voice of gladness, and a smile
And eloquence of beauty, and she glides
Into his darker musings, with a mild
And healing sympathy, that steals away
Their sharpness, ere he is aware. When thoughts
Of the last bitter hour come like a blight
Over thy spirit, and sad images
Of the stern agony, and shroud, and pall,

And breathless darkness, and the narrow house,
Make thee to shudder and grow sick at heart —
     Go forth, under the open sky, and list
To nature's teachings, while from all around —
Earth and her waters, and the depths of air —
     Comes a still voice. Yet a few days, and thee
     The all-beholding sun shall see no more
In all his course; nor yet in the cold ground,
Where thy pale form was laid, with many tears,
     Nor in the embrace of ocean, shall exist
Thy image. Earth, that nourished thee, shall claim
     Thy growth, to be resolved to earth again,
     And, lost each human trace, surrendering up
          Thine individual being, shalt thou go
          To mix forever with the elements,
          To be a brother to the insensible rock
And to the sluggish clod, which the rude swain
Turns with his share, and treads upon.   The oak
Shall send his roots abroad, and pierce thy mold.

          Yet not to thine eternal resting-place
     Shalt thou retire alone, nor couldst thou wish
Couch more magnificent.   Thou shalt lie down
With patriarchs of the infant world — with kings,
The powerful of the earth — the wise, the good,
     Fair forms, and hoary seers of ages past,

All in one mighty sepulchre.   The hills
Rock-ribbed and ancient as the sun — the vales
Stretching in pensive quietness between;
The venerable woods — rivers that move
In majesty, and the complaining brooks
That make the meadows green; and, poured round all,
Old ocean's gray and melancholy waste —
Are but the solemn decorations all
Of the great tomb of man. The golden sun,
The planets, all the infinite host of heaven,
Are shining on the sad abodes of death,
Through the still lapse of ages. All that tread
The globe are but a handful to the tribes
That slumber in its bosom. Take the wings
Of morning, pierce the Barcan wilderness,
Or lose thyself in the continuous woods
Where rolls the Oregon, and hears no sound,
Save his own dashings — yet the dead are there;
And millions in those solitudes, since first
The flight of years began, have laid them down
In their last sleep — the dead reign there alone.

So shalt thou rest, and what if thou withdraw
In silence from the living, and no friend
Take note of thy departure? All that breathe
Will share thy destiny.   The gay will laugh

When thou art gone, the solemn brood of care
Plod on, and each one as before will chase
His favorite phantom; yet all these shall leave
Their mirth and their employments, and shall come
And make their bed with thee.  As the long train
Of ages glides away, the sons of men,
The youth in life's fresh spring, and he who goes
In the full strength of years, matron and maid,
The speechless babe, and the gray-headed man —
Shall one by one be gathered to thy side,
By those who in their turn shall follow them.

So live, that when thy summons comes to join
The innumerable caravan, which moves
To that mysterious realm where each shall take
His chamber in the silent halls of death,
Thou go not, like the quarry-slave at night,
Scourged to his dungeon, but, sustained and soothed
By an unfaltering trust, approach thy grave,
Like one who wraps the drapery of his couch
About him, and lies down to pleasant dreams.

WILLIAM CULLEN BRYANT

## *Snake*

A snake came to my water-trough
On a hot, hot day, and I in pyjamas for the heat,
To drink there.

In the deep, strange-scented shade of the great dark carob-tree
I came down the steps with my pitcher
And must wait, must stand and wait, for there he was at the
trough before me.

He reached down from a fissure in the earth-wall in the
gloom
And trailed his yellow-brown slackness soft-bellied down,
over the edge of the stone trough
And rested his throat upon the stone bottom,
And where the water had dripped from the tap, in a small
clearness,
He sipped with his straight mouth,
Softly drank through his straight gums, into his slack long
body,
Silently.

Someone was before me at my water-trough,
And I, like a second comer, waiting.

He lifted his head from his drinking, as cattle do,
And looked at me vaguely, as drinking cattle do,
And flickered his two-forked tongue from his lips, and mused
    a moment,
And stooped and drank a little more,
Being earth-brown, earth-golden from the burning bowels of
    the earth
On the day of Sicilian July, with Etna smoking.

The voice of my education said to me
He must be killed,
For in Sicily the black, black snakes are innocent, the gold
    are venomous.
And voices in me said, If you were a man
You would take a stick and break him now, and finish him off.

But must I confess how I liked him,
How glad I was he had come like a guest in quiet, to drink at
    my water-trough
And depart peaceful, pacified, and thankless,
Into the burning bowels of this earth?

Was it cowardice, that I dared not kill him?
Was it perversity, that I longed to talk to him?
Was it humility, to feel so honoured?
I felt so honoured.

And yet those voices:
*If you were not afraid, you would kill him!*

And truly I was afraid, I was most afraid,
But even so, honoured still more
That he should seek my hospitality
From out the dark door of the secret earth.

He drank enough
And lifted his head, dreamily, as one who has drunken,
And flickered his tongue like a forked night on the air, so
    black,
Seeming to lick his lips,
And looked around like a god, unseeing, into the air,
And slowly turned his head,
And slowly, very slowly, as if thrice adream,
Proceeded to draw his slow length curving round
And climb again the broken bank of my wall-face.

And as he put his head into that dreadful hole,
And as he slowly drew up, snake-easing his shoulders, and
    entered further,
A sort of horror, a sort of protest against his withdrawing
    into that horrid black hole,
Deliberately going into the blackness, and slowly drawing
    himself after,
Overcame me now his back was turned.

I looked round, I put down my pitcher,
I picked up a clumsy log
And threw it at the water-trough with a clatter.
I think it did not hit him,
But suddenly that part of him that was left behind convulsed
    in undignified haste,
Writhed like lightning, and was gone
Into the black hole, the earth-lipped fissure in the wall-
    front,
At which, in the intense still noon, I stared with
    fascination.

And immediately I regretted it.
I thought how paltry, how vulgar, what a mean act!
I despised myself and the voices of my accursed human
    education.

And I thought of the albatross,
And I wished he would come back, my snake.

For he seemed to me again like a king,
Like a king in exile, uncrowned in the underworld,
Now due to be crowned again.

And so, I missed my chance with one of the lords
Of life.
And I have something to expiate:
A pettiness.

D. H. LAWRENCE

☙ • ❧

# Darest Thou Now, O Soul

Darest thou now, O soul,
Walk out with me toward the unknown region,
Where neither ground is for the feet nor any path to follow?

No map there, nor guide,
Nor voice sounding, nor touch of human hand,
Nor face with blooming flesh, nor lips, nor eyes are in that
    land.

I know it not O soul,
Nor dost thou, all is a blank before us,
All waits undream'd of in that region, that inaccessible land.

Till when the ties loosen,

All but the ties eternal, Time and Space,

Nor darkness, gravitation, sense, nor any bounds bounding
us.


Then we burst forth, we float,

In Time and Space O soul, prepared for them,

Equal, equipt at last, (O joy! O fruit of all!) them to fulfill O
soul.

WALT WHITMAN

ᘒ · ᘔ

## *After Great Pain, A Formal Feeling Comes*

After great pain, a formal feeling comes —
The Nerves sit ceremonious, like Tombs —
The stiff Heart questions was it He, that bore,
And Yesterday, or Centuries before?


The Feet, mechanical, go round —
Of Ground, or Air, or Ought —
A Wooden way
Regardless grown,

A Quartz contentment, like a stone —
This is the Hour of Lead —
Remembered, if outlived,
As Freezing persons recollect the Snow —
First — Chill — then Stupor — then the letting go —

EMILY DICKINSON

## To Emily Dickinson

You who desired so much — in vain to ask —
Yet fed your hunger like an endless task,
Dared dignify the labor, bless the quest —
Achieved that stillness ultimately best,

Being, of all, least sought for: Emily, hear!
O sweet, dead Silencer, most suddenly clear
When singing that Eternity possessed
And plundered momently in every breast;

— Truly no flower yet withers in your hand.
The harvest you descried and understand
Needs more than wit to gather, love to bind.
Some reconcilement of remotest mind —

Leaves Ormus rubyless, and Ophir chill.

Else tears heap all within one clay-cold hill.

HART CRANE

❧ • ☙

# *Remember*

Remember me when I am gone away,

    Gone far away into the silent land;

    When you can no more hold me by the hand,

Nor I half turn to go yet turning stay.

    Remember me when no more day by day

    You tell me of our future that you plann'd:

Only remember me; you understand

    It will be late to counsel then or pray.

    Yet if you should forget me for a while

And afterwards remember, do not grieve:

    For if the darkness and corruption leave

    A vestige of the thoughts that once I had,

Better by far you should forget and smile

    Than that you should remember and be sad.

CHRISTINA GEORGINA ROSSETTI

❧ • ☙

# A Dream Within A Dream

Take this kiss upon the brow!
And, in parting from you now,
Thus much let me avow —
You are not wrong, who deem
That my days have been a dream;
Yet if hope has flown away
In a night, or in a day,
In a vision, or in none,
Is it therefore the less gone?
All that we see or seem
Is but a dream within a dream.

I stand amid the roar
Of a surf-tormented shore,
And I hold within my hand
Grains of the golden sand —
How few! yet how they creep
Through my fingers to the deep,
While I weep — while I weep!
O God! can I not grasp
Them with a tighter clasp?

O God! can I not save
One from the pitiless wave?
Is all that we see or seem
But a dream within a dream?

EDGAR ALLAN POE

𝒟 • 𝒷

# Death
## AND
# Grief

## *Lux Est Umbra Dei*

Nay, Death, thou art a shadow! Even as light
Is but the shadow of invisible God,
And of that shade the shadow is thin Night,
Veiling the earth whereon our feet have trod;
So art Thou but the shadow of this life,
Itself the pale and unsubstantial shade
Of living God, fulfill'd by love and strife
Throughout the universe Himself hath made:
And as frail Night, following the flight of earth,
Obscures the world we breathe in, for a while,
So Thou, the reflex of our mortal birth,
Veilest the life wherein we weep and smile:
But when both earth and life are whirl'd away,
What shade can shroud us from God's deathless day?

JOHN ADDINGTON SYMONDS

*&* • *&*

## *On My First Son*

Farewell, thou child of my right hand, and joy;
My sin was too much hope of thee, lov'd boy.
Seven years thou wert lent to me, and I thee pay,
Exacted by thy fate, on the just day.

O, could I lose all father now! For why
Will man lament the state he should envy?
To have so soon 'scap'd world's and flesh's rage,
And if no other misery, yet age?
Rest in soft peace, and, ask'd, say, 'Here doth lie
Ben Jonson his best piece of poetry.'
For whose sake henceforth all his vows be such,
As what he loves may never like too much.

BEN JONSON

## In Beechwood Cemetery

Here the dead sleep — the quiet dead. No sound
Disturbs them ever, and no storm dismays.
Winter mid snow caresses the tired ground,
And the wind roars about the woodland ways.
Springtime and summer and red autumn pass,
With leaf and bloom and pipe of wind and bird,
And the old earth puts forth her tender grass,
By them unfelt, unheeded and unheard.
Our centuries to them are but as strokes
In the dim gamut of some far-off chime.
Unaltering rest their perfect being cloaks —

A thing too vast to hear or feel or see —
Children of Silence and Eternity,
They know no season but the end of time.

ARCHIBALD LAMPMAN

*E • B*

## *To One In Paradise*

Thou wast all that to me, love,
For which my soul did pine —
A green isle in the sea, love,
A fountain and a shrine,
All wreathed with fairy fruits and flowers,
And all the flowers were mine.

Ah, dream too bright to last!
Ah, starry Hope! that didst arise
But to be overcast!
A voice from out the Future cries,
'On! on!' — but o'er the Past
(Dim gulf!) my spirit hovering lies
Mute, motionless, aghast!

For, alas! alas! me
　　The light of Life is o'er!
'No more — no more — no more —'
　　(Such language holds the solemn sea
To the sands upon the shore)
　　Shall bloom the thunder-blasted tree
Or the stricken eagle soar!

And all my days are trances,
　　And all my nightly dreams
Are where thy grey eye glances,
　　And where thy footstep gleams —
In what ethereal dances,
　　By what eternal streams.

EDGAR ALLAN POE

ℰ • ℬ

## *To L. H. B.*

Last night for the first time since you were dead
　　I walked with you, my brother, in a dream.
　　We were at home again beside the stream
Fringed with tall berry bushes, white and red.
'Don't touch them: they are poisonous,' I said.

But your hand hovered, and I saw a beam
Of strange, bright laughter flying round your head,
And as you stooped I saw the berries gleam.
'Don't you remember? We called them Dead Man's Bread!'
I woke and heard the wind moan and the roar
Of the dark water tumbling on the shore.
Where — where is the path of my dream for my eager feet?
By the remembered stream my brother stands
Waiting for me with berries in his hands...
'These are my body. Sister, take and eat.'

KATHERINE MANSFIELD

ℐ • ℛ

## *She Dwelt Among The Untrodden Ways*

She dwelt among the untrodden ways
Beside the springs of Dove,
A Maid whom there were none to praise
And very few to love:

A violet by a mossy tone
    Half hidden from the eye!
— Fair as a star, when only one
    Is shining in the sky.

She lived unknown, and few could know
    When Lucy ceased to be;
But she is in her grave, and, oh,
    The difference to me!

WILLIAM WORDSWORTH

♉ • ♉

## *Remembrance*

Cold in the earth — and the deep snow piled above thee,
    Far, far removed, cold in the dreary grave!
    Have I forgot, my only Love, to love thee,
    Severed at last by Time's all-wearing wave?

Now, when alone, do my thoughts no longer hover
    Over the mountains, on that northern shore,
Resting their wings where heath and fern-leaves cover
    Thy noble heart for ever, ever more?

Cold in the earth — and fifteen wild Decembers,
From those brown hills, have melted into spring:
Faithful, indeed, is the spirit that remembers
After such years of change and suffering!

Sweet Love of youth, forgive, if I forget thee,
While the world's tide is bearing me along;
Sterner desires and darker hopes beset me,
Hopes which obscure, but cannot do thee wrong!

No other sun has lightened up my heaven,
No other star has ever shone for me;
All my life's bliss from thy dear life was given,
All my life's bliss is in the grave with thee.

But, when the days of golden dreams had perished,
And even Despair was powerless to destroy;
Then did I learn how existence could be cherished,
Strengthened, and fed without the aid of joy.

Then did I check the tears of useless passion —
Weaned my young soul from yearning after thine;
Sternly denied its burning wish to hasten
Down to that tomb already more than mine.

And, even yet, I dare not let it languish,
Dare not indulge in memory's rapturous pain;
Once drinking deep of that divinest anguish,
How could I seek the empty world again?

EMILY BRONTË

*𝒟 • 𝓑*

# *Surprised By Joy*

Surprised by joy — impatient as the wind
I turned to share the transport — Oh! with whom
But Thee, deep buried in the silent tomb,
That spot which no vicissitude can find?
Love, faithful love, recalled thee to my mind —
But how could I forget thee? Through what power,
Even for the least division of an hour,
Have I been so beguiled as to be blind
To my most grievous loss? — That thought's return
Was the worst pang that sorrow ever bore
Save one, one only, when I stood forlorn,
Knowing my heart's best treasure was no more;
That neither present time, nor years unborn,
Could to my sight that heavenly face restore.

WILLIAM WORDSWORTH

*𝒟 • 𝓑*

# *O Captain! My Captain!*

## I

O Captain! my Captain! our fearful trip is done;

The ship has weather'd every rack, the prize we sought is
 won;

The port is near, the bells I hear, the people all exulting,

While follow eyes the steady keel, the vessel grim and daring:

  But O heart! heart! heart!

    O the bleeding drops of red,

      Where on the deck my Captain lies,

       Fallen cold and dead.

## II

O Captain! my Captain! rise up and hear the bells;

Rise up — for you the flag is flung — for you the bugle trills;

For you bouquets and ribbon'd wreaths — for you the shores
 a-crowding;

For you they call, the swaying mass, their eager faces
 turning;

  Here Captain! dear father!

    This arm beneath your head;

      It is some dream that on the deck,

       You've fallen cold and dead.

### III

My Captain does not answer, his lips are pale and still;

My father does not feel my arm, he has no pulse nor will;

The ship is anchor'd safe and sound, its voyage closed and
done;

From fearful trip the victor ship comes in with object won;

Exult, O shores, and ring, O bells!

But I, with mournful tread,

Walk the deck my Captain lies,

Fallen cold and dead.

WALT WHITMAN

*𝒟 • ℬ*

## *Prospice*

Fear death? — to feel the fog in my throat,

The mist in my face,

When the snows begin, and the blasts denote

I am nearing the place,

The power of the night, the press of the storm,

The post of the foe;

Where he stands, the Arch Fear in a visible form,

Yet the strong man must go:

For the journey is done and the summit attained,
    And the barriers fall,
Though a battle's to fight ere the guerdon be gained,
    The reward of it all.
I was ever a fighter, so — one fight more,
    The best and the last!

I would hate that death bandaged my eyes, and forbore,
    And bade me creep past.
No! let me taste the whole of it, fare like my peers,
    The heroes of old,
Bear the brunt, in a minute pay glad life's arrears
    Of pain, darkness and cold.
For sudden the worst turns the best to the brave.
    The black minute's at end,
And the elements' rage, the fiend-voices that rave,
    Shall dwindle, shall blend,
Shall change, shall become first a peace out of pain.
    Then a light, then thy breast,
O thou soul of my soul! I shall clasp thee again,
    And with God be the rest!

ROBERT BROWNING

*R • B*

## *We Too Shall Sleep*

Not, not for thee,
Beloved child, the burning grasp of life
Shall bruise the tender soul. The noise, and strife,
And clamor of midday thou shalt not see;
But wrapped for ever in thy quiet grave,
Too little to have known the earthly lot.
Time's clashing hosts above thine innocent head,
Wave upon wave,
Shall break, or pass as with an army's tread,
And harm thee not.

A few short years
We of the living flesh and restless brain
Shall plumb the deeps of life and know the strain,
The fleeting gleams of joy, the fruitless tears;
And then at last when all is touched and tried,
Our own immutable night shall fall, and deep
In the same silent plot, O little friend,
Side by thy side,
In peace that changeth not, nor knoweth end,
We too shall sleep.

ARCHIBALD LAMPMAN

## *The Chariot*

Because I could not stop for Death,
He kindly stopped for me;
The carriage held but just ourselves
And Immortality.

We slowly drove, he knew no haste,
And I had put away
My labor, and my leisure too,
For his civility.

We passed the school where children played,
Their lessons scarcely done;
We passed the fields of gazing grain,
We passed the setting sun.

We paused before a house that seemed
A swelling of the ground;
The roof was scarcely visible,
The cornice but a mound.

Since then 't is centuries; but each
Feels shorter than the day
I first surmised the horses' heads
Were toward eternity.

EMILY DICKINSON

E • D

## *Requiescat*

Tread lightly, she is near
    Under the snow,
Speak gently, she can hear
    The daisies grow.

All her bright golden hair
    Tarnished with rust,
She that was young and fair
    Fallen to dust.

Lily-like, white as snow,
    She hardly knew
She was a woman, so
    Sweetly she grew.

Coffin-board, heavy stone,
    Lie on her breast,
I vex my heart alone,
    She is at rest.

Peace, Peace, she cannot hear
    Lyre or sonnet,
All my life's buried here,
    Heap earth upon it.

OSCAR WILDE

## The Dead

How great unto the living seem the dead!
How sacred, solemn; how heroic grown;
How vast and vague, as they obscurely tread
The shadowy confines of the dim unknown! —
For they have met the monster that we dread,
Have learned the secret not to mortal shown.
E'en as gigantic shadows on the wall
The spirit of the daunted child amaze,
So on us thoughts of the departed fall,
And with phantasma fill our gloomy gaze.
Awe and deep wonder lend the living lines,
And hope and ecstasy the borrowed beams;
While fitful fancy the full form divines,
And all is what imagination dreams.

CHARLES HEAVYSEGE

*&* • *B*

## Bredon Hill

In summertime on Bredon
The bells they sound so clear;
Round both the shires they ring them
In steeples far and near,

A happy noise to hear.
Here of a Sunday morning
My love and I would lie,
And see the coloured counties,
And hear the larks so high
About us in the sky.
The bells would ring to call her
In valleys miles away;
'Come all to church, good people;
Good people, come and pray.'
But here my love would stay.
And I would turn and answer
Among the springing thyme,
'Oh, peal upon our wedding,
And we will hear the chime,
And come to church in time.'
But when the snows at Christmas
On Bredon top were strown,
My love rose up so early
And stole out unbeknown
And went to church alone.
They tolled the one bell only,
Groom there was none to see,
The mourners followed after,
And so to church went she,

And would not wait for me.
The bells they sound on Bredon,
And still the steeples hum,
'Come all to church, good people.'
Oh, noisy bells, be dumb;
I hear you, I will come.


A. E. HOUSMAN

*Y • B*


## When I Have Fears That I May Cease To Be

When I have fears that I may cease to be
Before my pen has glean'd my teeming brain,
Before high-piled books, in charactry,
Hold like rich garners the full-ripen'd grain;
When I behold, upon the night's starr'd face,
Huge cloudy symbols of a high romance,
And think that I may never live to trace
Their shadows, with the magic hand of chance;
And when I feel, fair creature of an hour,
That I shall never look upon thee more,
Never have relish in the faery power
Of unreflecting love; — then on the shore

Of the wide world I stand alone, and think
    Till Love and Fame to nothingness do sink.

JOHN KEATS

✣ • ✣

## *The Grave Of Keats*

Rid of the world's injustice, and his pain,
   He rests at last beneath God's veil of blue:
   Taken from life when life and love were new
The youngest of the martyrs here is lain,
Fair as Sebastian, and as early slain.
   No cypress shades his grave, no funeral yew,
   But gentle violets weeping with the dew
Weave on his bones an ever-blossoming chain.
O proudest heart that broke for misery!
   O sweetest lips since those of Mitylene!
   O poet-painter of our English Land!
Thy name was writ in water — it shall stand:
   And tears like mine will keep thy memory green,
   As Isabella did her Basil-tree.

OSCAR WILDE

✣ • ✣

# *The Death Of The Flowers*

The melancholy days are come, the saddest of the year,
Of wailing winds, and naked woods, and meadows brown
   and sear.
Heaped in the hollows of the grove the autumn leaves lie
   dead;
They rustle to the eddying gust and to the rabbit's tread.
The robin and the wren are flown, and from the shrubs the
   jay,
And from the wood-top calls the crow through all the gloomy
   day.

Where are the flowers, the fair young flowers, that lately
   sprang and stood
In brighter light and softer airs, a beauteous sisterhood?
Alas! they all are in their graves; the gentle race of flowers
Are lying in their lowly beds, with the fair and good of ours.
The rain is falling where they lie; but the cold November rain
Calls not from out the gloomy earth the lovely ones again.

The wind-flower and the violet, they perished long ago,
And the brier-rose and the orchis died amid the summer
   glow;

But on the hill the golden-rod, and the aster in the wood,
And the yellow sunflower by the brook in autumn beauty
stood,
Till fell the frost from the clear cold heaven, as falls the
plague on men,
And the brightness of their smile was gone from upland,
glade, and glen.

And now, when comes the calm mild day, as still such days
will come,
To call the squirrel and the bee from out their winter home;
When the sound of dropping nuts is heard, though all the
trees are still,
And twinkle in the smoky light the waters of the rill,
The south-wind searches for the flowers whose fragrance late
he bore,
And sighs to find them in the wood and by the stream no
more.

And then I think of one who in her youthful beauty died,
The fair meek blossom that grew up and faded by my side.
In the cold moist earth we laid her, when the forests cast the
leaf,
And we wept that one so lovely should have a life so brief;

Yet not unmeet it was that one, like that young friend of
  ours,
So gentle and so beautiful, should perish with the flowers.

WILLIAM CULLEN BRYANT

*Ʒ • Ƀ*

# *To Mary: It Is The Evening Hour*

It is the evening hour,
How silent all doth lie,
The horned moon he shows his face
In the river with the sky.
Just by the path on which we pass,
The flaggy lake lies still as glass.

Spirit of her I love,
Whispering to me,
Stories of sweet visions, as I rove,
Here stop, and crop with me
Sweet flowers that in the still hour grew,
We'll take them home, nor shake off the bright dew.

Mary, or sweet spirit of thee,
As the bright sun shines tomorrow.
Thy dark eyes these flowers shall see,
Gathered by me in sorrow.

In the still hour when my mind was free
To walk alone — yet wish I walked with thee.

JOHN CLARE

*ℰ • ℬ*

# *Grief*

I tell you, hopeless grief is passionless;
    That only men incredulous of despair,
    Half-taught in anguish, through the midnight air
Beat upward to God's throne in loud access
Of shrieking and reproach. Full desertness,
    In souls as countries, lieth silent-bare
    Under the blanching, vertical eye-glare
Of the absolute Heavens. Deep-hearted man, express
Grief for thy Dead in silence like to death —
    Most like a monumental statue set
In everlasting watch and moveless woe
Till itself crumble to the dust beneath.
    Touch it; the marble eyelids are not wet:
If it could weep, it could arise and go.

ELIZABETH BARRETT BROWNING

*ℰ • ℬ*

# *The Funeral*

Whoever comes to shroud me, do not harm,
      Nor question much,
That subtle wreath of hair, which crowns my arm;
The mystery, the sign, you must not touch;
      For 'tis my outward soul,
Viceroy to that, which then to heaven being gone,
      Will leave this to control
And keep these limbs, her provinces, from dissolution.

For if the sinewy thread my brain lets fall
      Through every part
Can tie those parts, and make me one of all,
Those hairs which upward grew, and strength and art
      Have from a better brain,
Can better do it; except she meant that I
      By this should know my pain,
As prisoners then are manacled, when they're condemn'd to die.

Whate'er she meant by it, bury it with me,
      For since I am
Love's martyr, it might breed idolatry,
If into other hands these relics came.

As 'twas humility
To afford to it all that a soul can do,
So 'tis some bravery,
That since you would have none of me, I bury some of you.

JOHN DONNE

## *They Are All Gone Into The World Of Light*

They are all gone into the world of light!
And I alone sit ling'ring here;
Their very memory is fair and bright,
And my sad thoughts doth clear.

It glows and glitters in my cloudy breast,
Like stars upon some gloomy grove,
Or those faint beams in which this hill is drest,
After the sun's remove.

I see them walking in an air of glory,
Whose light doth trample on my days:
My days, which are at best but dull and hoary,
Mere glimmering and decays.

O holy Hope! and high Humility,
    High as the heavens above!
These are your walks, and you have show'd them me
    To kindle my cold love.

Dear, beauteous Death! the jewel of the just,
    Shining nowhere, but in the dark;
What mysteries do lie beyond thy dust
    Could man outlook that mark!

He that hath found some fledg'd bird's nest, may know
    At first sight, if the bird be flown;
But what fair well or grove he sings in now,
    That is to him unknown.

And yet as angels in some brighter dreams
    Call to the soul, when man doth sleep:
So some strange thoughts transcend our wonted themes
    And into glory peep.

If a star were confin'd into a tomb,
    Her captive flames must needs burn there;
But when the hand that lock'd her up, gives room,
    She'll shine through all the sphere.

O Father of eternal life, and all
    Created glories under thee!
Resume thy spirit from this world of thrall
    Into true liberty.

Either disperse these mists, which blot and fill
    My perspective still as they pass,
Or else remove me hence unto that hill,
    Where I shall need no glass.

HENRY VAUGHAN

*E · R*

# *Requiescat*

Strew on her roses, roses,
    And never a spray of yew!
In quiet she reposes;
    Ah, would that I did too!

Her mirth the world required;
    She bathed it in smiles of glee.
But her heart was tired, tired,
    And now they let her be.

Her life was turning, turning,
  In mazes of heat and sound.
But for peace her soul was yearning,
  And now peace laps her round.

Her cabin'd, ample spirit,
  It flutter'd and fail'd for breath.
To-night it doth inherit
  The vasty hall of death.

MATTHEW ARNOLD

*❦ • ❦*

# *Like As The Waves Make Towards The Pebbl'd Shore*

Like as the waves make towards the pebbl'd shore,
So do our minutes hasten to their end;
Each changing place with that which goes before,
In sequent toil all forwards do contend.
Nativity, once in the main of light,
Crawls to maturity, wherewith being crown'd,
Crooked eclipses 'gainst his glory fight,
And Time that gave doth now his gift confound.
Time doth transfix the flourish set on youth
And delves the parallels in beauty's brow,

Feeds on the rarities of nature's truth,
And nothing stands but for his scythe to mow:
    And yet to times in hope my verse shall stand,
    Praising thy worth, despite his cruel hand.

WILLIAM SHAKESPEARE

    *&#x00B7;*

## *When All Is Done*

When all is done, and my last word is said,
And ye who loved me murmur, 'He is dead,'
Let no one weep, for fear that I should know,
And sorrow too that ye should sorrow so.

When all is done and in the oozing clay,
Ye lay this cast-off hull of mine away,
Pray not for me, for, after long despair,
The quiet of the grave will be a prayer.

For I have suffered loss and grievous pain,
The hurts of hatred and the world's disdain,
And wounds so deep that love, well-tried and pure,
Had not the pow'r to ease them or to cure.

When all is done, say not my day is o'er,
And that thro' night I seek a dimmer shore:
Say rather that my morn has just begun, —
I greet the dawn and not a setting sun,
When all is done.

PAUL LAURENCE DUNBAR

# Nature
## AND
# the Seasons

# On The Companionship With Nature

Let us be much with Nature; not as they
That labour without seeing, that employ
Her unloved forces, blindly without joy;
Nor those whose hands and crude delights obey
The old brute passion to hunt down and slay;
But rather as children of one common birth,
Discerning in each natural fruit of earth
Kinship and bond with this diviner clay.
Let us be with her wholly at all hours,
With the fond lover's zest, who is content
If his ear hears, and if his eye but sees;
So shall we grow like her in mould and bent,
Our bodies stately as her blessèd trees,
Our thoughts as sweet and sumptuous as her flowers.

ARCHIBALD LAMPMAN

*ℰ • ℬ*

# Ode To A Nightingale

My heart aches, and a drowsy numbness pains
My sense, as though of hemlock I had drunk,
Or emptied some dull opiate to the drains
One minute past, and Lethe-wards had sunk:

'Tis not through envy of thy happy lot,
  But being too happy in thy happiness, —
    That thou, light-winged Dryad of the trees,
     In some melodious plot
  Of beechen green, and shadows numberless,
    Singest of summer in full-throated ease.


O for a draught of vintage, that hath been
  Cooled a long age in the deep-delved earth,
Tasting of Flora and the country green,
  Dance, and Provençal song, and sunburnt mirth!
O for a beaker full of the warm South,
  Full of the true, the blushful Hippocrene,
    With beaded bubbles winking at the brim
    And purple-stained mouth;
That I might drink, and leave the world unseen,
  And with thee fade away into the forest dim:


Fade far away, dissolve, and quite forget
  What thou among the leaves hast never known,
The weariness, the fever, and the fret
  Here, where men sit and hear each other groan;
Where palsy shakes a few, sad, last grey hairs,
  Where youth grows pale, and spectre-thin, and dies;

Where but to think is to be full of sorrow
And leaden-eyed despairs;
Where Beauty cannot keep her lustrous eyes,
Or new Love pine at them beyond tomorrow.

Away! away! for I will fly to thee,
Not charioted by Bacchus and his pards,
But on the viewless wings of Poesy,
Though the dull brain perplexes and retards:
Already with thee! tender is the night,
And haply the Queen-Moon is on her throne,
Clustered around by all her starry fays;
But here there is no light
Save what from heaven is with the breezes blown
Through verdurous glooms and winding
mossy ways.

I cannot see what flowers are at my feet,
Nor what soft incense hangs upon the boughs,
But, in embalmed darkness, guess each sweet
Wherewith the seasonable month endows
The grass, the thicket, and the fruit-tree wild;
White hawthorn, and the pastoral eglantine;
Fast-fading violets covered up in leaves;
And mid-May's eldest child

The coming musk-rose, full of dewy wine,
>> The murmurous haunt of flies on summer eves.

Darkling I listen; and for many a time
> I have been half in love with easeful Death,
Called him soft names in many a mused rhyme,
> To take into the air my quiet breath;
Now more than ever seems it rich to die,
> To cease upon the midnight with no pain,
>> While thou art pouring forth thy soul abroad
>> In such an ecstasy!
> Still wouldst thou sing, and I have ears in vain —
>> To thy high requiem become a sod.

Thou wast not born for death, immortal Bird!
> No hungry generations tread thee down;
The voice I hear this passing night was heard
> In ancient days by emperor and clown:
Perhaps the selfsame song that found a path
> Through the sad heart of Ruth, when, sick for home,
>> She stood in tears amid the alien corn;
>>> The same that oft-times hath
> Charmed magic casements, opening on the foam
>> Of perilous seas, in faery lands forlorn.

Forlorn! the very word is like a bell
    To toll me back from thee to my sole self!
Adieu! the fancy cannot cheat so well
    As she is famed to do, deceiving elf.
Adieu! adieu! thy plaintive anthem fades
    Past the near meadows, over the still stream,
        Up the hill-side; and now 'tis buried deep
        In the next valley-glades:
    Was it a vision, or a waking dream?
        Fled is that music: do I wake or sleep?

JOHN KEATS

❧ • ❧

## *Trees*

I think that I shall never see
A poem lovely as a tree.

A tree whose hungry mouth is prest
Against the earth's sweet flowing breast;

A tree that looks at God all day,
And lifts her leafy arms to pray;

A tree that may in Summer wear
A nest of robins in her hair;

Upon whose bosom snow has lain;
Who intimately lives with rain.

Poems are made by fools like me,
But only God can make a tree.

JOYCE KILMER

*J • R*

## *Ode To The West Wind*

I

O wild West Wind, thou breath of Autumn's being,
Thou, from whose unseen presence the leaves dead
Are driven, like ghosts from an enchanter fleeing,

Yellow, and black, and pale, and hectic red,
Pestilence-stricken multitudes: O thou,
Who chariotest to their dark wintry bed

The wingèd seeds, where they lie cold and low,
Each like a corpse within its grave, until
Thine azure sister of the Spring shall blow

Her clarion o'er the dreaming earth, and fill
(Driving sweet buds like flocks to feed in air)
With living hues and odours plain and hill:

Wild Spirit, which art moving everywhere;
Destroyer and preserver; hear, oh, hear!

## II

Thou on whose stream, 'mid the steep sky's commotion,
Loose clouds like earth's decaying leaves are shed,
Shook from the tangled boughs of heaven and ocean,

Angels of rain and lightning; there are spread
On the blue surface of thine airy surge,
Like the bright hair uplifted from the head

Of some fierce Maenad, even from the dim verge
Of the horizon to the zenith's height –
The locks of the approaching storm. Thou dirge

Of the dying year, to which this closing night
Will be the dome of a vast sepulchre,
Vaulted with all thy congregated might

Of vapours, from whose solid atmosphere
Black rain, and fire, and hail, will burst: oh, hear!

### III

Thou who didst waken from his summer dreams,
The blue Mediterranean, where he lay,
Lulled by the coil of his crystalline streams,

Beside a pumice isle in Baiae's bay,
And saw in sleep old palaces and towers
Quivering within the wave's intenser day,

All overgrown with azure moss and flowers
So sweet, the sense faints picturing them! Thou
For whose path the Atlantic's level powers

Cleave themselves into chasms, while far below
The sea-blooms and the oozy woods which wear
The sapless foliage of the ocean, know

Thy voice, and suddenly grow grey with fear,
And tremble and despoil themselves: oh, hear!

### IV

If I were a dead leaf thou mightest bear;
If I were a swift cloud to fly with thee;
A wave to pant beneath thy power, and share

The impulse of thy strength, only less free
Than thou, O uncontrollable! If even
I were as in my boyhood, and could be

The comrade of thy wanderings over Heaven,
As then, when to outstrip thy skiey speed
Scarce seemed a vision, I would ne'er have striven

As thus with thee in prayer in my sore need.
O, lift me as a wave, a leaf, a cloud!
I fall upon the thorns of life! I bleed!

A heavy weight of hours has chained and bowed
One too like thee: tameless, and swift, and proud.

V

Make me thy lyre, even as the forest is:
What if my leaves are falling like its own!
The tumult of thy mighty harmonies

Will take from both a deep autumnal tone,
Sweet though in sadness. Be thou, Spirit fierce,
My spirit! be thou me, impetuous one!

Drive my dead thoughts over the universe
Like withered leaves, to quicken a new birth;
And, by the incantation of this verse,

Scatter, as from an unextinguished hearth
Ashes and sparks, my words among mankind!
Be through my lips to unawakened earth

The trumpet of a prophecy! O Wind,
If Winter comes, can Spring be far behind?

PERCY BYSSHE SHELLEY

℘ • ℘

# On The Grasshopper And Cricket

The poetry of earth is never dead:
When all the birds are faint with the hot sun,
And hide in cooling trees, a voice will run
From hedge to hedge about the new-mown mead;
That is the Grasshopper's — he takes the lead
In summer luxury, — he has never done
With his delights; for when tired out with fun
He rests at ease beneath some pleasant weed.
The poetry of earth is ceasing never:
On a lone winter evening, when the frost
Has wrought a silence, from the stove there shrills
The Cricket's song, in warmth increasing ever,
And seems to one in drowsiness half-lost,
The Grasshopper's among the grassy hills.

JOHN KEATS

℘ • ℘

## Quiet Work

One lesson, Nature, let me learn of thee,
One lesson which in every wind is blown,
One lesson of two duties kept at one
Though the loud world proclaim their enmity —
Of toil unsevered from tranquillity!
Of labour, that in lasting fruit outgrows
Far noisier schemes, accomplish'd in repose,
Too great for haste, too high for rivalry!

Yes, while on earth a thousand discords ring,
Man's fitful uproar mingling with his toil,
Still do thy sleepless ministers move on,
Their glorious tasks in silence perfecting;
Still working, blaming still our vain turmoil,
Labourers that shall not fail, when man is gone.

MATTHEW ARNOLD

# *Nature*

O nature I do not aspire
To be the highest in thy quire,
To be a meteor in the sky
Or comet that may range on high,
Only a zephyr that may blow
Among the reeds by the river low.
Give me thy most privy place
Where to run my airy race.
In some withdrawn unpublic mead
Let me sigh upon a reed,
Or in the woods with leafy din
Whisper the still evening in,
For I had rather be thy child
And pupil in the forest wild
Than be the king of men elsewhere
And most sovereign slave of care
To have one moment of thy dawn
Than share the city's year forlorn.
Some still work give me to do
Only be it near to you.

HENRY DAVID THOREAU

# *The Mower To The Glowworms*

### I

Ye living Lamps, by whose dear light
The Nightingale does sit so late,
And studying all the Summer night,
Her matchless Songs does meditate;

### II

Ye Country Comets, that portend
No War, nor Prince's funeral,
Shining unto no higher end
Than to presage the Grass's fall;

### III

Ye Glowworms, whose officious Flame
To wandring Mowers shows the way,
That in the Night have lost their aim,
And after foolish Fires do stray;

### IV

Your courteous Lights in vain you waste,
Since Juliana here is come,
For She my Mind hath so displac'd
That I shall never find my home.

ANDREW MARVELL

*𝒜 • ℬ*

## *To Daffodils*

Fair Daffodils, we weep to see
     You haste away so soon;
As yet the early-rising sun
     Has not attained his noon.
     Stay, stay,
     Until the hasting day
     Has run
     But to the even-song;
And, having prayed together, we
     Will go with you along.

We have short time to stay, as you,
     We have as short a Spring!
As quick a growth to meet decay,
     As you, or any thing.
     We die,
     As your hours do, and dry
     Away,
     Like to the Summer's rain;
Or as the pearls of morning's dew,
     Ne'er to be found again.

ROBERT HERRICK

323

## *The Sick Rose*

O rose, thou art sick:
The invisible worm
That flies in the night,
In the howling storm,

Has found out thy bed
Of crimson joy,
And his dark secret love
Does thy life destroy.

WILLIAM BLAKE

*𝒟 · ℬ*

## *The Lily*

White Lady of the silvered lakes,
Chaste goddess of the sweet, still shrine,
The jocund river fitful makes
By sudden, deep-gloomed brakes,
Close sheltered by close warp and woof of vine,
Spilling a shadow gloomy-rich as wine
Into the silver throne where thou dost sit,
Thy silken leaves all dusky round thee knit!

Mild Soul of the unsalted wave,
White bosom holding golden fire,
Deep as some ocean-hidden cave
Are fixed the roots of thy desire,
Through limpid currents stealing up,
And rounding to the pearly cup.
Thou dost desire,
With all thy trembling heart of sinless fire,
But to be filled
With dew distilled
From clear, fond skies that in their gloom
Hold, floating high, thy sister moon,
Pale chalice of a sweet perfume.
Whiter-breasted than a dove,
To thee the dew is — love!

ISABELLA VALANCY CRAWFORD

*❦ · ❦*

## Reverie: The Orchard On The Slope

Thin ridges of land unploughed
Along the tree-rows
Covered with long cream grasses
Wind-torn.

Brown sand between them,
Blue boughs above.

Row and row of waves ever
In the breaking;
Ever in arching and convulsed
Imminence;
Roll of muddy sea between;
Low clouds down-pressing
And pallid and streaming rain.

RAYMOND KNISTER

## The Passionate Shepherd To His Love

Come live with me, and be my Love,
And we will all the pleasures prove
That hills and valleys, dale and field,
And all the craggy mountains yield.

There we will sit upon the rocks,
And see the shepherds feed their flocks,
By shallow rivers, to whose falls
Melodious birds sing madrigals.

And I will make thee beds of roses
With a thousand fragrant posies,
A cap of flowers and a kirtle
Embroidered all with leaves of myrtle.

A gown made of the finest wool,
Which from our pretty lambs we pull,
Fair-linèd slippers for the cold,
With buckles of the purest gold.

A belt of straw and ivy buds,
With coral clasps and amber studs:
And if these pleasures may thee move,
Come live with me, and be my Love.

Thy silver dishes for thy meat
As precious as the gods do eat,
Shall on an ivory table be
Prepared each day for thee and me.

The shepherd swains shall dance and sing
For thy delight each May-morning:
If these delights thy mind may move,
Then live with me, and be my Love.

CHRISTOPHER MARLOWE

$\mathcal{D} \cdot \mathcal{B}$

## *Her Reply*

If all the world and love were young,
And truth in every shepherd's tongue,
These pretty pleasures might me move
To live with thee and be thy Love.

But Time drives flocks from field to fold,
When rivers rage and rocks grow cold;
And Philomel becometh dumb;
The rest complain of cares to come.

The flowers do fade, and wanton fields
To wayward winter reckoning yields:
A honey tongue, a heart of gall,
Is fancy's spring, but sorrow's fall.

Thy gowns, thy shoes, thy beds of roses,
Thy cap, thy kirtle, and thy posies,
Soon break, soon wither, soon forgotten, —
In folly ripe, in reason rotten.

Thy belt of straw and ivy buds,
Thy coral clasps and amber studs, —
All these in me no means can move
To come to thee and be thy Love.

But could youth last, and love still breed,
Had joys no date, nor age no need,
Then these delights my mind might move
To live with thee and be thy Love.

SIR WALTER RALEIGH

## To A Skylark

Hail to thee, blithe Spirit!
Bird thou never wert,
That from Heaven or near it
Pourest thy full heart
In profuse strains of unpremeditated art.

Higher still and higher
　From the earth thou springest,
Like a cloud of fire;
　The blue deep thou wingest,
And singing still dost soar, and soaring ever singest.

In the golden lightning
　Of the sunken sun,
O'er which clouds are bright'ning,
　Thou dost float and run,
Like an unbodied joy whose race is just begun.

The pale purple even
　Melts around thy flight;
Like a star of heaven,
　In the broad daylight
Thou art unseen, but yet I hear thy shrill delight:

Keen as are the arrows
　Of that silver sphere,
Whose intense lamp narrows
　In the white dawn clear,
Until we hardly see — we feel that it is there.

All the earth and air
   With thy voice is loud,
As when night is bare,
   From one lonely cloud
The moon rains out her beams, and heaven is overflowed.

What thou art we know not;
   What is most like thee?
From rainbow clouds there flow not
   Drops so bright to see,
As from thy presence showers a rain of melody.

Like a poet hidden
   In the light of thought,
Singing hymns unbidden,
   Till the world is wrought
To sympathy with hopes and fears it heeded not:

Like a high-born maiden
   In a palace tower,
Soothing her love-laden
   Soul in secret hour
With music sweet as love, which overflows her bower:

Like a glow-worm golden
  In a dell of dew,
Scattering unbeholden
  Its aerial hue
Among the flowers and grass which screen it from the view:

Like a rose embowered
  In its own green leaves,
By warm winds deflowered,
  Till the scent it gives
Makes faint with too much sweet these heavy-winged thieves.

Sound of vernal showers
  On the twinkling grass,
Rain-awakened flowers,
  All that ever was
Joyous, and clear, and fresh, thy music doth surpass.

Teach us, sprite or bird,
  What sweet thoughts are thine:
I have never heard
  Praise of love or wine
That panted forth a flood of rapture so divine.

Chorus hymeneal,
　Or triumphal chaunt,
Matched with thine would be all
　But an empty vaunt
A thing wherein we feel there is some hidden want.

What objects are the fountains
　Of thy happy strain?
What fields, or waves, or mountains?
　What shapes of sky or plain?
What love of thine own kind? what ignorance of pain?

With thy clear keen joyance
　Languor cannot be:
Shadow of annoyance
　Never came near thee:
Thou lovest, but ne'er knew love's sad satiety.

Waking or asleep,
　Thou of death must deem
Things more true and deep
　Than we mortals dream,
Or how could thy notes flow in such a crystal stream?

We look before and after,
   And pine for what is not:
Our sincerest laughter
   With some pain is fraught;
Our sweetest songs are those that tell of saddest thought.

Yet, if we could scorn
   Hate and pride and fear,
If we were things born
   Not to shed a tear,
I know not how thy joy we ever should come near.

Better than all measures
   Of delightful sound,
Better than all treasures
   That in books are found,
Thy skill to poet were, thou scorner of the ground!

Teach me half the gladness
   That thy brain must know,
Such harmonious madness
   From my lips would flow,
The world should listen then, as I am listening now.

PERCY BYSSHE SHELLEY

## *To The Man-of-War Bird*

Thou who hast slept all night upon the storm,

Waking renewed on thy prodigious pinions,

(Burst the wild storm? above it thou ascended'st,

And rested on the sky, thy slave that cradled thee,)

Now a blue point, far, far in heaven floating,

As to the light emerging here on deck I watch thee,

(Myself a speck, a point on the world's floating vast.)


Far, far at sea,

After the night's fierce drifts have strewn the shore with
wrecks,

With re-appearing day as now so happy and serene,

The rosy and elastic dawn, the flashing sun,

The limpid spread of air cerulean,

Thou also re-appearest.


Thou born to match the gale, (thou art all wings,)

To cope with heaven and earth and sea and hurricane,

Thou ship of air that never furl'st thy sails,

Days, even weeks untired and onward, through spaces,
realms gyrating,

At dusk that look'st on Senegal, at morn America,

That sport'st amid the lightning-flash and thunder-cloud,
    In them, in thy experiences, had'st thou my soul,
        What joys! what joys were thine!

WALT WHITMAN

𝒜 • ℬ

## *Robin Redbreast*

Good-bye, good-bye to Summer!
    For Summer's nearly done;
The garden smiling faintly,
    Cool breezes in the sun;
Our thrushes now are silent,
    Our swallows flown away, —
But Robin's here in coat of brown,
    And scarlet breast-knot gay.
        Robin, Robin Redbreast,
           O Robin dear!
        Robin sings so sweetly
           In the falling of the year.

Bright yellow, red, and orange,
    The leaves come down in hosts;
The trees are Indian princes,

But soon they'll turn to ghosts;
The scanty pears and apples
Hang russet on the bough;
It's autumn, autumn, autumn late,
'Twill soon be Winter now.
Robin, Robin Redbreast,
O Robin dear!
And what will this poor Robin do?
For pinching days are near.

The fireside for the cricket,
The wheat-stack for the mouse,
When trembling night-winds whistle
And moan all round the house.
The frosty ways like iron,
The branches plumed with snow, —
Alas! in Winter dead and dark,
Where can poor Robin go?
Robin, Robin Redbreast,
O Robin dear!
And a crumb of bread for Robin,
His little heart to cheer.

WILLIAM ALLINGHAM

## Sunrise Along The Shore

Athwart the harbour lingers yet
The ashen gleam of breaking day,
And where the guardian cliffs are set
The noiseless shadows steal away;
But all the winnowed eastern sky
Is flushed with many a tender hue,
And spears of light are smiting through
The ranks where huddled sea-mists fly.

Across the ocean, wan and gray,
Gay fleets of golden ripples come,
For at the birth hour of the day
The roistering, wayward winds are dumb.

The rocks that stretch to meet the tide
Are smitten with a ruddy glow,
And faint reflections come and go
Where fishing boats at anchor ride.

All life leaps out to greet the light —
The shining sea-gulls dive and soar,
The swallows wheel in dizzy flight,
And sandpeeps flit along the shore.

From every purple landward hill
The banners of the morning fly,
But on the headlands, dim and high,
The fishing hamlets slumber still.

One boat alone beyond the bar
Is sailing outward blithe and free,
To carry sturdy hearts afar
Across those wastes of sparkling sea,
Staunchly to seek what may be won
From out the treasures of the deep,
To toil for those at home who sleep
And be the first to greet the sun.

L. M. MONTGOMERY

* · *

## *The Coming Of Morn*

See how the Morn awakes. Along the sky
Proceeds she with her pale, increasing light,
And, from the depths of the dim canopy,
Drives out the shadows of departing night.
Lo, the clouds break, and gradually more wide
Morn openeth her bright, rejoicing gates;

And ever, as the orient valves divide,
A costlier aspect on their breadth awaits.

Lo, the clouds break, and in each opened schism
The coming Phoebus lays huge beams of gold,
And roseate fire and glories that the prism
Would vainly strive before us to unfold;
And, while I gaze, from out the bright abysm
A flaming disc is to the horizon rolled.

CHARLES HEAVYSEGE

♔ · ♕

## *The Morning Land*

The light rains grandly from the distant wood,
For in the wood the hermit sun is hid;
So night draws back her curtains ebon-hued,
To close them round some eastern pyramid.

The listless dew lies shining on the grass,
And o'er the streams the light darts quick away,
And through the fields the morning sunbeams pass,
Shot from the opening portals of the day.

Still upward mounts the tireless eremite,
    (While all the herald birds make loud acclaim)
Till o'er the woods he rounds upon our sight,
    And, lo! the western world is all aflame.

From out the landscape lying 'neath the sun
    The last sea-smelling, cloud-like mists arise;
The smoky woods grow clear, and, one by one,
    The meadow blossoms open their winking eyes.

Now pleased fancy starts with eager mien —
    A-tiptoe, looking o'er the silent fields,
Where all the land is fresh and calm and green,
    And every flow'r its balmy incense yields.

And I, who am upon no business bent,
    A simple stroller through these dewy ways,
Feel that all things are with my future blent,
    Yet see them in the light of by-gone days.

CHARLES MAIR

    *❦ • ❦*

# *Indian Summer*

By the purple haze that lies
    On the distant rocky height,
By the deep blue of the skies,
    By the smoky amber light
Through the forest arches streaming,
Where Nature on her throne sits dreaming,
And the sun is scarcely gleaming
    Through the cloudlets, snowy white, —
Winter's lovely herald greets us,
Ere the ice-crowned tyrant meets us.

This dreamy Indian Summer day
    Attunes the soul to tender sadness;
We love — but joy not in the ray;
    It is not summer's fervid gladness,
But a melancholy glory,
    Hovering softly round decay, —
Like swan that sings her own sad story,
    Ere she floats in death away.

SUSANNA MOODIE

*ℐ • ℛ*

## *Loveliest Of Trees*

Loveliest of trees, the cherry now
Is hung with bloom along the bough,
And stands about the woodland ride
Wearing white for Eastertide.

Now, of my threescore years and ten,
Twenty will not come again,
And take from seventy springs a score,
It only leaves me fifty more.

And since to look at things in bloom
Fifty springs are little room,
About the woodlands I will go
To see the cherry hung with snow.

A. E. HOUSMAN

*&  •  &*

## *Indian Summer*

Along the line of smoky hills
The crimson forest stands,
And all the day the blue-jay calls
Throughout the autumn lands.

Now by the brook the maple leans
    With all his glory spread,
And all the sumachs on the hills
    Have turned their green to red.

Now by great marshes wrapt in mist,
    Or past some river's mouth,
Throughout the long, still autumn day
    Wild birds are flying south.

WILFRED CAMPBELL

## October's Bright Blue Weather

O Suns and skies and clouds of June,
    And flowers of June together,
Ye cannot rival for one hour
    October's bright blue weather.

When loud the humblebee makes haste,
    Belated, thriftless vagrant,
And Golden-Rod is dying fast,
    And lanes with grapes are fragrant;

When Gentians roll their fringes tight
     To save them for the morning,
And chestnuts fall from satin burrs
     Without a sound of warning;

When on the ground red apples lie
     In piles like jewels shining,
And redder still on old stone walls
     Are leaves of woodbine twining;

When all the lovely wayside things
     Their white-winged seeds are sowing,
And in the fields, still green and fair,
     Late aftermaths are growing;

When springs run low, and on the brooks,
     In idle golden freighting,
Bright leaves sink noiseless in the hush
     Of woods, for winter waiting;

When comrades seek sweet country haunts,
     By twos and twos together,
And count like misers, hour by hour,
     October's bright blue weather.

O suns and skies and flowers of June,
Count all your boasts together,
Love loveth best of all the year
October's bright blue weather.

HELEN HUNT JACKSON

ℰ • ℬ

## *October*

October's peace hath fallen on everything.
In the far west, above the pine-crowned hill,
With red and purple yet the heavens thrill —
The passing of the sun remembering.
A crow sails by on heavy, flapping wing,
(In some land, surely the young Spring hath her will!)
Below, the little city lieth still;
And on the river's breast the mist-wreaths cling.
Here, on this slope that yet hath known no plough,
The cattle wander homeward slowly now;
In shapeless clumps the ferns are brown and dead.
Among the fir-trees dusk is swiftly born;
The maples will be desolate by morn.
The last word of the summer hath been said.

FRANCIS SHERMAN

ℰ • ℬ

## *To Autumn*

Season of mists and mellow fruitfulness,
Close bosom-friend of the maturing sun;
Conspiring with him how to load and bless
With fruit the vines that round the thatch-eves run;
To bend with apples the moss'd cottage-trees,
And fill all fruit with ripeness to the core;
To swell the gourd, and plump the hazel shells
With a sweet kernel; to set budding more,
And still more, later flowers for the bees,
Until they think warm days will never cease,
For summer has o'er-brimm'd their clammy cells.

Who hath not seen thee oft amid thy store?
Sometimes whoever seeks abroad may find
Thee sitting careless on a granary floor,
Thy hair soft-lifted by the winnowing wind;
Or on a half-reap'd furrow sound asleep,
Drows'd with the fume of poppies, while thy hook
Spares the next swath and all its twined flowers:
And sometimes like a gleaner thou dost keep
Steady thy laden head across a brook;
Or by a cyder-press, with patient look,
Thou watchest the last oozings hours by hours.

Where are the songs of spring? Ay, where are they?
Think not of them, thou hast thy music too, —
While barred clouds bloom the soft-dying day,
And touch the stubble-plains with rosy hue;
Then in a wailful choir the small gnats mourn
Among the river sallows, borne aloft
Or sinking as the light wind lives or dies;
And full-grown lambs loud bleat from hilly bourn;
Hedge-crickets sing; and now with treble soft
The red-breast whistles from a garden-croft;
And gathering swallows twitter in the skies.

JOHN KEATS

## A Song Of Autumn

'Where shall we go for our garlands glad
At the falling of the year,
When the burnt-up banks are yellow and sad,
When the boughs are yellow and sere?
Where are the old ones that once we had,
And when are the new ones near?
What shall we do for our garlands glad

At the falling of the year?'
'Child! can I tell where the garlands go?
    Can I say where the lost leaves veer
On the brown-burnt banks, when the wild winds blow,
    When they drift through the dead-wood drear?
Girl! when the garlands of next year glow,
    *You* may gather again, my dear —
But *I* go where the last year's lost leaves go
    At the falling of the year.'

ADAM LINDSAY GORDON

*ℰ • ℬ*

## The Fall Of The Leaf

Earnest and sad the solemn tale
    That the sighing winds give back,
Scatt'ring the leaves with mournful wail
    O'er the forest's faded track;
Gay summer birds have left us now
    For a warmer, brighter clime,
Where no leaden sky or leafless bough
    Tell of change and winter-time.

Reapers have gathered golden store
    Of maize and ripened grain,

And they'll seek the lonely fields no more
    Till the springtide comes again.
But around the homestead's blazing hearth
    Will they find sweet rest from toil,
And many an hour of harmless mirth
    While the snow-storm piles the soil.

Then, why should we grieve for summer skies —
    For its shady trees — its flowers,
Or the thousand light and pleasant ties
    That endeared the sunny hours?
A few short months of snow and storm,
    Of winter's chilling reign,
And summer, with smiles and glances warm,
    Will gladden our earth again.

ROSANNA LEPROHON

*∂ • ℛ*

## *In Memorabilia Mortis*

I marked the slow withdrawal of the year.
Out on the hills the scarlet maples shone —
The glad, first herald of triumphant dawn.
A robin's song fell through the silence — clear
    As long ago it rang when June was here.
Then, suddenly, a few grey clouds were drawn

Across the sky; and all the song was gone,

And all the gold was quick to disappear.

That day the sun seemed loth to come again;

And all day long the low wind spoke of rain,

Far off, beyond the hills; and moaned, like one

Wounded, among the pines: as though the Earth,

Knowing some giant grief had come to birth,

Had wearied of the Summer and the Sun.

FRANCIS SHERMAN

$\mathscr{T} \cdot \mathscr{B}$

## *The Winter Galaxy*

The stars are glittering in the frosty sky,

Numerous as pebbles on a broad sea-coast;

And o'er the vault the cloud-like galaxy

Has marshalled its innumerable host.

Alive all heaven seems! with wondrous glow

Tenfold refulgent every star appears,

As if some wide, celestial gale did blow,

And thrice illume the ever-kindled spheres.

Orbs, with glad orbs rejoicing, burning, beam

Ray-crowned, with lambent lustre in their zones,

Till o'er the blue, bespangled spaces seem

Angels and great archangels on their thrones;
A host divine, whose eyes are sparkling gems,
And forms more bright than diamond diadems.

CHARLES HEAVYSEGE

*ℰ • ℬ*

# *Winter Evening*

To-night the very horses springing by
Toss gold from whitened nostrils. In a dream
The streets that narrow to the westward gleam
Like rows of golden palaces; and high
From all the crowded chimneys tower and die
A thousand aureoles.  Down in the west
The brimming plains beneath the sunset rest,
One burning sea of gold.  Soon, soon shall fly
The glorious vision, and the hours shall feel
A mightier master; soon from height to height,
With silence and the sharp unpitying stars,
Stern creeping frosts, and winds that touch like steel,
Out of the depth beyond the eastern bars,
Glittering and still shall come the awful night.

ARCHIBALD LAMPMAN

*ℰ • ℬ*

## The Snow Storm

Announced by all the trumpets of the sky,
Arrives the snow, and, driving o'er the fields,
Seems nowhere to alight: the whited air
Hides hills and woods, the river, and the heaven,
And veils the farmhouse at the garden's end.
The sled and traveller stopped, the courier's feet
Delayed, all friends shut out, the housemates sit
Around the radiant fireplace, enclosed
In a tumultuous privacy of storm.

Come see the north wind's masonry.
Out of an unseen quarry evermore
Furnished with tile, the fierce artificer
Curves his white bastions with projected roof
Round every windward stake, or tree, or door.
Speeding, the myriad-handed, his wild work
So fanciful, so savage, nought cares he
For number or proportion. Mockingly,
On coop or kennel he hangs Parian wreaths;
A swan-like form invests the hidden thorn;
Fills up the farmer's lane from wall to wall,
Maugre the farmer's sighs; and at the gate
A tapering turret overtops the work.
And when his hours are numbered, and the world

Is all his own, retiring, as he were not,
Leaves, when the sun appears, astonished Art
To mimic in slow structures, stone by stone,
Built in an age, the mad wind's night-work,
The frolic architecture of the snow.

RALPH WALDO EMERSON

❧ • ☙

## *The Quiet Snow*

The quiet snow
Will splotch
Each in the row of cedars
With a fine
And patient hand;
Numb the harshness,
Tangle of that swamp.
It does not say, The sun
Does these things another way.

Even on hats of walkers,
The air of noise
And street-car ledges
It does not know
There should be hurry.

RAYMOND KNISTER

❧ • ☙

## *December*

The woods that summer loved are grey and bare;
The sombre trees stretch up their arms on high,
In mute appeal, against the leaden sky;
A flurry faint of snow is in the air.
All day the clouds have hung in heavy fold
Above the valley, where grey shadows steal;
And I, who sit and watch them, seem to feel
A touch of sadness as the day grows old.
But o'er my fancy comes a tender face,
A dream of curls that float like sunlight golden —
A subtle fragrance, filling all the place,
The whisper of a story that is olden —
Till breaks the sun through dull December skies,
And all the world is springtime in the deep blue of her eyes.

STUART LIVINGSTONE

*ℰ • ℬ*

## *A January Morning*

The glittering roofs are still with frost; each worn
Black chimney builds into the quiet sky
Its curling pile to crumble silently.
Far out to westward on the edge of morn,

The slender misty city towers up-borne
Glimmer faint rose against the pallid blue;
And yonder on those northern hills, the hue
Of amethyst, hang fleeces dull as horn.
And here behind me come the woodmen's sleighs
With shouts and clamorous squeakings; might and main
Up the steep slope the horses stamp and strain,
Urged on by hoarse-tongued drivers — cheeks ablaze,
Iced beards and frozen eyelids — team by team,
With frost-fringed flanks, and nostrils jetting steam.

ARCHIBALD LAMPMAN

ℰ · ℬ

## *January*

The soft blue touch of turquoise, crystal clear,
Curves o'er white hills and rivers' frozen flow,
Draped in a virgin robe of dazzling snow
That veils the silent landscape far and near,
Swathing the withered herbage brown and sere,
And the tall dusky pines that — sweeping low
Their long dark branches — violet  shadows throw
Across the stainless marble of the mere.

Hark! through the stillness break the glad sleigh-bells
In silvery cadence through the frosty air;
Of happy hearts their merry music tells; —
Of glad home-comings — meetings  everywhere;
But late we owned the sway of Christmas spells;
Now New Year chimes ring out the call to prayer!

AGNES MAULE MACHAR

*ᕮ • ᕮ*

## *The Winter Lakes*

Out in a world of death far to the northward lying,
    Under the sun and the moon, under the dusk and the
        day;
Under the glimmer of stars and the purple of sunsets dying,
    Wan and waste and white, stretch the great lakes
        away.

Never a bud of spring, never a laugh of summer,
    Never a dream of love, never a song of bird;
But only the silence and white, the shores that grow chiller
    and dumber,
        Wherever the ice winds sob, and the griefs of winter
            are heard.

Crags that are black and wet out of the grey lake looming,
> Under the sunset's flush and the pallid, faint glimmer
> > of dawn;
Shadowy, ghost-like shores, where midnight surfs are booming
> Thunders of wintry woe over the spaces wan.

Lands that loom like spectres, whited regions of winter,
> Wastes of desolate woods, deserts of water and shore;
A world of winter and death, within these regions who enter,
> Lost to summer and life, go to return no more.

Moons that glimmer above, waters that lie white under,
> Miles and miles of lake far out under the night;
Foaming crests of waves, surfs that shoreward thunder,
> Shadowy shapes that flee, haunting the spaces white.

Lonely hidden bays, moon-lit, ice-rimmed, winding,
> Fringed by forests and crags, haunted by shadowy
> > shores;
Hushed from the outward strife, where the mighty surf is
grinding
> Death and hate on the rocks, as sandward and landward
> > it roars.

WILFRED CAMPBELL

*ℐ • ℬ*

## *The Heart Of Night*

When all the stars are sown
Across the night-blue space,
With the immense unknown,
    In silence face to face.

We stand in speechless awe
While Beauty marches by,
And wonder at the Law
Which wears such majesty.

How small a thing is man
In all that world-sown vast,
That he should hope or plan
Or dream his dream could last!

O doubter of the light,
Confused by fear and wrong,
Lean on the heart of night
And let love make thee strong!

The Good that is the True
Is clothed with Beauty still.
Lo, in their tent of blue,
The stars above the hill!

BLISS CARMAN

*B · B*

# A Canadian Summer Evening

The rose-tints have faded from out of the West,
From the Mountain's high peak, from the river's broad
breast.
And, silently shadowing valley and rill,
The twilight steals noiselessly over the hill.
Behold, in the blue depths of ether afar,
Now softly emerging each glittering star;
While, later, the moon, placid, solemn and bright,
Floods earth with her tremulous, silvery light.

Hush! list to the Whip-poor-will's soft plaintive notes,
As up from the valley the lonely sound floats,
Inhale the sweet breath of yon shadowy wood
And the wild flowers blooming in hushed solitude.
Start not at the whispering, 'tis but the breeze,
Low rustling, 'mid maple and lonely pine trees,
Or willows and alders that fringe the dark tide
Where canoes of the red men oft silently glide.

See, rising from out of that copse, dark and damp,
The fire-flies, each bearing a flickering lamp!
Like meteors, gleaming and streaming, they pass
O'er hillside and meadow, and dew-laden grass,

Contrasting with ripple on river and stream,
Alternately playing in shadow and beam,
Till fullness of beauty fills hearing and sight
Throughout the still hours of a calm summer's night.

ROSANNA LEPROHON

☙ • ❧

# *A Thunderstorm*

A moment the wild swallows like a flight
Of withered gust-caught leaves, serenely high,
Toss in the wind-rack up the muttering sky.
The leaves hang still. Above the weird twilight,
The hurrying centres of the storm unite
And spreading with huge trunk and rolling fringe,
Each wheeled upon its own tremendous hinge,
Tower darkening on. And now from heaven's height,
With the long roar of elm-trees swept and swayed,
And pelted waters, on the vanished plain
Plunges the blast. Behind the wild white flash
That splits abroad the pealing thunder-crash,
Over bleared fields and gardens disarrayed,
Column on column comes the drenching rain.

ARCHIBALD LAMPMAN

☙ • ❧

## *Marigolds*

The marigolds are nodding;
I wonder what they know.
Go, listen very gently;
You may persuade them so.

Go, be their little brother,
As humble as the grass,
And lean upon the hill-wind,
And watch the shadows pass.

Put off the pride of knowledge,
Put by the fear of pain;
You may be counted worthy
To live with them again.

Be Darwin in your patience,
Be Chaucer in your love;
They may relent and tell you
What they are thinking of.

BLISS CARMAN

## Fire-Flowers

And only where the forest fires have sped,
     Scorching relentlessly the cool north lands,
A sweet wild flower lifts its purple head,
And, like some gentle spirit sorrow-fed,
     It hides the scars with almost human hands.

And only to the heart that knows of grief,
     Of desolating fire, of human pain,
There comes some purifying sweet belief,
Some fellow-feeling, beautiful, if brief.
     And life revives and blossoms once again.

E. PAULINE JOHNSON

## Beyond The Sunset

Hushed in a calm beyond mine utterance,
See in the western sky the evening spread;
Suspended in its pale, serene expanse,
Like scattered flames, the glowing cloudlets red.
Clear are those clouds, and that pure sky's profound,

Transparent as a lake of hyaline;
Nor motion, nor the faintest breath of sound,
Disturbs the steadfast beauty of the scene.
Far o'er the vault the winnowed welkin wide,
From the bronzed east unto the whitened west,
Moored, seem, in their sweet, tranquil, roseate pride,
Those clouds the fabled islands of the blest; —
The lands where pious spirits breathe in joy,
And love and worship all their hours employ.

CHARLES HEAVYSEGE

*❦ • ❧*

## *The Vesper Star*

Unfold thy pinions, drooping to the sun,
Just plunged behind the round-browed mountain, deep
Crowned with the snows of hawthorn, avalanched
All down its sloping shoulder with the bloom
Of orchards, blushing to the ardent South,
And to the evening oriflamme of rose
That arches the blue concave of the sky.

O rosy Star, thy trembling glory part
From the great sunset splendour that its tides
Sends rushing in swift billows to the east,
And on their manes of fire outswell thy sails
Of light-spun gold; and as the glory dies,
Throbbing thro' changeful rose to silver mist,
Laden with souls of flowers wooed abroad
From painted petals by the ardent Night,
Possess the heavens for one short splendid hour —
Sole jewel on the Egypt brow of Night,
Who steals, dark giant, to caress the Earth,
And gathers from the glassy mere and sea
The silver foldings of his misty robe,
And hangs upon the air with brooding wings
Of shadow, shadow, stretching everywhere.

ISABELLA VALANCY CRAWFORD

*ℐ • ℬ*

# To A Mouse, On Turning Up Her Nest With The Plough

Wee, sleekit, cow'rin, tim'rous beastie,
O, what a panic's in thy breastie!
Thou need na start awa sae hasty,
Wi' bickering brattle!

I wad be laith to rin an' chase thee,
    Wi' murd'ring pattle!

I'm truly sorry man's dominion,
Has broken nature's social union,
An' justifies that ill opinion,
    Which makes thee startle
At me, thy poor, earth-born companion,
    An' fellow-mortal!

I doubt na, whiles, but thou may thieve;
What then? poor beastie, thou maun live!
A daimen icker in a thrave
    'S a sma' request;
I'll get a blessin wi' the laive,
    An' never miss't!

Thy wee bit housie, too, in ruin!
It's silly wa's the win's are strewin!
An' naething, now, to big a new ane,
    O' foggage green!
An' bleak December's winds ensuin,
    Baith snell an' keen!

Thou saw the fields laid bare an' waste,
An' weary winter comin fast,
An' cozie here, beneath the blast,
Thou thought to dwell —
Till crash! the cruel coulter past
Out thro' thy cell.

That wee bit heap o' leaves an' stibble,
Has cost thee mony a weary nibble!
Now thou's turn'd out, for a' thy trouble,
But house or hald,
To thole the winter's sleety dribble,
An' cranreuch cauld!

But, Mousie, thou art no thy lane,
In proving foresight may be vain;
The best-laid schemes o' mice an' men
Gang aft a-gley,
An'lea'e us nought but grief an' pain,
For promis'd joy!

Still thou art blest, compar'd wi' me
The present only toucheth thee:

But, Och! I backward cast my e'e
On prospects drear!
An' forward, tho' I canna see,
I guess an' fear!

ROBERT BURNS

*𝒯 • 𝒝*

## *The Tiger*

Tiger, tiger, burning bright
In the forests of the night,
What immortal hand or eye
Could frame thy fearful symmetry?

In what distant deeps or skies
Burnt the fire of thine eyes?
On what wings dare he aspire?
What the hand dare seize the fire?

And what shoulder, and what art,
Could twist the sinews of thy heart?
And, when thy heart began to beat,
What dread hand, and what dread feet?

What the hammer? what the chain?
In what furnace was thy brain?
What the anvil? what dread grasp
Dare its deadly terrors clasp?

When the stars threw down their spears,
And watered heaven with their tears,
Did he smile his work to see?
Did he who made the lamb make thee?

Tiger, tiger, burning bright
In the forests of the night,
What immortal hand or eye
Dare frame thy fearful symmetry?

WILLIAM BLAKE

*The Darkling Thrush*

I leant upon a coppice gate
When Frost was spectre-grey,
And Winter's dregs made desolate
The weakening eye of day.

The tangled bine-stems scored the sky
  Like strings from broken lyres,
And all mankind that haunted nigh
  Had sought their household fires.

The land's sharp features seemed to be
  The Century's corpse outleant;
His crypt the cloudy canopy,
  The wind his death-lament.
The ancient pulse of germ and birth
  Was shrunken hard and dry,
And every spirit upon earth
  Seemed fervourless as I.

At once a voice burst forth among
  The bleak twigs overhead
In a full-hearted evensong
  Of joy unlimited;
An aged thrush, frail, gaunt and small,
  In blast-beruffled plume,
Had chosen thus to fling his soul
  Upon the growing gloom.

So little cause for carolings
  Of such ecstatic sound
Was written on terrestrial things
  Afar or nigh around,

That I could think there trembled through
    His happy good-night air
Some blessed hope, whereof he knew
    And I was unaware.

THOMAS HARDY

# *A Noiseless Patient Spider*

A noiseless patient spider
I mark'd, where, on a little promontory, it stood isolated;
Mark'd how, to explore the vacant vast surrounding,
It launch'd forth filament, filament, filament, out of itself;
Ever unreeling them — ever tirelessly speeding them.

And you, O my soul, where you stand,
Surrounded, surrounded, in measureless oceans of space,
Ceaselessly musing, venturing, throwing, — seeking the
    spheres, to connect them;
Till the bridge you will need, be form'd — till the ductile
    anchor hold
Till the gossamer thread you fling, catch somewhere, O my
    soul.

WALT WHITMAN

# *Moonset*

Idles the night wind through the dreaming firs,
That waking murmur low,
As some lost melody returning stirs
The love of long ago;
And through the far, cool distance, zephyr fanned.
The moon is sinking into shadow-land.

The troubled night-bird, calling plaintively,
Wanders on restless wing;
The cedars, chanting vespers to the sea,
Await its answering,
That comes in wash of waves along the strand,
The while the moon slips into shadow-land.

O! soft responsive voices of the night
I join your minstrelsy,
And call across the fading silver light
As something calls to me;
I may not all your meaning understand,
But I have touched your soul in shadow-land.

E. PAULINE JOHNSON

## The Last Rose Of Summer

'Tis the last rose of summer,
           Left blooming alone;
All her lovely companions
           Are faded and gone;
No flower of her kindred,
           No rosebud is nigh,
To reflect back her blushes,
           Or give sigh for sigh!

I'll not leave thee, thou lone one,
           To pine on the stem;
Since the lovely are sleeping,
           Go sleep thou with them.
Thus kindly I scatter
           Thy leaves o'er the bed,
Where thy mates of the garden
           Lie scentless and dead.

So soon may I follow,
           When friendships decay,
And from Love's shining circle
           The gems drop away.
When true hearts lie wither'd,

And fond ones are flown,
Oh! who would inhabit
This bleak world alone?

THOMAS MOORE

# Humour

## AND

# Nonsense

# *Jabberwocky*

'Twas brillig, and the slithy toves
Did gyre and gimble in the wabe;
All mimsy were the borogoves,
And the mome raths outgrabe.

'Beware the Jabberwock, my son!
The jaws that bite, the claws that catch!
Beware the Jubjub bird, and shun
The frumious Bandersnatch!'

He took his vorpal sword in hand:
Long time the manxome foe he sought —
So rested he by the Tumtum tree,
And stood awhile in thought.

And as in uffish thought he stood,
The Jabberwock, with eyes of flame,
Came whiffling through the tulgey wood,
And burbled as it came!

One, two! One, two! And through and through
The vorpal blade went snicker-snack!
He left it dead, and with its head
He went galumphing back.

'And hast thou slain the Jabberwock?
Come to my arms, my beamish boy!
O frabjous day! Callooh! Callay!'
He chortled in his joy.

'Twas brillig, and the slithy toves
Did gyre and gimble in the wabe;
All mimsy were the borogoves,
And the mome raths outgrabe.

LEWIS CARROLL

*A Sonnet*

O lovely O most charming pug
Thy gracefull air and heavenly mug
The beauties of his mind do shine
And every bit is shaped so fine
Your very tail is most devine
Your teeth is whiter than the snow
You are a great buck and a bow
Your eyes are of so fine a shape
More like a christains then an ape
His cheeks is like the roses blume

Your hair is like the raven's plume

His noses cast is of the roman

He is a very pretty weomen

I could not get a rhyme for roman

And was oblidged to call it weoman.

MARJORY FLEMING

𝒟 • ℬ

## *The Walrus And The Carpenter*

The sun was shining on the sea,

Shining with all his might:

He did his very best to make

The billows smooth and bright —

And this was odd, because it was

The middle of the night.

The moon was shining sulkily,

Because she thought the sun

Had got no business to be there

After the day was done —

'It's very rude of him,' she said,

'To come and spoil the fun.'

The sea was wet as wet could be,
The sands were dry as dry.
You could not see a cloud, because
No cloud was in the sky:
No birds were flying overhead —
There were no birds to fly.

The Walrus and the Carpenter
Were walking close at hand;
They wept like anything to see
Such quantities of sand:
'If this were only cleared away,'
They said, 'it would be grand.'

'If seven maids with seven mops
Swept it for half a year,
Do you suppose,' the Walrus said,
'That they could get it clear?'
'I doubt it,' said the Carpenter,
And shed a bitter tear.

'O Oysters, come and walk with us!'
The Walrus did beseech.
'A pleasant walk, a pleasant talk,

Along the briny beach:
We cannot do with more than four,
To give a hand to each.'

The eldest Oyster looked at him,
But never a word he said:
The eldest Oyster winked his eye,
And shook his heavy head —
Meaning to say he did not choose
To leave the oyster-bed.

But four young Oysters hurried up,
All eager for the treat:
Their coats were brushed, their faces washed,
Their shoes were clean and neat —
And this was odd, because, you know,
They hadn't any feet.

Four other Oysters followed them,
And yet another four;
And thick and fast they came at last,
And more, and more, and more —
All hopping through the frothy waves,
And scrambling to the shore.

The Walrus and the Carpenter
Walked on a mile or so,
And then they rested on a rock
Conveniently low:
And all the little Oysters stood
And waited in a row.

'The time has come,' the Walrus said,
'To talk of many things:
Of shoes — and ships — and sealing-wax —
Of cabbages — and kings —
And why the sea is boiling hot —
And whether pigs have wings.'

'But wait a bit,' the Oysters cried,
'Before we have our chat;
For some of us are out of breath,
And all of us are fat!'
'No hurry!' said the Carpenter.
They thanked him much for that.

'A loaf of bread,' the Walrus said,
'Is what we chiefly need:
Pepper and vinegar besides

Are very good indeed —
Now if you're ready, Oysters dear,
We can begin to feed.'

'But not on us!' the Oysters cried,
Turning a little blue.
'After such kindness, that would be
A dismal thing to do!'
'The night is fine,' the Walrus said,
'Do you admire the view?

'It was so kind of you to come!
And you are very nice!'
The Carpenter said nothing but
'Cut us another slice:
I wish you were not quite so deaf —
I've had to ask you twice!'

'It seems a shame,' the Walrus said,
'To play them such a trick,
After we've brought them out so far,
And made them trot so quick!'
The Carpenter said nothing but
'The butter's spread too thick!'

'I weep for you,' the Walrus said:
'I deeply sympathise.'
With sobs and tears he sorted out
Those of the largest size,
Holding his pocket-handkerchief
Before his streaming eyes.

'O Oysters,' said the Carpenter,
'You've had a pleasant run!
Shall we be trotting home again?'
But answer came there none —
And this was scarcely odd, because
They'd eaten every one.

LEWIS CARROLL

## *The Pig*

It was an evening in November,
As I very well remember.
I was walking down the street in drunken pride,
And my knees were all a-flutter,
So I landed in the gutter,
And a pig walked up and laid down at my side.

Yes, I lay there in the gutter,
Thinking thoughts I could not utter,
When a colleen passing by did softly say,
'You can tell the man that boozes
By the company he chooses...'
At that, the pig got up and walked away.

ANONYMOUS

𝒟 • ℬ

## *A Terrible Infant*

I recollect a nurse call'd Ann,
Who carried me about the grass,
And one fine day a fine young man
Came up, and kiss'd the pretty lass.
She did not make the least objection.
Thinks I, *'Aha!*
*When I can talk I'll tell Mama'*
— And that's my earliest recollection.

FREDERICK LOCKER-LAMPSON

𝒟 • ℬ

# The Owl And The Pussy-Cat

## I

The Owl and the Pussy-cat went to sea
    In a beautiful pea-green boat,
They took some honey, and plenty of money,
    Wrapped up in a five-pound note.
The Owl looked up to the stars above,
    And sang to a small guitar,
'O lovely Pussy! O Pussy, my love,
    What a beautiful Pussy you are,
        You are,
        You are!
    What a beautiful Pussy you are!'

## II

Pussy said to the Owl, 'You elegant fowl!
    How charmingly sweet you sing!
O let us be married! too long we have tarried:
    But what shall we do for a ring?'
They sailed away, for a year and a day,
    To the land where the Bong-tree grows
And there in a wood a Piggy-wig stood
    With a ring at the end of his nose,
        His nose,
        His nose,
    With a ring at the end of his nose.

### III

'Dear Pig, are you willing to sell for one shilling
      Your ring?' Said the Piggy, 'I will.'
So they took it away, and were married next day
      By the Turkey who lives on the hill.
They dined on mince, and slices of quince,
      Which they ate with a runcible spoon;
And hand in hand, on the edge of the sand,
      They danced by the light of the moon,
          The moon,
          The moon,
      They danced by the light of the moon.

EDWARD LEAR

## How Pleasant To Know Mr Lear

'How pleasant to know Mr Lear!'
      Who has written such volumes of stuff!
Some think him ill-tempered and queer,
      But a few think him pleasant enough.

His mind is concrete and fastidious,
     His nose is remarkably big;
His visage is more or less hideous,
     His beard it resembles a wig.

He has ears, and two eyes, and ten fingers,
     Leastways if you reckon two thumbs;
Long ago he was one of the singers,
     But now he is one of the dumbs.

He sits in a beautiful parlour,
     With hundreds of books on the wall;
He drinks a great deal of Marsala,
     But never gets tipsy at all.

He has many friends, lay-men and clerical,
     Old Foss is the name of his cat;
His body is perfectly spherical,
     He weareth a runcible hat.

When he walks in waterproof white,
     The children run after him so!
Calling out, 'He's come out in his night-
     gown, that crazy old Englishman, oh!'

He weeps by the side of the ocean,
　　He weeps on the top of the hill;
He purchases pancakes and lotion,
　　And chocolate shrimps from the mill.

He reads, but he cannot speak, Spanish,
　　He cannot abide ginger beer:
Ere the days of his pilgrimage vanish,
　　How pleasant to know Mr Lear!

EDWARD LEAR

ℰ • ℬ

# *Fable*

The mountain and the squirrel
　　Had a quarrel;
And the former called the latter 'Little Prig';
　　Bun replied,
'You are doubtless very big;
But all sorts of things and weather
　　Must be taken in together
　　To make up a year
　　And a sphere.
And I think it no disgrace

To occupy my place.
If I'm not so large as you,
You are not so small as I,
And not half so spry.
I'll not deny you make
A very pretty squirrel track;
Talents differ: all is well and wisely put;
If I cannot carry forests on my back,
Neither can you crack a nut.'

RALPH WALDO EMERSON

## *The Elephant, Or The Force of Habit*

A tail behind, a trunk in front,
Complete the usual elephant.
The tail in front, the trunk behind
Is what you very seldom find.

If you for specimens should hunt
With trunks behind and tails in front,
That hunt would occupy you long;
The force of habit is so strong.

A. E. HOUSMAN

## *When Lovely Woman*

When lovely woman wants a favor,
And finds, too late, that man won't bend,
What earthly circumstance can save her
From disappointment in the end?

The only way to bring him over,
The last experiment to try,
Whether a husband or a lover,
If he have feeling, is, to cry!

PHOEBE CARY

☙ • ❧

## *Thy Heart*

Thy heart is like some icy lake,
On whose cold brink I stand;
Oh, buckle on my spirit's skate,
And lead, thou living saint, the way
To where the ice is thin —
That it may break beneath my feet
And let a lover in!

ANONYMOUS

☙ • ❧

# *Miniver Cheevy*

Miniver Cheevy, child of scorn,
 Grew lean while he assailed the seasons;
He wept that he was ever born,
 And he had reasons.

Miniver loved the days of old
 When swords were bright and steeds were prancing;
The vision of a warrior bold
 Would send him dancing.

Miniver sighed for what was not,
 And dreamed, and rested from his labors;
He dreamed of Thebes and Camelot,
 And Priam's neighbors.

Miniver mourned the ripe renown
 That made so many a name so fragrant;
He mourned Romance, now on the town,
 And Art, a vagrant.

Miniver loved the Medici,
 Albeit he had never seen one;
He would have sinned incessantly
 Could he have been one.

Miniver cursed the commonplace
    And eyed a khaki suit with loathing:
He missed the medieval grace
    Of iron clothing.

Miniver scorned the gold he sought,
    But sore annoyed was he without it;
Miniver thought, and thought, and thought,
    And thought about it.

Miniver Cheevy, born too late,
    Scratched his head and kept on thinking;
Miniver coughed, and called it fate,
    And kept on drinking.

EDWIN ARLINGTON ROBINSON

*E · B*

## The Pessimist

Nothing to do but work,
    Nothing to eat but food,
Nothing to wear but clothes,
    To keep one from going nude.

Nothing to breathe but air,
    Quick as a flash 'tis gone;
Nowhere to fall but off,
    Nowhere to stand but on.

Nothing to comb but hair,
    Nowhere to sleep but in bed,
Nothing to weep but tears,
    Nothing to bury but dead.

Nothing to sing but songs,
    Ah, well, alas! alack!
Nowhere to go but out,
    Nowhere to come but back.

Nothing to see but sights,
    Nothing to quench but thirst,
Nothing to have but what we've got,
    Thus through life we are cursed.

Nothing to strike but a gait;
    Everything moves that goes.
Nothing at all but common sense
    Can ever withstand these woes.

BEN KING

## *Excelsior*

The shades of night were falling fast
And the rain was falling faster,
When through an Alpine village passed
An Alpine village pastor;
A youth who bore mid snow and ice
A bird that wouldn't chirrup,
And a banner, with the strange device —
'Mrs. Winslow's soothing syrup.

'Beware the pass,' the old man said,
'My bold and desperate fellah;
Dark lowers the tempest overhead,
And you'll want your umberella;
And the roaring torrent is deep and wide —
You may hear how it washes.'
But still that clarion voice replied:
'I've got my old goloshes.'

'Oh stay,' the maiden said, 'and rest
(For the wind blows from the nor'ward)
Thy weary head upon my breast —
And please don't think me forward.'

A tear stood in his bright blue eye
And gladly he would have tarried;
But still he answered with a sigh:
'Unhappily I'm married.'

A. E. HOUSMAN

## Ode On The Death Of A Favourite Cat, Drowned In A Tub Of Gold Fishes

'Twas on a lofty vase's side,
Where China's gayest art had dyed
The azure flowers that blow,
Demurest of the tabby kind,
The pensive Selima, reclined,
Gazed on the lake below.

Her conscious tail her joy declared;
The fair round face, the snowy beard,
The velvet of her paws,
Her coat, that with the tortoise vies,
Her ears of jet, and emerald eyes,
She saw; and purred applause.

Still had she gazed; but 'midst the tide
Two angel forms were seen to glide,
The genii of the stream:
Their scaly armour's Tyrian hue
Through richest purple to the view
Betrayed a golden gleam.

The hapless nymph with wonder saw:
A whisker first, and then a claw,
With many an ardent wish,
She stretched, in vain, to reach the prize.
What female heart can gold despise?
What cat's averse to fish?

Presumptuous maid! with looks intent
Again she stretched, again she bent,
Nor knew the gulf between:
(Malignant Fate sat by, and smiled)
The slippery verge her feet beguiled,
She tumbled headlong in.

Eight times emerging from the flood
She mewed to ev"y wat'ry god
Some speedy aid to send.

No dolphin came, no nereid stirred;
Nor cruel Tom, nor Susan heard.
A fav'rite has no friend!

From hence, ye beauties undeceived,
Know, one false step is ne'er retrieved,
And be with caution bold.
Not all that tempts your wand'ring eyes
And heedless hearts is lawful prize;
Nor all that glisters, gold.

THOMAS GRAY

*Ð • Ɓ*

## *Elegy On The Death Of A Mad Dog*

Good people all, of every sort,
Give ear unto my song;
And if you find it wond'rous short,
It cannot hold you long.

In Islington there was a man,
Of whom the world might say,
That still a godly race he ran,
Whene'er he went to pray.

A kind and gentle heart he had,
　　To comfort friends and foes;
The naked every day he clad,
　　When he put on his clothes.

And in that town a dog was found,
　　As many dogs there be,
Both mongrel, puppy, whelp and hound,
　　And curs of low degree.

This dog and man at first were friends;
　　But when a pique began,
The dog, to gain some private ends,
　　Went mad and bit the man.

Around from all the neighbouring streets
　　The wond'ring neighbours ran,
And swore the dog had lost its wits,
　　To bite so good a man.

The wound it seemed both sore and sad
　　To every Christian eye;
And while they swore the dog was mad,
　　They swore the man would die.

But soon a wonder came to light,
  That showed the rogues they lied:
The man recovered of the bite,
  The dog it was that died.

OLIVER GOLDSMITH

&sect; · &sect;

## *Phyllis's Age*

How old may Phyllis be, you ask,
Whose beauty thus all hearts engages?
 To answer is no easy task;
 For she has really two ages.

Stiff in brocard, and pinch'd in stays,
 Her patches, paint, and jewels on;
 All day let envy view her face;
 And Phyllis is but twenty-one.

Paint, patches, jewels laid aside,
 At night astronomers agree,
 The evening has the day belied;
 And Phyllis is some forty-three.

MATTHEW PRIOR

&sect; · &sect;

## *Jenny Kiss'd Me*

Jenny kiss'd me when we met,
>        Jumping from the chair she sat in;
Time, you thief, who love to get
>        Sweets into your list, put that in!
Say I'm weary, say I'm sad,
>        Say that health and wealth have miss'd me,
Say I'm growing old, but add —
>        Jenny kiss'd me!

LEIGH HUNT

*ℰ · ℬ*

## *How Doth The Little Crocodile*

How doth the little crocodile
Improve his shining tail,
And pour the waters of the Nile
On every golden scale!

How cheerfully he seems to grin
How neatly spreads his claws,
And welcomes little fishes in,
With gently smiling jaws!

LEWIS CARROLL

*ℰ · ℬ*

# *The Jumblies*

They went to sea in a Sieve, they did,
    In a Sieve they went to sea:
In spite of all their friends could say,
    On a winter's morn, on a stormy day,
In a Sieve they went to sea!
    And when the Sieve turned round and round,
And every one cried, 'You'll all be drowned!'
    They called aloud, 'Our Sieve ain't big,
But we don't care a button! we don't care a fig!
    In a Sieve we'll go to sea!'
        Far and few, far and few,
            Are the lands where the Jumblies live;
            Their heads are green, and their hands are blue,
            And they went to sea in a Sieve.

They sailed away in a Sieve, they did,
    In a Sieve they sailed so fast,
With only a beautiful pea-green veil
    Tied with a riband by way of a sail,
To a small tobacco-pipe mast;
    And every one said, who saw them go,
'O won't they be soon upset, you know!
    For the sky is dark, and the voyage is long,

And happen what may, it's extremely wrong
   In a Sieve to sail so fast!'
      Far and few, far and few,
         Are the lands where the Jumblies live;
      Their heads are green, and their hands are blue,
         And they went to sea in a Sieve.

The water it soon came in, it did,
   The water it soon came in;
So to keep them dry, they wrapped their feet
   In a pinky paper all folded neat,
And they fastened it down with a pin.
   And they passed the night in a crockery-jar,
And each of them said, 'How wise we are!
   Though the sky be dark, and the voyage be long,
Yet we never can think we were rash or wrong,
   While round in our Sieve we spin!'
      Far and few, far and few,
         Are the lands where the Jumblies live;
      Their heads are green, and their hands are blue,
         And they went to sea in a Sieve.

And all night long they sailed away;
   And when the sun went down,

They whistled and warbled a moony song
   To the echoing sound of a coppery gong,
In the shade of the mountains brown.
   'O Timballo! How happy we are,
When we live in a Sieve and a crockery-jar,
   And all night long in the moonlight pale,
We sail away with a pea-green sail,
   In the shade of the mountains brown!'
      Far and few, far and few,
        Are the lands where the Jumblies live;
      Their heads are green, and their hands are blue,
        And they went to sea in a Sieve.

They sailed to the Western Sea, they did,
   To a land all covered with trees,
And they bought an Owl, and a useful Cart,
   And a pound of Rice, and a Cranberry Tart,
And a hive of silvery Bees.
   And they bought a Pig, and some green Jack-daws,
And a lovely Monkey with lollipop paws,
   And forty bottles of Ring-Bo-Ree,
And no end of Stilton Cheese.
   Far and few, far and few,
      Are the lands where the Jumblies live;
    Their heads are green, and their hands are blue,
      And they went to sea in a Sieve.

And in twenty years they all came back,
    In twenty years or more,
And every one said, 'How tall they've grown!
    For they've been to the Lakes, and the Torrible Zone,
And the hills of the Chankly Bore!'
    And they drank their health, and gave them a feast
Of dumplings made of beautiful yeast;
    And every one said, 'If we only live,
We too will go to sea in a Sieve, —
    To the hills of the Chankly Bore!'
      Far and few, far and few,
        Are the lands where the Jumblies live;
      Their heads are green, and their hands are blue,
        And they went to sea in a Sieve.

EDWARD LEAR

*E • B*

## Wynken, Blynken, And Nod

Wynken, Blynken, and Nod one night
    Sailed off in a wooden shoe —
Sailed on a river of crystal light,
    Into a sea of dew.
'Where are you going, and what do you wish?'

The old moon asked the three.
'We have come to fish for the herring fish
That live in this beautiful sea;
Nets of silver and gold have we!'
Said Wynken,
Blynken,
And Nod.

The old moon laughed and sang a song,
As they rocked in the wooden shoe,
And the wind that sped them all night long
Ruffled the waves of dew.
The little stars were the herring fish
That lived in that beautiful sea —
'Now cast your nets wherever you wish —
Never afeard are we';
So cried the stars to the fishermen three:
Wynken,
Blynken,
And Nod.

All night long their nets they threw
To the stars in the twinkling foam —
Then down from the skies came the wooden shoe,
Bringing the fishermen home;

'Twas all so pretty a sail it seemed
    As if it could not be,
And some folks thought 'twas a dream they'd dreamed
    Of sailing that beautiful sea —
    But I shall name you the fishermen three:
        Wynken,
        Blynken,
        And Nod.

Wynken and Blynken are two little eyes,
    And Nod is a little head,
And the wooden shoe that sailed the skies
    Is a wee one's trundle-bed.
So shut your eyes while Mother sings
    Of wonderful sights that be,
And you shall see the beautiful things
    As you rock on the misty sea,
    Where the old shoe rocked the fishermen three:
        Wynken,
        Blynken,
        And Nod.

EUGENE FIELD

## *Old Nick In Sorel*

Old Nick took a fancy, as many men tell,
To come for a winter to live in Sorel.
Yet the snow fell so deep as he came in his sleigh,
That his fingers and toes were frost-nipt on the way.

In truth, said the demon, who'd ever suppose,
I must go back again with the loss of all those;
In either extreme, sure it matters me not,
If I freeze upon earth or at home I'm too hot;

So he put back his sleigh, for he thought it amiss,
His clime to compare to a climate like this;
And now 'tis resolved that this frightful new-comer
Will winter in hell and be here in the summer.

STANDISH O'GRADY

## The Boy Of Quebec

There was a young boy of Quebec
Who fell into the ice to his neck.
When asked, 'Are you friz?'
He replied, 'Yes, I is,
But we don't call this cold in Quebec.'

RUDYARD KIPLING

❧ • ❧

## The Camel's Hump

The Camel's hump is an ugly lump
Which well you may see at the Zoo;
But uglier yet is the hump we get
From having too little to do.

Kiddies and grown-ups too-oo-oo,
If we haven't enough to do-oo-oo,
We get the hump —
Cameelious hump —
The hump that is black and blue!

We climb out of bed with a frouzly head,
And a snarly-yarly voice.
We shiver and scowl and we grunt and we growl
At our bath and our boots and our toys;

And there ought to be a corner for me
(And I know there is one for you)
When we get the hump —
Cameelious hump —
The hump that is black and blue!

The cure for this ill is not to sit still,
Or frowst with a book by the fire;
But to take a large hoe and a shovel also,
And dig till you gently perspire;

And then you will find that the sun and the wind,
And the Djinn of the Garden too,
Have lifted the hump —
The horrible hump —
The hump that is black and blue!

I get it as well as you-oo-oo,
If I haven't enough to do-oo-oo!
We all get hump —
Cameelious hump —
Kiddies and grown-ups too!

RUDYARD KIPLING

$\mathcal{O} \cdot \mathcal{B}$

## *The Lazy Writer*

In summer I'm disposed to shirk,

As summer is no time to work.

In winter inspiration dies

For lack of out-door exercise.

In spring I'm seldom in the mood,

Because of vernal lassitude.

The fall remains. But such a fall!

We've really had no fall at all.

BERT LESTON TAYLOR

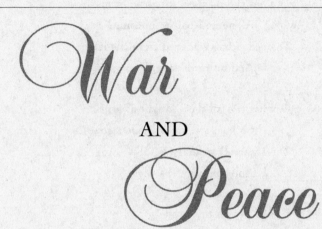

War

AND

Peace

## *La Belle Dame Sans Merci*

O what can ail thee, knight-at-arms,
    Alone and palely loitering?
The sedge has withered from the lake,
    And no birds sing.

O what can ail thee, knight-at-arms,
    So haggard and so woebegone?
The squirrel's granary is full,
    And the harvest's done.

I see a lily on thy brow
    With anguish moist and fever dew,
And on thy cheek a fading rose
    Fast withereth too.

I met a lady in the meads,
    Full beautiful — a faery's child,
Her hair was long, her foot was light,
    And her eyes were wild.

I made a garland for her head,
    And bracelets too, and fragrant zone;
She looked at me as she did love,
    And made sweet moan.

I set her on my pacing steed,
        And nothing else saw all day long,
For sidelong would she bend, and sing
        A faery's song.

She found me roots of relish sweet,
        And honey wild, and manna dew,
And sure in language strange she said
        'I love thee true.'

She took me to her elfin grot,
        And there she wept, and sighed full sore,
And there I shut her wild wild eyes
        With kisses four.

And there she lulled me asleep,
        And there I dreamed —Ah! woe betide!
The latest dream I ever dreamed
        On the cold hill's side.

I saw pale kings and princes too,
        Pale warriors, death-pale were they all;
They cried — 'La Belle Dame sans Merci
        Hath thee in thrall!'

I saw their starved lips in the gloam,
>With horrid warning gaped wide,
And I awoke and found me here,
>On the cold hill's side.

And this is why I sojourn here,
>Alone and palely loitering,
Though the sedge has withered from the lake,
>And no birds sing.

JOHN KEATS

## To Lucasta, On Going To The Wars

Tell me not, Sweet, I am unkind,
>That from the nunnery
Of thy chaste breast, and quiet mind,
>To war and arms I fly.

True, a new mistress now I chase,
>The first foe in the field;
And with a stronger faith embrace
>A sword, a horse, a shield.

Yet this inconstancy is such,
　　As you too shall adore;
I could not love thee, Dear, so much,
　　Loved I not honour more.

RICHARD LOVELACE

*Ꮽ • Ꮬ*

# *Concord Hymn*

By the rude bridge that arched the flood,
　　Their flag to April's breeze unfurled,
Here once the embattled farmers stood
And fired the shot heard round the world.

　　The foe long since in silence slept;
　　Alike the conqueror silent sleeps;
　　And Time the ruined bridge has swept
Down the dark stream that seaward creeps.

On this green bank, by this soft stream,
　　We set today a votive stone;
That memory may their deed redeem,
When, like our sires, our sons are gone.

Spirit, that made those heroes dare
To die, and leave their children free,
Bid Time and Nature gently spare
The shaft we raise to them and thee.

RALPH WALDO EMERSON

ℐ • ℬ

## The Burial Of Sir John Moore After Corunna

Not a drum was heard, not a funeral note,
As his corse to the rampart we hurried;
Not a soldier discharged his farewell shot
O'er the grave where our hero we buried.

We buried him darkly at dead of night,
The sods with our bayonets turning,
By the struggling moonbeam's misty light
And the lanthorn dimly burning.

No useless coffin enclosed his breast,
Not in sheet or in shroud we wound him;
But he lay like a warrior taking his rest
With his martial cloak around him.
Few and short were the prayers we said,

And we spoke not a word of sorrow;
But we steadfastly gazed on the face that was dead,
And we bitterly thought of the morrow.

We thought, as we hollow'd his narrow bed
And smooth'd down his lonely pillow,
That the foe and the stranger would tread o'er his head,
And we far away on the billow!

Lightly they'll talk of the spirit that's gone,
And o'er his cold ashes upbraid him
But little he'll reck, if they let him sleep on
In the grave where a Briton has laid him.

But half of our heavy task was done
When the clock struck the hour for retiring;
And we heard the distant and random gun
That the foe was sullenly firing.

Slowly and sadly we laid him down,
From the field of his fame fresh and gory;
We carved not a line, and we raised not a stone,
But we left him alone with his glory.

CHARLES WOLFE

                    * • *

# *Brock*

One voice, one people, one in heart
And soul and feeling and desire.
Re-light the smouldering martial fire
And sound the mute trumpet! Strike the lyre!
The hero deed cannot expire:
The dead still play their part.

Raise high the monumental stone!
A nation's fealty is theirs,
And we are the rejoicing heirs,
The honoured sons of sires whose cares
We take upon us unawares
As freely as our own.

We boast not of the victory,
But render homage, deep and just,
To his — to their — immortal dust,
Who proved so worthy of their trust;
No lofty pile nor sculptured bust
Can herald their degree.

No tongue need blazon forth their fame—
The cheers that stir the sacred hill

Are but mere promptings of the will
That conquered then, that conquers still;
And generations yet shall thrill
At Brock's remembered name.

Some souls are the Hesperides
Heaven sends to guard the golden age,
Illuming the historic page
With record of their pilgrimage.
True martyr, hero, poet, sage, —
And he was one of these.

Each in his lofty sphere, sublime,
Sits crowned above the common throng:
Wrestling with some pythonic wrong
In prayer, in thunder, thought or song,
Briareus-limbed, they sweep along,
The Typhons of the time.

CHARLES SANGSTER

𝒟 • ℬ

# The Charge Of The Light Brigade

Half a league, half a league,

Half a league onward,

All in the valley of Death

Rode the six hundred.

'Forward, the Light Brigade!

Charge for the guns!' he said:

Into the valley of Death

Rode the six hundred.


'Forward, the Light Brigade!'

Was there a man dismayed?

Not though the soldier knew

Some one had blundered:

Their's not to make reply,

Their's not to reason why,

Their's but to do and die:

Into the valley of Death

Rode the six hundred.


Cannon to right of them,

Cannon to left of them,

Cannon in front of them

Volleyed and thundered;
Stormed at with shot and shell,
Boldly they rode and well,
Into the jaws of Death,
Into the mouth of Hell
Rode the six hundred.

Flashed all their sabres bare,
Flashed as they turned in air
Sabring the gunners there,
Charging an army, while
All the world wondered:
Plunged in the battery-smoke
Right through the line they broke;
Cossack and Russian
Reeled from the sabre-stroke
Shattered and sundered.
Then they rode back, but not,
Not the six hundred.

Cannon to right of them,
Cannon to left of them,
Cannon behind them
Volleyed and thundered;

Stormed at with shot and shell,
While horse and hero fell,
They that had fought so well
Came through the jaws of Death
Back from the mouth of Hell,
All that was left of them,
Left of six hundred.

When can their glory fade?
O the wild charge they made!
All the world wondered.
Honour the charge they made!
Honour the Light Brigade,
Noble six hundred!

ALFRED, LORD TENNYSON

$\mathscr{E} \cdot \mathscr{B}$

## *Cavalry Crossing A Ford*

A line in long array, where they wind betwixt green islands;
They take a serpentine course — their arms flash in the sun
   — Hark to the musical clank;
Behold the silvery river—in it the splashing horses, loitering,
   stop to drink;

Behold the brown-faced men — each group, each person, a
   picture — the negligent rest on the saddles;
Some emerge on the opposite bank — others are just
   entering the ford — while,
Scarlet, and blue, and snowy white,
The guidon flags flutter gaily in the wind.

WALT WHITMAN

## *When I Was Small, A Woman Died*

When I was small, a woman died.
To-day her only boy
Went up from the Potomac,
His face all victory,

To look at her; how slowly
The seasons must have turned
Till bullets clipt an angle,
And he passed quickly round!

If pride shall be in Paradise
I never can decide;
Of their imperial conduct,
No person testified.

But proud in apparition,
That woman and her boy
Pass back and forth before my brain,
As ever in the sky.

EMILY DICKINSON

## Your Letter, Lady, Came Too Late

Your letter, lady, came too late,
For Heaven had claimed its own.
Ah, sudden change — from prison rats
Unto the great white throne!
And yet I think he would have stayed
To live for his disdain,
Could he have read the careless words
Which you have sent in vain.

So full of patience did he wait
Through many a weary hour,
That o'er his simple soldier faith
Not even death had power.

And you — did others whisper low
Their homage in your ear,
As though among their shadowy throng
His spirit had a peer.


I would that you were by me now,
To draw the sheet aside,
And see how pure the look he wore
The moment when he died.
The sorrow that you gave him
Had left its weary trace,
As 'twere the shadow of the cross
Upon his pallid face.


'Her love,' he said, 'could change for me
The winter's cold to spring.'
Ah, trust of fickle maiden's love,
Thou art a bitter thing!
For when these valleys bright in May
Once more with blossoms wave,
The northern violets shall blow
Above his humble grave.

Your dole of scanty words had been
But one more pang to bear,
For him who kissed unto the last
Your tress of golden hair.
I did not put it where he said,
For when the angels come
I would not have them find the sign
Of falsehood in the tomb.

I've seen your letter and I know
The wiles that you have wrought
To win that noble heart of his,
And gained it — cruel thought!
What lavish wealth men sometimes give
For what is worthless all:
What manly bosoms beat for them
In folly's falsest thrall.

You shall not pity him, for now
His sorrow has an end,
Yet would that you could stand with me
Beside my fallen friend.
And I forgive you for his sake
As he — if it be given —

May even be pleading grace for you
Before the court of Heaven.

Tonight the cold wind whistles by
As I, my vigil keep
Within the prison dead house, where
Few mourners come to weep.
A rude plank coffin holds his form,
Yet death exalts his face
And I would rather see him thus
Than clasped in your embrace.

Tonight your home may shine with lights
And ring with merry song,
And you be smiling as your soul
Had done no deadly wrong.
Your hand so fair that none would think
It penned these words of pain;
Your skin so white — would God, your heart
Were half as free from stain.

I'd rather be my comrade dead,
Than you in life supreme:
For yours the sinner's waking dread,

And his the martyr's dream.
Whom serve we in this life, we serve
In that which is to come:
He chose his way, you yours; let God
Pronounce the fitting doom.

W. S. HAWKINS

$\mathcal{I} \cdot \mathcal{B}$

## *The Unknown Dead*

The rain is plashing on my sill,
But all the winds of Heaven are still;
And so it falls with that dull sound
Which thrills us in the church-yard ground,
When the first spadeful drops like lead
Upon the coffin of the dead.
Beyond my streaming window-pane,
I cannot see the neighboring vane,
Yet from its old familiar tower
The bell comes, muffled, through the shower
What strange and unsuspected link
Of feeling touched, has made me think —
While with a vacant soul and eye
I watch that gray and stony sky —

Of nameless graves on battle-plains
Washed by a single winter's rains,
Where, some beneath Virginian hills,
And some by green Atlantic rills,
Some by the waters of the West,
A myriad unknown heroes rest.
Ah! not the chiefs, who, dying, see
Their flags in front of victory,
Or, at their life-blood's noble cost
Pay for a battle nobly lost,
Claim from their monumental beds
The bitterest tears a nation sheds.

Beneath yon lonely mound — the spot
By all save some fond few forgot —
Lie the true martyrs of the fight
Which strikes for freedom and for right.
Of them, their patriot zeal and pride,
The lofty faith that with them died,
No grateful page shall farther tell
Than that so many bravely fell;
And we can only dimly guess
What worlds of all this world's distress,
What utter woe, despair, and dearth,
Their fate has brought to many a hearth.

Just such a sky as this should weep
Above them, always, where they sleep;
Yet, haply, at this very hour,
Their graves are like a lover's bower;
And Nature's self, with eyes unwet,
Oblivious of the crimson debt
To which she owes her April grace,
Laughs gayly o'er their burial-place.

HENRY TIMROD

*ℐ · ℛ*

# *He Fought Like Those Who've Nought To Lose*

He fought like those Who've nought to lose —
Bestowed Himself to Balls
As One who for a further Life
Had not a further Use —

Invited Death — with bold attempt —
But Death was Coy of Him
As Other Men, were Coy of Death —
To Him — to live — was Doom —

His Comrades, shifted like the Flakes
When Gusts reverse the Snow —
But He — was left alive Because
Of Greediness to die —

EMILY DICKINSON

❧ • ❦

## *The Wound Dresser*

### I

An old man bending I come among new faces,

Years looking backward resuming in answer to children,

Come tell us old man, as from young men and maidens that
love me;

(Arous'd and angry, I'd thought to beat the alarum, and urge
relentless war,

But soon my fingers fail'd me, my face droop'd and I resign'd
myself,

To sit by the wounded and soothe them, or silently watch the
dead

Years hence of these scenes, of these furious passions, these
chances,

Of unsurpass'd heroes, (was one side so brave? the other was
equally brave

Now be witness again—paint the mightiest armies of earth;
Of those armies so rapid so wondrous what saw you to tell
  us?
What stays with you latest and deepest? of curious panics,
Of hard-fought engagements or sieges tremendous what
  deepest remains?

## II

O maidens and young men I love, and that love me,
What you ask of my days those the strangest and sudden
  your talking recalls;
Soldier alert I arrive after a long march cover'd with sweat
  and dust;
In the nick of time I come, plunge in the fight, loudly shout
  in the rush of successful charge;
Enter the captur'd works — yet lo! like a swift-running river,
  they fade;
Pass and are gone they fade — I dwell not on soldiers' perils
  or soldiers' joys;
(Both I remember well — many the hardships, few the joys,
  yet I was content).

But in silence, in dreams' projections,
While the world of gain and appearance and mirth goes on,

So soon what is over forgotten, and waves wash the imprints
    off the sand,
With hinged knees returning I enter the doors — (while for
    you up there,
Whoever you are, follow me without noise and be of strong
    heart).

### III

Bearing the bandages, water and sponge,
Straight and swift to my wounded I go,
Where they lie on the ground after the battle brought in;
Where their priceless blood reddens the grass, the ground;
Or to the rows of the hospital tent, or under the roof'd
    hospital;
To the long rows of cots up and down each side, I return;
To each and all one after another I draw near — not one do
    I miss;
An attendant follows holding a tray — he carries a refuse pail,
Soon to be fill'd with clotted rags and blood, emptied and
    fill'd again.

I onward go, I stop,
With hinged knees and steady hand to dress wounds;
I am firm with each — the pangs are sharp yet unavoidable;
One turns to me his appealing eyes — (poor boy! I never
    knew you,

Yet I think I could not refuse this moment to die for you, if
    that would save you).

### III

On, on I go! (open doors of time! open hospital doors!)
The crush'd head I dress (poor crazed hand tear not the
    bandage away
The neck of the cavalry-man with the bullet through and
    through, I examine;
Hard the breathing rattles, quite glazed already the eye, yet
    life struggles hard;
(Come sweet death! be persuaded O beautiful death!
In mercy come quickly).

From the stump of the arm, the amputated hand,
I undo the clotted lint, remove the slough, wash off the
    matter and blood;
Back on his pillow the soldier bends with curv'd neck and
    side-falling head;
His eyes are closed, his face is pale, he dares not look on the
    bloody stump,
And has not yet look'd on it.

I dress a wound in the side, deep, deep;
But a day or two more—for see the frame all wasted, and
    sinking,

And the yellow-blue countenance see.

I dress the perforated shoulder, the foot with the bullet
  wound,

Cleanse the one with a gnawing and putrid gangrene, so sick-
  ening, so offensive,

While the attendant stands behind aside me holding the tray
  and pail.

I am faithful, I do not give out;

The fractur'd thigh, the knee, the wound in the abdomen,

These and more I dress with impassive hand (yet deep in my
  breast a fire, a burning flame).

## IV

Thus in silence in dreams' projections,

Returning, resuming, I thread my way through the hospitals;

The hurt and wounded I pacify with soothing hand,

I sit by the restless all the dark night—some are so young;

Some suffer so much—I recall the experience sweet and sad;

(Many a soldier's loving arms about this neck have cross'd
  and rested,

Many a soldier's kiss dwells on these bearded lips).

WALT WHITMAN

                                                 * • *

# *The Blue And The Gray*

By the flow of the inland river,
Whence the fleets of iron have fled,
Where the blades of the grave-grass quiver,
Asleep are the ranks of the dead:
Under the sod and the dew,
Waiting the judgment-day;
Under the one, the Blue,
Under the other, the Gray.

These in the robings of glory,
Those in the gloom of defeat,
All with the battle-blood gory,
In the dusk of eternity meet:
Under the sod and the dew,
Waiting the judgment-day;
Under the laurel, the Blue,
Under the willow, the Gray.

From the silence of sorrowful hours
The desolate mourners go,
Lovingly laden with flowers
Alike for the friend and the foe:

Under the sod and the dew,
Waiting the judgment-day;
Under the roses, the Blue,
Under the lilies, the Gray.

So with an equal splendor,
The morning sunrays fall,
With a touch impartially tender,
On the blossoms blooming for all:
Under the sod and the dew,
Waiting the judgment-day;
Broidered with gold, the Blue,
Mellowed with gold, the Gray.

So, when the summer calleth,
On forest and field of grain,
With an equal murmur falleth
The cooling drip of the rain:
Under the sod and the dew,
Waiting the judgment-day;
Wet with the rain, the Blue,
Wet with the rain, the Gray.

Sadly, but not with upbraiding,
The generous deed was done,
In the storm of the years that are fading
No braver battle was won:
Under the sod and the dew,
Waiting the judgment-day;
Under the blossoms, the Blue,
Under the garlands, the Gray.

No more shall the war-cry sever,
Or the winding rivers be red;
They banish our anger forever
When they laurel the graves of our dead!
Under the sod and the dew,
Waiting the judgment-day;
Love and tears for the Blue,
Tears and love for the Gray.

FRANCIS MILES FINCH

$\mathscr{B} \cdot \mathscr{B}$

## *Reconciliation*

Word over all, beautiful as the sky!

Beautiful that war, and all its deeds of carnage, must in time
be utterly lost;

That the hands of the sisters Death and Night, incessantly
softly wash again, and ever again, this soil'd world:

For my enemy is dead — a man divine as myself is dead;

I look where he lies, white-faced and still, in the coffin — I
draw near;

I bend down, and touch lightly with my lips the white face in
the coffin.

WALT WHITMAN

## *War Is Kind*

Do not weep, maiden, for war is kind.
Because your lover threw wild hands toward the sky
And the affrighted steed ran on alone,
Do not weep.
War is kind.

Hoarse, booming drums of the regiment,
Little souls who thirst for fight,

These men were born to drill and die.
The unexplained glory flies above them,
Great is the battle-god, great, and his kingdom —
A field where a thousand corpses lie.

Do not weep, babe, for war is kind.
Because your father tumbled in the yellow trenches,
Raged at his breast, gulped and died,
Do not weep.
War is kind.

Swift blazing flag of the regiment,
Eagle with crest of red and gold,
These men were born to drill and die.
Point for them the virtue of slaughter,
Make plain to them the excellence of killing
And a field where a thousand corpses lie.

Mother whose heart hung humble as a button
On the bright splendid shroud of your son,
Do not weep.
War is kind.

STEPHEN CRANE

℘ • ℬ

## *The Unconquered Dead*

Not we the conquered! Not to us the blame
    Of them that flee, of them that basely yield;
Nor ours the shout of victory, the fame
    Of them that vanquish in a stricken field.


That day of battle in the dusty heat
    We lay and heard the bullets swish and sing
Like scythes amid the over-ripened wheat,
    And we the harvest of their garnering.


Some yielded, No, not we! Not we, we swear
    By these our wounds; this trench upon the hill
Where all the shell-strewn earth is seamed and bare,
    Was ours to keep; and lo! we have it still.


We might have yielded, even we, but death
    Came for our helper; like a sudden flood
The crashing darkness fell; our painful breath
    We drew with gasps amid the choking blood.


The roar fell faint and farther off, and soon
    Sank to a foolish humming in our ears,

Like crickets in the long, hot afternoon
    Among the wheat fields of the olden years.

Before our eyes a boundless wall of red
    Shot through by sudden streaks of jagged pain!
Then a slow-gathering darkness overhead
    And rest came on us like a quiet rain.

Not we the conquered! Not to us the shame,
    Who hold our earthen ramparts, nor shall cease
To hold them ever; victors we, who came
    In that fierce moment to our honoured peace.

JOHN McCRAE

## *The Man He Killed*

Had he and I but met
    By some old ancient inn,
We should have set us down to wet
    Right many a nipperkin!

    But ranged as infantry,
    And staring face to face,
I shot at him as he at me,
    And killed him in his place.

    I shot him dead because—
    Because he was my foe,
Just so: my foe of course he was;
    That's clear enough; although

    He thought he'd 'list, perhaps,
    Off-hand like — just as I—
Was out of work — had sold his traps—
    No other reason why.

    Yes; quaint and curious war is!
    You shoot a fellow down
You'd treat, if met where any bar is,
    Or help to half a crown.

THOMAS HARDY

## *The Soldier*

If I should die, think only this of me:
    That there's some corner of a foreign field
That is for ever England. There shall be
    In that rich earth a richer dust concealed;
A dust whom England bore, shaped, made aware,
    Gave, once, her flowers to love, her ways to roam,
A body of England's, breathing English air,
    Washed by the rivers, blest by suns of home.

And think, this heart, all evil shed away,
    A pulse in the eternal mind, no less
      Gives somewhere back the thoughts by England given;
Her sights and sounds; dreams happy as her day;
    And laughter, learnt of friends; and gentleness,
      In hearts at peace, under an English heaven.

RUPERT BROOKE

*ℐ • ℬ*

## Anthem For Doomed Youth

What passing-bells for these who die as cattle?
      Only the monstrous anger of the guns.
      Only the stuttering rifles' rapid rattle
Can patter out their hasty orisons.
No mockeries for them from prayers or bells,
      Nor any voice of mourning save the choirs, —
The shrill, demented choirs of wailing shells;
      And bugles calling for them from sad shires.

What candles may be held to speed them all?
      Not in the hands of boys, but in their eyes
Shall shine the holy glimmers of good-byes.
      The pallor of girls' brows shall be their pall;
Their flowers the tenderness of silent minds,
And each slow dusk a drawing-down of blinds.

WILFRED OWEN

               *Ð • Ð*

# In Time Of 'The Breaking Of Nations'

Only a man harrowing clods
In a slow silent walk
With an old horse that stumbles and nods
Half asleep as they stalk.

Only thin smoke without flame
From the heaps of couch-grass;
Yet this will go onward the same
Though Dynasties pass.

Yonder a maid and her wight
Go whispering by:
War's annals will fade into night
Ere their story die.

THOMAS HARDY

𝒢 • ℬ

## The Armed Liner

The dull gray paint of war
Covering the shining brass and gleaming decks
That once re-echoed to the steps of youth.
That was before
The storms of destiny made ghastly wrecks
Of peace, the Right of Truth.
Impromptu dances, colored lights and laughter,
Lovers watching the phosphorescent waves,
Now gaping guns, a whistling shell; and after
So mans wandering graves.

H. SMALLEY SARSON

## In Memoriam (Easter, 1915)

The flowers left thick at nightfall in the wood
This Eastertide call into mind the men,
Now far from home, who, with their sweethearts, should
Have gathered them and will do never again.

EDWARD THOMAS

447

# Channel Firing

That night your great guns, unawares,
Shook all our coffins as we lay,
And broke the chancel window-squares,
We thought it was the Judgment-day

And sat upright. While drearisome
Arose the howl of wakened hounds:
The mouse let fall the altar-crumb,
The worms drew back into the mounds,

The glebe cow drooled. Till God called, 'No;
It's gunnery practice out at sea
Just as before you went below;
The world is as it used to be:

'All nations striving strong to make
Red war yet redder. Mad as hatters
They do no more for Christés sake
Than you who are helpless in such matters.

'That this is not the judgment-hour
For some of them's a blessed thing,
For if it were they'd have to scour
Hell's floor for so much threatening....

'Ha, ha. It will be warmer when
I blow the trumpet (if indeed
I ever do; for you are men,
And rest eternal sorely need).'

So down we lay again. 'I wonder,
Will the world ever saner be,'
Said one, 'than when He sent us under
In our indifferent century!'

And many a skeleton shook his head.
'Instead of preaching forty year,'
My neighbour Parson Thirdly said,
'I wish I had stuck to pipes and beer.'

Again the guns disturbed the hour,
Roaring their readiness to avenge,
As far inland as Stourton Tower,
And Camelot, and starlit Stonehenge.

THOMAS HARDY

# The Parable Of The Old Man And The Young

So Abram rose, and clave the wood, and went,
    And took the fire with him, and a knife.
And as they sojourned both of them together,
Isaac the first-born spake and said, My Father,
    Behold the preparations, fire and iron,
    But where the lamb for this burnt-offering?
Then Abram bound the youth with belts and straps,
    And builded parapets and trenches there,
    And stretchèd forth the knife to slay his son.
When lo! an Angel called him out of heaven,
    Saying, Lay not thy hand upon the lad,
    Neither do anything to him, thy son.
    Behold! Caught in a thicket by its horns,
    A Ram. Offer the Ram of Pride instead.

But the old man would not so, but slew his son,
    And half the seed of Europe, one by one.

WILFRED OWEN

✶ • ✶

## Here Dead Lie We

Here dead lie we
Because we did not choose
To live and shame the land
From which we sprung.

Life, to be sure,
Is nothing much to lose,
But young men think it is,
And we were young.

A. E. HOUSMAN

⌀ • ℬ

## Strange Meeting

It seemed that out of the battle I escaped
Down some profound dull tunnel, long since scooped
Through granites which Titanic wars had groined.
Yet also there encumbered sleepers groaned,
Too fast in thought or death to be bestirred.
Then, as I probed them, one sprang up, and stared
With piteous recognition in fixed eyes,
Lifting distressful hands as if to bless.
And by his smile, I knew that sullen hall;
By his dead smile I knew we were in hell.

With a thousand fears that vision's face was grained;
Yet no blood reached there from the upper ground,
And no guns thumped, or down the flues made moan.
'Strange friend,' I said, 'Here is no cause to mourn.'
'None,' said the other, 'Save the undone years,
The hopelessness. Whatever hope is yours,
Was my life also; I went hunting wild
After the wildest beauty in the world,
Which lies not calm in eyes, or braided hair,
But mocks the steady running of the hour,
And if it grieves, grieves richlier than here.
For by my glee might many men have laughed,
And of my weeping something had been left,
Which must die now. I mean the truth untold,
The pity of war, the pity war distilled.
Now men will go content with what we spoiled.
Or, discontent, boil bloody, and be spilled.
They will be swift with swiftness of the tigress,
None will break ranks, though nations trek from progress.
Courage was mine, and I had mystery;
Wisdom was mine, and I had mastery;
To miss the march of this retreating world
Into vain citadels that are not walled.
Then, when much blood had clogged their chariot-wheels
I would go up and wash them from sweet wells,

Even with truths that lie too deep for taint.

I would have poured my spirit without stint

But not through wounds; not on the cess of war.

Foreheads of men have bled where no wounds were.

I am the enemy you killed, my friend.

I knew you in this dark; for so you frowned

Yesterday through me as you jabbed and killed.

I parried; but my hands were loath and cold.

Let us sleep now...'

WILFRED OWEN

*ℐ • ℛ*

## *All The Hills And Vales Along*

All the hills and vales along

Earth is bursting into song,

And the singers are the chaps

Who are going to die perhaps.

O sing, marching men,

Till the valleys ring again.

Give your gladness to earth's keeping,

So be glad, when you are sleeping.

Cast away regret and rue,
Think what you are marching to.
Little live, great pass.
Jesus Christ and Barabbas
Were found the same day.
This died, that went his way.
>> So sing with joyful breath,
>> For why, you are going to death.
>> Teeming earth will surely store
>> All the gladness that you pour.

Earth that never doubts nor fears,
Earth that knows of death, not tears,
Earth that bore with joyful ease
Hemlock for Socrates,
Earth that blossomed and was glad
'Neath the cross that Christ had,
Shall rejoice and blossom too
When the bullet reaches you.
>> Wherefore, men marching
>> On the road to death, sing!
>> Pour your gladness on earth's head,
>> So be merry, so be dead.

From the hills and valleys earth
Shouts back the sound of mirth,
Tramp of feet and lilt of song
Ringing all the road along.
All the music of their going,
Ringing, swinging, glad song-throwing,
Earth will echo still, when foot
Lies numb and voice mute.

On, marching men, on
To the gates of death with song.
Sow your gladness for earth's reaping,
So you may be glad, though sleeping.
Strew your gladness on earth's bed,
So be merry, so be dead.

CHARLES HAMILTON SORLEY

*C • B*

# *I Have A Rendezvous With Death*

I have a rendezvous with Death
At some disputed barricade,
When Spring comes back with rustling shade
And apple-blossoms fill the air —
I have a rendezvous with Death
When Spring brings back blue days and fair.

It may be he shall take my hand
And lead me into his dark land
And close my eyes and quench my breath—
It may be I shall pass him still.
I have a rendezvous with Death
On some scarred slope of battered hill,
When Spring comes round again this year
And the first meadow-flowers appear.

God knows 'twere better to be deep
Pillowed in silk and scented down,
Where love throbs out in blissful sleep,
Pulse nigh to pulse, and breath to breath,
Where hushed awakenings are dear...
But I've a rendezvous with Death
At midnight in some flaming town,
When Spring trips north again this year,
And I to my pledged word am true,
I shall not fail that rendezvous.

ALAN SEEGER

## *I Tracked A Dead Man Down A Trench*

I tracked a dead man down a trench,
I knew not he was dead.
They told me he had gone that way,
And there his foot-marks led.

The trench was long and close and curved,
It seemed without an end;
And as I threaded each new bay
I thought to see my friend.

I went there stooping to the ground.
For, should I raise my head,
Death watched to spring; and how should then
A dead man find the dead?

At last I saw his back. He crouched
As still as still could be,
And when I called his name aloud
He did not answer me.

The floor-way of the trench was wet
Where he was crouching dead;
The water of the pool was brown,
And round him it was red.

I stole up softly where he stayed
With head hung down all slack,
And on his shoulders laid my hands
And drew him gently back.
And then, as I had guessed, I saw
His head, and how the crown—
I saw then why he crouched so still,
And why his head hung down.

W. S. S. LYON

*A · B*

## Apologia Pro Poemate Meo

I, too, saw God through mud—
The mud that cracked on cheeks when wretches smiled.
War brought more glory to their eyes than blood,
And gave their laughs more glee than shakes a child.

Merry it was to laugh there—
Where death becomes absurd and life absurder.
For power was on us as we slashed bones bare
Not to feel sickness or remorse of murder.

I, too, have dropped off fear—
Behind the barrage, dead as my platoon,
And sailed my spirit surging, light and clear,
Past the entanglement where hopes lie strewn;

And witnessed exultation—
Faces that used to curse me, scowl for scowl,
Shine and lift up with passion of oblation,
Seraphic for an hour, though they were foul.

I have made fellowships—
Untold of happy lovers in old song.
For love is not the binding of fair lips
With the soft silk of eyes that look and long.

By joy, whose ribbon slips, —
But wound with war's hard wire whose stakes are strong;
Bound with the bandage of the arm that drips;
Knit in the welding of the rifle-thong.

I have perceived much beauty
In the hoarse oaths that kept our courage straight;
Heard music in the silentness of duty;
Found peace where shell-storms spouted reddest spate.

Nevertheless, except you share
With them in hell the sorrowful dark of hell,
Whose world is but a trembling of a flare
And heaven but a highway for a shell,

You shall not hear their mirth:
You shall not come to think them well content
By any jest of mine. These men are worth
Your tears: You are not worth their merriment.

WILFRED OWEN

$\mathcal{O} \cdot \mathcal{B}$

# *The Shell*

Shrieking its message the flying death
Cursed the resisting air,
Then buried its nose by a battered church,
A skeleton gaunt and bare.

The brains of science, the money of fools
Had fashioned an iron slave
Destined to kill, yet the futile end
Was a child's uprooted grave.

H. SMALLEY SARSON

$\mathcal{O} \cdot \mathcal{B}$

# When You See Millions Of The Mouthless Dead

When you see millions of the mouthless dead
Across your dreams in pale battalions go,
Say not soft things as other men have said,
That you'll remember.   For you need not so.
Give them not praise.   For, deaf, how should they know
It is not curses heaped on each gashed head?
Nor tears.   Their blind eyes see not your tears flow.
Nor honour.   It is easy to be dead.
Say only this, 'They are dead.'   Then add thereto,
'Yet many a better one has died before.'
Then, scanning all the o'ercrowded mass, should you
Perceive one face that you loved heretofore,
It is a spook.   None wears the face you knew.
Great death has made all his for evermore.

CHARLES HAMILTON SORLEY

𝒮 • 𝒮

# *The Anxious Dead*

O guns, fall silent till the dead men hear
    Above their heads the legions pressing on:
(These fought their fight in time of bitter fear,
    And died not knowing how the day had gone.)

O flashing muzzles, pause, and let them see
    The coming dawn that streaks the sky afar
Then let your mighty chorus witness be
    To them, and Caesar, that we still make war.

Tell them, O guns, that we have heard their call,
    That we have sworn, and will not turn aside,
That we will onward till we win or fall,
    That we will keep the faith for which they died.

Bid them be patient, and some day, anon,
    They shall feel earth enwrapt in silence deep;
Shall greet, in wonderment, the quiet dawn,
    And in content may turn them to their sleep.

JOHN McCRAE

# *Futility*

Move him into the sun—
Gently its touch awoke him once,
At home, whispering of fields unsown.
Always it woke him, even in France,
Until this morning and this snow.
If anything might rouse him now
The kind old sun will know.

Think how it wakes the seeds—
Woke, once, the clays of a cold star.
Are limbs so dear-achieved, are sides
Full-nerved — still warm — too hard to stir?
Was it for this the clay grew tall?
— O what made fatuous sunbeams toil
To break earth's sleep at all?

WILFRED OWEN

# *God! How I Hate You, You Young Cheerful Men*

God! How I hate you, you young cheerful men,

Whose pious poetry blossoms on your graves

As soon as you are in them, nurtured up

By the salt of your corruption, and the tears

Of mothers, local vicars, college deans,

And flanked by prefaces and photographs

From all your minor poet friends — the fools—

Who paint their sentimental elegies

Where sure, no angel treads; and, living, share

The dead's brief immortality.

                        Oh Christ!

To think that one could spread the ductile wax

Of his fluid youth to Oxford's glowing fires

And take her seal so ill! Hark how one chants—

'Oh happy to have lived these epic days'—

'These epic days'! And *he'd* been to France,

And seen the trenches, glimpsed the huddled dead

In the periscope, hung in the rusting wire:

Choked by their sickly foetor, day and night

Blown down his throat: stumbled through ruined hearths,

Proved all that muddy brown monotony,

Where blood's the only coloured thing. Perhaps

Had seen a man killed, a sentry shot at night,
Hunched as he fell, his feet on the firing-step,
His neck against the back slope of the trench,
And the rest doubled up between, his head
Smashed like an egg-shell, and the warm grey brain
Spattered all bloody on the parados:
Had flashed a torch on his face, and known his friend,
Shot, breathing hardly, in ten minutes — gone!
Yet still God's in His heaven, all is right
In the best possible of worlds. The woe,
Even His scaled eyes *must* see, is partial, only
A seeming woe, we cannot understand.
God loves us, God looks down on this our strife
And smiles in pity, blows a pipe at times
And calls some warriors home. We do not die,
God would not let us, He is too 'intense',
Too 'passionate', a whole day sorrows He
Because a grass-blade dies. How rare life is!
On earth, the love and fellowship of men,
Men sternly banded: banded for what end?
Banded to maim and kill their fellow men—
For even Huns are men. In heaven above
A genial umpire, a good judge of sport,
Won't let us hurt each other! Let's rejoice
God keeps us faithful, pens us still in fold.

Ah, what a faith is ours (almost, it seems,
Large as a mustard-seed) — we trust and trust,
Nothing can shake us! Ah, how good God is
To suffer us be born just now, when youth
That else would rust, can slake his blade in gore,
Where very God Himself does seem to walk
The bloody fields of Flanders He so loves!

ARTHUR GRAHAM WEST

## *Ici Repose*

A little cross of weather-silvered wood,
Hung with a garish wreath of tinselled wire,
And on it carved a legend — thus it runs:
*'Ici repose* — ' Add what name you will,
And multiply by thousands: in the fields,
Along the roads, beneath the trees — one here,
A dozen there, to each its simple tale
Of one more jewel threaded star-like on
The sacrificial rosary of France.

And as I read and read again those words,
Those simple words, they took a mystic sense;
And from the glamour of an alien tongue
They wove insistent music in my brain,
Which, in a twilight hour, when all the guns
Were silent, shaped itself to song.

*O happy dead! Who sleep embalmed in glory,*
  *Safe from corruption, purified by fire, —*
*Ask you our pity? — ours, mud-grimed and gory,*
  *Who still must firmly strive, grimly desire?*

*You have outrun the reach of our endeavour,*
  *Have flown beyond our most exalted quest, —*
*Who prate of Faith and Freedom, knowing ever*
  *That all we really fight for's just — a rest,*

*The rest that only Victory can bring us —*
  *Or Death, which throws us brother-like by you —*
*The civil commonplace in which 'twill fling us*
  *To neutralize our then too martial hue.*

*But you have rest from every tribulation*
  *Even in the midst of war; you sleep serene,*
*Pinnacled on the sorrow of a nation,*
  *In cerements of sacrificial sheen.*

*Oblivion cannot claim you: our heroic*
    *War-lustred moment, as our youth, will pass*
*To swell the dusty hoard of Time the Stoic,*
    *That gathers cobwebs in the nether glass.*

*We shall grow old, and tainted with the rotten*
    *Effluvia of the peace we fought to win,*
*The bright deeds of our youth will be forgotten,*
    *Effaced by later failure, sloth, or sin;*

*But you have conquered Time, and sleep forever,*
    *Like gods, with a white halo on your brows —*
*Your souls our lode-stars, your death-crowned endeavour*
    *The spur that holds the nations to their vows.*

BERNARD FREEMAN TROTTER

## *Spring Offensive*

Halted against the shade of a last hill,
They fed, and, lying easy, were at ease
And, finding comfortable chests and knees
Carelessly slept. But many there stood still
To face the stark, blank sky beyond the ridge,
Knowing their feet had come to the end of the world.

Marvelling they stood, and watched the long grass swirled
By the May breeze, murmurous with wasp and midge,
For though the summer oozed into their veins
Like the injected drug for their bones' pains,
Sharp on their souls hung the imminent line of grass,
Fearfully flashed the sky's mysterious glass.

Hour after hour they ponder in the warm field, —
And the far valley behind, where the buttercups
Had blessed with gold their slow boots coming up,
Where even the little brambles would not yield
But clutched and clung to them like sorrowing hands.
They breathe like trees unstirred.

Till like a cold gust thrilled the little word
At which each body and its soul begird
And tighten them for battle. No alarms
Of bugles, no high flags, no clamorous haste —
Only a lift and flare of eyes that faced
The sun, like a friend with whom their love is done.
O larger shone that smile against the sun, —
Mightier than his whose bounty these have spurned.

So, soon they topped the hill, and raced together
Over an open stretch of herb and heather

Exposed. And instantly the whole sky burned
With fury against them; earth set sudden cups
In thousands for their blood; and the green slope
Chasmed and steepened sheer to infinite space.

Of them who running on that last high place
Leapt to swift unseen bullets, or went up
On the hot blast and fury of hell's upsurge,
Or plunged and fell away past this world's verge,
Some say God caught them even before they fell.

But what say such as from existence's brink
Ventured but drave too swift to sink,
The few who rushed in the body to enter hell,
And there outfiending all its fiends and flames
With superhuman inhumanities,
Long-famous glories, immemorial shames —
And crawling slowly back, have by degrees
Regained cool peaceful air in wonder —
Why speak they not of comrades that went under?

WILFRED OWEN

$\mathscr{E} \cdot \mathscr{B}$

## *War*

To end the dreary day,
The sun brought fire
And smote the grey
Of the heavens away
In his desire
That the evening sky might glow as red
As showed the earth with blood and ire.

The distant cannons' boom
In a land oppressed
Still spake the gloom
Of a country's doom,
Denying rest.
'War!' — called the frightened rooks and flew
From the crimson East to the crimson West.

Then, lest the dark might mar
The sky o'erhead,
There shone a star,
In the night afar
O'er each man's bed,
A symbol of undying peace,
The peace encompassing the dead.

RICHARD DENNYS

*Ǝ • Ɓ*

## The Song Of Sheffield

Shells, shells, shells!
> The song of the city of steel;
Hammer and turn, and file,
> Furnace, and lathe, and wheel.
>> Tireless machinery,
>> Man's ingenuity,
Making a way for the martial devil's meal.

Shells, shells, shells!
> Out of the furnace blaze;
Roll, roll, roll,
> Into the workshop's maze.
>> Ruthless machinery
>> Boring eternally, .
Boring a hole for the shattering charge that stays.

Shells, shells, shells!
> The song of the city of steel;
List to the devils' mirth,
> Hark to their laughters' peal:
>> Sheffield's machinery
>> Crushing humanity
Neath devil-ridden death's impassive heel.

HAROLD BECKH

## *To My Daughter Betty,*
## *The Gift Of God*

In wiser days, my darling rosebud, blown
To beauty proud as was your mother's prime,
In that desired, delayed, incredible time,
You'll ask why I abandoned you, my own,
And the dear heart that was your baby throne,
To dice with death. And oh! they'll give you rhyme
And reason: some will call the thing sublime,
And some decry it in a knowing tone.
So here, while the mad guns curse overhead,
And tired men sigh with mud for couch and floor,
Know that we fools, now with the foolish dead,
Died not for flag, nor King, nor Emperor,
But for a dream, born in a herdsman's shed,
And for the secret Scripture of the poor.

T. M. KETTLE

# *Disabled*

He sat in a wheeled chair, waiting for dark,
And shivered in his ghastly suit of grey,
Legless, sewn short at elbow. Through the park
Voices of boys rang saddening like a hymn,
Voices of play and pleasure after day,
Till gathering sleep had mothered them from him.

About this time Town used to swing so gay
When glow-lamps budded in the light-blue trees,
And girls glanced lovelier as the air grew dim,
– In the old times, before he threw away his knees.
Now he will never feel again how slim
Girls' waists are, or how warm their subtle hands,
All of them touch him like some queer disease.

There was an artist silly for his face,
For it was younger than his youth, last year.
Now, he is old; his back will never brace;
He's lost his colour very far from here,
Poured it down shell-holes till the veins ran dry,
And half his lifetime lapsed in the hot race,
And leap of purple spurted from his thigh.

One time he liked a bloodsmear down his leg,
 After the matches, carried shoulder-high.
It was after football, when he'd drunk a peg,
He thought he'd better join. – He wonders why.
 Someone had said he'd look a god in kilts.
That's why; and maybe, too, to please his Meg,
 Aye, that was it, to please the giddy jilts
 He asked to join. He didn't have to beg;
Smiling they wrote his lie: aged nineteen years.
Germans he scarcely thought of; all their guilt
And Austria's, did not move him. And no fears
Of Fear came yet. He thought of jewelled hilts
 For daggers in plaid socks; of smart salutes;
And care of arms; and leave; and pay arrears;
 *Esprit de corps*; and hints for young recruits.
And soon, he was drafted out with drums and cheers.

Some cheered him home, but not as crowds cheer Goal.
 Only a solemn man who brought him fruits
*Thanked* him; and then enquired about his soul.

Now, he will spend a few sick years in institutes,
 And do what things the rules consider wise,
 And take whatever pity they may dole.
Tonight he noticed how the women's eyes

Passed from him to the strong men that were whole.

How cold and late it is! Why don't they come

And put him into bed? Why don't they come?

WILFRED OWEN

℘ • ℘

## *Break Of Day In The Trenches*

The darkness crumbles away.

It is the same old druid Time as ever,

Only a live thing leaps my hand,

A queer sardonic rat,

As I pull the parapet's poppy

To stick behind my ear.

Droll rat, they would shoot you if they knew

Your cosmopolitan sympathies.

Now you have touched this English hand

You will do the same to a German

Soon, no doubt, if it be your pleasure

To cross the sleeping green between.

It seems you inwardly grin as you pass

Strong eyes, fine limbs, haughty athletes,

Less chanced than you for life,

Bonds to the whims of murder,

Sprawled in the bowels of the earth,
The torn fields of France.
What do you see in our eyes
At the shrieking iron and flame
Hurled through still heavens?
What quaver — what heart aghast?
Poppies whose roots are in man's veins
Drop, and are ever dropping;
But mine in my ear is safe —
Just a little white with the dust.

ISAAC ROSENBERG

𝒪 · 𝒫

## *As The Team's Head-Brass*

As the team's head-brass flashed out on the turn
The lovers disappeared into the wood.
I sat among the boughs of the fallen elm
That strewed the angle of the fallow, and
Watched the plough narrowing a yellow square
Of charlock. Every time the horses turned
Instead of treading me down, the ploughman leaned
Upon the handles to say or ask a word,
About the weather, next about the war.

Scraping the share he faced towards the wood,
And screwed along the furrow till the brass flashed
Once more.

The blizzard felled the elm whose crest
I sat in, by a woodpecker's round hole,
The ploughman said. 'When will they take it away?'
'When the war's over.' So the talk began —
One minute and an interval of ten,
A minute more and the same interval.
'Have you been out?' 'No.' 'And don't want to, perhaps?'
'If I could only come back again, I should.
I could spare an arm. I shouldn't want to lose
A leg. If I should lose my head, why, so,
I should want nothing more... Have many gone
From here?' 'Yes.' 'Many lost?' 'Yes, a good few.
Only two teams work on the farm this year.
One of my mates is dead. The second day
In France they killed him. It was back in March,
The very night of the blizzard, too. Now if
He had stayed here we should have moved the tree.'
'And I should not have sat here. Everything
Would have been different. For it would have been
Another world.' 'Ay, and a better, though
If we could see all all might seem good.' Then

The lovers came out of the wood again;
The horses started and for the last time
I watched the clods crumble and topple over
After the ploughshare and the stumbling team.

EDWARD THOMAS
*ℰ · ℬ*

## *Returning, We Hear the Larks*

Sombre the night is.
And though we have our lives, we know
What sinister threat lies there.

Dragging these anguished limbs, we only know
This poison-blasted track opens on our camp—
On a little safe sleep.

But hark! joy — joy — strange joy.
Lo! heights of night ringing with unseen larks.
Music showering our upturned list'ning faces.

Death could drop from the dark
As easily as song—
But song only dropped,
Like a blind man's dreams on the sand

By dangerous tides,
Like a girl's dark hair for she dreams no ruin lies there,
Or her kisses where a serpent hides.

ISAAC ROSENBERG

℘ • ℬ

## *Mental Cases*

Who are these? Why sit they here in twilight?
Wherefore rock they, purgatorial shadows,
Drooping tongues from jaws that slob their relish,
Baring teeth that leer like skulls' teeth wicked?
Stroke on stroke of pain, — but what slow panic,
Gouged these chasms round their fretted sockets?
Ever from their hair and through their hands' palms
Misery swelters. Surely we have perished
Sleeping, and walk hell; but who these hellish?

— These are men whose minds the Dead have ravished.
Memory fingers in their hair of murders,
Multitudinous murders they once witnessed.
Wading sloughs of flesh these helpless wander,

Treading blood from lungs that had loved laughter.
Always they must see these things and hear them,
Batter of guns and shatter of flying muscles,
Carnage incomparable and human squander
Rucked too thick for these men's extrication.

Therefore still their eyeballs shrink tormented
Back into their brains, because on their sense
Sunlight seems a bloodsmear; night comes blood-black;
Dawn breaks open like a wound that bleeds afresh
— Thus their heads wear this hilarious, hideous,
Awful falseness of set-smiling corpses.
— Thus their hands are plucking at each other;
Picking at the rope-knouts of their scourging;
Snatching after us who smote them, brother,
Pawing us who dealt them war and madness.

WILFRED OWEN

## Light After Darkness

Once more the Night, like some great dark drop-scene
Eclipsing horrors for a brief *entr'acte*,
Descends, lead-weighty. Now the space between,
Fringed with the eager eyes of men, is racked
By spark-tailed lights, curvetting far and high,
Swift smoke-flecked coursers, raking the black sky.

And as each sinks in ashes grey, one more
Rises to fall, and so through all the hours
They strive like petty empires by the score,
Each confident of his success and powers,
And, hovering at its zenith, each will show
Pale, rigid faces, lying dead, below.

There shall they lie, tainting the innocent air,
Until the dawn, deep veiled in mournful grey,
Sadly and quietly shall lay them bare,
The broken heralds of a doleful day.

E. WYNDHAM TENNANT

## *Dead Man's Dump*

The plunging limbers over the shattered track
Racketed with their rusty freight,
Stuck out like many crowns of thorns,
And the rusty stakes like sceptres old
To stay the flood of brutish men
Upon our brothers dear.

The wheels lurched over sprawled dead
But pained them not, though their bones crunched,
Their shut mouths made no moan,
They lie there huddled, friend and foeman,
Man born of man, and born of woman,
And shells go crying over them
From night till night and now.

Earth has waited for them
All the time of their growth
Fretting for their decay:
Now she has them at last!
In the strength of their strength
Suspended — stopped and held.

What fierce imaginings their dark souls lit?
Earth! have they gone into you?
Somewhere they must have gone,
And flung on your hard back
Is their souls' sack,
Emptied of God-ancestralled essences.
Who hurled them out? Who hurled?

None saw their spirits' shadow shake the grass,
Or stood aside for the half-used life to pass
Out of those doomed nostrils and the doomed mouth,
When the swift iron burning bee
Drained the wild honey of their youth.

What of us who, flung on the shrieking pyre,
Walk, our usual thoughts untouched,
Our lucky limbs as on ichor fed,
Immortal seeming ever?
Perhaps when the flames beat loud on us,
A fear may choke in our veins
And the startled blood may stop.

The air is loud with death,
The dark air spurts with fire

The explosions ceaseless are.
Timelessly now, some minutes past,
These dead strode time with vigorous life,
Till the shrapnel called 'an end!'
But not to all. In bleeding pangs
Some borne on stretchers dreamed of home,
Dear things, war-blotted from their hearts.

Maniac Earth! howling and flying, your bowel
Seared by the jagged fire, the iron love,
The impetuous storm of savage love.
Dark Earth! dark Heavens! swinging in chemic smoke,
What dead are born when you kiss each soundless soul
With lightning and thunder from your mined heart,
Which man's self dug, and his blind fingers loosed?

A man's brains splattered on
A stretcher-bearer's face;
His shook shoulders slipped their load,
But when they bent to look again
The drowning soul was sunk too deep
For human tenderness.

They left this dead with the older dead,
Stretched at the cross roads.

Burnt black by strange decay,
Their sinister faces lie;
The lid over each eye,
The grass and coloured clay
More motion have than they,
Joined to the great sunk silences.

Here is one not long dead;
His dark hearing caught our far wheels,
And the choked soul stretched weak hands
To reach the living word the far wheels said,
The blood-dazed intelligence beating for light,
Crying through the suspense of the far torturing wheels
Swift for the end to break,
Or the wheels to break,
Cried as the tide of the world broke over his sight.

Will they come? Will they ever come?
Even as the mixed hoofs of the mules,
The quivering-bellied mules,
And the rushing wheels all mixed
With his tortured upturned sight,

So we crashed round the bend,
We heard his weak scream,
We heard his very last sound,
And our wheels grazed his dead face.

ISAAC ROSENBERG
*I · R*

## *Dulce Et Decorum Est*

Bent double, like old beggars under sacks,
Knock-kneed, coughing like hags, we cursed through sludge,
Till on the haunting flares we turned our backs,
And towards our distant rest began to trudge.
Men marched asleep. Many had lost their boots,
But limped on, blood-shod. All went lame, all blind;
Drunk with fatigue; deaf even to the hoots
Of gas-shells dropping softly behind.

Gas! GAS! Quick, boys! — An ecstasy of fumbling
Fitting the clumsy helmets just in time,
But someone still was yelling out and stumbling
And flound'ring like a man in fire or lime. —
Dim through the misty panes and thick green light,
As under a green sea, I saw him drowning.

In all my dreams, before my helpless sight
He plunges at me, guttering, choking, drowning.

If in some smothering dreams, you too could pace
Behind the wagon that we flung him in,
And watch the white eyes writhing in his face,
His hanging face, like a devil's sick of sin,
If you could hear, at every jolt, the blood
Come gargling from the froth-corrupted lungs
Bitten as the cud
Of vile, incurable sores on innocent tongues, —
My friend, you would not tell with such high zest
To children ardent for some desperate glory,
The old Lie: *Dulce et decorum est*
*Pro patria mori.*

WILFRED OWEN

## *In Flanders Fields*

In Flanders fields the poppies blow
Between the crosses, row on row,
That mark our place; and in the sky
The larks, still bravely singing, fly
Scarce heard amid the guns below.

We are the Dead. Short days ago
We lived, felt dawn, saw sunset glow,
Loved, and were loved, and now we lie
     In Flanders fields.

Take up our quarrel with the foe:
To you from failing hands we throw
The torch; be yours to hold it high.
If ye break faith with us who die
We shall not sleep, though poppies grow
     In Flanders fields.

JOHN McCRAE

# *The Man With The Wooden Leg*

There was a man lived quite near us;

He had a wooden leg and a goldfinch in a green cage.

His name was Farkey Anderson,

And he'd been in a war to get his leg.

We were very sad about him,

Because he had such a beautiful smile

And was such a big man to live in a very small house.

When he walked on the road his leg did not matter so much;

But when he walked in his little house

It made an ugly noise.

Little Brother said his goldfinch sang the loudest of all birds,

So that he should not hear his poor leg

And feel too sorry about it.

KATHERINE MANSFIELD

*J · B*

# Inspiration AND Joy

# *Kubla Khan*

In Xanadu did Kubla Khan
A stately pleasure-dome decree:
Where Alph, the sacred river, ran
Through caverns measureless to man
     Down to a sunless sea.

So twice five miles of fertile ground
With walls and towers were girdled round:
And there were gardens bright with sinuous rills,
Where blossomed many an incense-bearing tree;
And here were forests ancient as the hills,
Enfolding sunny spots of greenery.

But oh! that deep romantic chasm which slanted
Down the green hill athwart a cedarn cover!
A savage place! as holy and enchanted
As e'er beneath a waning moon was haunted
By woman wailing for her demon-lover!
And from this chasm, with ceaseless turmoil seething,
As if this earth in fast thick pants were breathing,
A mighty fountain momently was forced:
Amid whose swift half-intermitted burst
Huge fragments vaulted like rebounding hail,

Or chaffy grain beneath the thresher's flail:
And 'mid these dancing rocks at once and ever
It flung up momently the sacred river.
Five miles meandering with a mazy motion
Through wood and dale the sacred river ran,
Then reached the caverns measureless to man,
And sank in tumult to a lifeless ocean:
And 'mid this tumult Kubla heard from far
Ancestral voices prophesying war!

    The shadow of the dome of pleasure
    Floated midway on the waves;
    Where was heard the mingled measure
    From the fountain and the caves.
It was a miracle of rare device,
A sunny pleasure-dome with caves of ice!

    A damsel with a dulcimer
    In a vision once I saw:
    It was an Abyssinian maid,
    And on her dulcimer she played,
    Singing of Mount Abora.
    Could I revive within me
    Her symphony and song,
    To such a deep delight 'twould win me,

That with music loud and long,
I would build that dome in air,
That sunny dome! those caves of ice!
And all who heard should see them there,
And all should cry, Beware! Beware!
His flashing eyes, his floating hair!
Weave a circle round him thrice,
And close your eyes with holy dread,
For he on honey-dew hath fed,
And drunk the milk of Paradise.

SAMUEL TAYLOR COLERIDGE

*S • B*

# *If —*

If you can keep your head when all about you

Are losing theirs and blaming it on you;
If you can trust yourself when all men doubt you,

But make allowance for their doubting too;
If you can wait and not be tired by waiting,

Or, being lied about, don't deal in lies,
Or, being hated, don't give way to hating,

And yet don't look too good, nor talk too wise;

If you can dream — and not make dreams your master;

If you can think — and not make thoughts your aim;

If you can meet with Triumph and Disaster
  And treat those two impostors just the same;
If you can bear to hear the truth you've spoken
  Twisted by knaves to make a trap for fools,
Or watch the things you gave your life to, broken,
  And stoop and build 'em up with worn-out tools;

If you can make one heap of all your winnings
  And risk it on one turn of pitch-and-toss,
And lose, and start again at your beginnings
  And never breathe a word about your loss;
If you can force your heart and nerve and sinew
  To serve your turn long after they are gone,
And so hold on when there is nothing in you
  Except the Will which says to them: 'Hold on';

If you can talk with crowds and keep your virtue,
  Or walk with Kings — nor lose the common touch;
If neither foes nor loving friends can hurt you;
  If all men count with you, but none too much;
If you can fill the unforgiving minute
  With sixty seconds' worth of distance run —
Yours is the Earth and everything that's in it,
  And — which is more — you'll be a Man, my son!

RUDYARD KIPLING

*ℐ • ℬ*

# *Solitude*

Laugh, and the world laughs with you;
Weep, and you weep alone.
For the sad old earth must borrow its mirth,
But has trouble enough of its own.
Sing, and the hills will answer;
Sigh, it is lost on the air.
The echoes bound to a joyful sound,
But shrink from voicing care.

Rejoice, and men will seek you;
Grieve, and they turn and go.
They want full measure of all your pleasure,
But they do not need your woe.
Be glad, and your friends are many;
Be sad, and you lose them all.
There are none to decline your nectared wine,
But alone you must drink life's gall.

Feast, and your halls are crowded;
Fast, and the world goes by.
Succeed and give, and it helps you live,
But no man can help you die.
There is room in the halls of pleasure

For a long and lordly train,
But one by one we must all file on
Through the narrow aisles of pain.

ELLA WHEELER WILCOX

℘ • ℬ

## *My Heart Leaps Up*

My heart leaps up when I behold
 A rainbow in the sky:
So was it when my life began,
So is it now I am a man,
So be it when I shall grow old
 Or let me die!
The child is father of the man;
And I could wish my days to be
Bound each to each by natural piety.

WILLIAM WORDSWORTH

℘ • ℬ

# *A Birthday*

My heart is like a singing bird
Whose nest is in a watered shoot;
My heart is like an apple tree
Whose boughs are bent with thick-set fruit;
My heart is like a rainbow shell
That paddles in a halcyon sea;
My heart is gladder than all these,
Because my love is come to me.

Raise me a dais of silk and down;
Hang it with vair and purple dyes;
Carve it in doves and pomegranates,
And peacocks with a hundred eyes;
Work it in gold and silver grapes,
In leaves and silver fleurs-de-lys;
Because the birthday of my life
Is come, my love is come to me.

CHRISTINA GEORGINA ROSSETTI

$\mathcal{O} \cdot \mathcal{B}$

# Up-Hill

Does the road wind up-hill all the way?
>    *Yes, to the very end.*
Will the day's journey take the whole long day?
>    *From morn to night, my friend.*

But is there for the night a resting-place?
>    *A roof for when the slow dark hours begin.*
May not the darkness hide it from my face?
>    *You cannot miss that inn.*

Shall I meet other wayfarers at night?
>    *Those who have gone before.*
Then must I knock, or call when just in sight?
>    *They will not keep you standing at that door.*

Shall I find comfort, travel-sore and weak?
>    *Of labour you shall find the sum.*
Will there be beds for me and all who seek?
>    *Yea, beds for all who come.*

CHRISTINA GEORGINA ROSSETTI

# *I Hear America Singing*

I hear America singing, the varied carols I hear;

Those of mechanics—each one singing his, as it should be,
  blithe and strong;

The carpenter singing his, as he measures his plank or beam,

The mason singing his, as he makes ready for work, or leaves
  off work;

The boatman singing what belongs to him in his boat—the
  deckhand singing on the steamboat deck;

The shoemaker singing as he sits on his bench—the hatter
  singing as he stands;

The wood-cutter's song—the ploughboy's, on his way in the
  morning, or at the noon intermission, or at sundown;

The delicious singing of the mother—or of the young wife at
  work—or of the girl sewing or washing,

Each singing what belongs to him or her, and to none else;

The day what belongs to the day—At night, the party of
  young fellows, robust, friendly,

Singing, with open mouths, their strong melodious songs.

WALT WHITMAN

# Love's Land

Oh! Love builds on the azure sea,
    And Love builds on the golden strand,
And Love builds on the rose-winged cloud,
    And sometimes Love builds on the land.

Oh! if Love build on sparkling sea,
    And if Love build on golden strand,
And if Love build on rosy cloud,
    To Love these are the solid land.

Oh! Love will build his lily walls,
    And Love his pearly roof will rear
On cloud, or land, or mist, or sea —
    Love's solid land is everywhere!

ISABELLA VALANCY CRAWFORD

## The Song My Paddle Sings

West wind, blow from your prairie nest
Blow from the mountains, blow from the west.
The sail is idle, the sailor too;
O! wind of the west, we wait for you.
Blow, blow!
I have wooed you so,
But never a favour you bestow.
You rock your cradle the hills between,
But scorn to notice my white lateen.

I stow the sail, unship the mast:
I wooed you long but my wooing's past;
My paddle will lull you into rest.
O! drowsy wind of the drowsy west,
Sleep, sleep,
By your mountain steep,
Or down where the prairie grasses sweep!
Now fold in slumber your laggard wings,
For soft is the song my paddle sings.

August is laughing across the sky,
Laughing while paddle, canoe and I,
Drift, drift,
Where the hills uplift
On either side of the current swift.

The river rolls in its rocky bed;
My paddle is plying its way ahead;
Dip, dip,
While the waters flip
In foam as over their breast we slip.


And oh, the river runs swifter now;
The eddies circle about my bow.
Swirl, swirl!
How the ripples curl
In many a dangerous pool awhirl!


And forward far the rapids roar,
Fretting their margin for evermore.
Dash, dash,
With a mighty crash,
They seethe, and boil, and bound, and splash.


Be strong, O paddle! be brave, canoe!
The reckless waves you must plunge into.
Reel, reel.
On your trembling keel,
But never a fear my craft will feel.

We've raced the rapid, we're far ahead!
The river slips through its silent bed.
Sway, sway,
As the bubbles spray
And fall in tinkling tunes away.

And up on the hills against the sky,
A fir tree rocking its lullaby,
Swings, swings,
Its emerald wings,
Swelling the song that my paddle sings.

E. PAULINE JOHNSON

## Over The Wintry Threshold

Over the wintry threshold
Who comes with joy today,
So frail, yet so enduring,
To triumph o'er dismay?

Ah, quick her tears are springing,
And quickly they are dried,

For sorrow walks before her,
      But gladness walks beside.

She comes with gusts of laughter, —
      The music as it rills;
With tenderness and sweetness,
      The wisdom of the hills.

Her hands are strong to comfort,
      Her heart is quick to heed;
She knows the signs of sadness,
      She knows the voice of need;

There is no living creature,
      However poor or small,
But she will know its trouble,
      And hearken to its call.

Oh, well they fare forever,
      By mighty dreams possessed,
Whose hearts have lain a moment
      On that eternal breast.

BLISS CARMAN

## *Dreams*

What dreams we have and how they fly
Like rosy clouds across the sky;
    Of wealth, of fame, of sure success,
    Of love that comes to cheer and bless;
And how they wither, how they fade,
The waning wealth, the jilting jade —
    The fame that for a moment gleams,
    Then flies forever, —dreams, ah —dreams!

O burning doubt and long regret
O tears with which our eyes are wet,
    Heart-throbs, heart-aches, the glut of pain,
    The somber cloud, the bitter rain,
You were not of those dreams — ah! well,
Your full fruition who can tell?
    Wealth, fame, and love, ah! love that beams
    Upon our souls, all dreams — ah! dreams.

PAUL LAURENCE DUNBAR

# *Change*

I shall not wonder more, then,
But I shall know.

Leaves change, and birds, flowers,
And after years are still the same.

The sea's breast heaves in sighs to the moon,
But they are moon and sea forever.

As in other times the trees stand tense and lonely,
And spread a hollow moan of other times.

You will be you yourself,
I'll find you more, not else,
For vintage of the woeful years.

The sea breathes, or broods, or loudens,
Is bright or is mist and the end of the world;
And the sea is constant to change.

I shall not wonder more, then,
But I shall know.

RAYMOND KNISTER

## *Frowns And Smiles*

I thought the world was cold and dull,
That clouds on clouds were darkly piled,
All bleak and sombre, anguish-full—
I fancied this till Cathos smiled.

I thought the world was warm and bright,
That mirth and laughter floated round
The heart's bright chambers day and night—
I fancied this Cathos frowned.

She frowns, she smiles, by turns my heart
Is sad, is glad — its ev'ry tone
Of gay or grave she doth impart
By that strange magic all her own.

But let me only laugh and weep,
I would not have another gain
Those frowns, those smiles which she doth keep
To woo my tears, to ease my pain.

CHARLES MAIR

# *Return*

I have a sea-going spirit haunts my sleep,

Not a sad spirit wearisome to follow,

Less like a tenant of the mystic deep

Than the good fairy of the hazel hollow;

Full often at the midwatch of the night

I see departing in his silver bark

This spirit, steering toward an Eastern light,

Calling me to him from the Western dark.

'Spirit!' I ask, 'say, whither bound away?'

'Unto the old Hesperides!' he cries.

'Oh, Spirit, take me in thy bark, I pray.'

'For thee I came,' he joyfully replies;

'Exile! no longer shalt thou absent mourn,

For I the Spirit am men call — RETURN.'

THOMAS D'ARCY McGEE

*∂ • ℬ*

## Song Of The Axe

High grew the snow beneath the low-hung sky,
And all was silent in the wilderness;
In trance of stillness Nature heard her God
Rebuilding her spent fires, and veil'd her face
While the Great Worker brooded o'er His work.

'Bite deep and wide, O Axe, the tree!
What doth thy bold voice promise me?'

'I promise thee all joyous things
That furnish forth the lives of kings!

'For ev'ry silver ringing blow
Cities and palaces shall grow!'

'Bite deep and wide, O Axe, the tree!
Tell wider prophecies to me.'

'When rust hath gnaw'd me deep and red.
A nation strong shall lift his head!

'His crown the very Heav'ns shall smite,
Æons shall build him in his might!'

'Bite deep and wide, O Axe, the tree!
Bright Seer, help on thy prophecy!'

Max smote the snow-weigh'd tree, and lightly laugh'd.
'See, friend,' he cried to one that look'd and smil'd,
'My axe and I — we do immortal tasks —
We build up nations — this my axe and I!'

ISABELLA VALANCY CRAWFORD

$\mathcal{I} \cdot \mathcal{B}$

## *Ye Mariners Of England*

Ye Mariners of England
    That guard our native seas!
Whose flag has braved a thousand years
    The battle and the breeze —
Your glorious standard launch again
    To match another foe;
And sweep through the deep,
    While the stormy winds do blow!
While the battle rages loud and long
    And the stormy winds do blow.

The spirits of your fathers
    Shall start from every wave —

For the deck it was their field of fame,
    And Ocean was their grave.
Where Blake and mighty Nelson fell
    Your manly hearts shall glow,
As ye sweep through the deep,
    While the stormy winds do blow!
While the battle rages loud and long
    And the stormy winds do blow.

Britannia needs no bulwarks,
    No towers along the steep;
Her march is o'er the mountain-waves,
    Her home is on the deep.
The thunders from her native oak
    She quells the floods below,
As they roar on the shore,
    When the stormy winds do blow!
When the battle rages loud and long,
    And the stormy winds do blow.

The meteor flag of England
    Shall yet terrific burn;
Till danger's troubled night depart
    And the star of peace return.
Then, then, ye ocean-warriors!

Our song and feast shall flow
To the fame of your name,
When the storm has ceased to blow!
When the fiery fight is heard no more,
And the storm has ceased to blow.

THOMAS CAMPBELL

*I · B*

# *Ode*

We are the music-makers,
And we are the dreamers of dreams,
Wandering by lone sea-breakers,
And sitting by desolate streams;
World-losers and world-forsakers,
On whom the pale moon gleams:
Yet we are the movers and shakers
Of the world for ever, it seems.

With wonderful deathless ditties
We build up the world's great cities,
And out of a fabulous story
We fashion an empire's glory:
One man with a dream, at pleasure,
Shall go forth and conquer a crown;

And three with a new song's measure
    Can trample an empire down.

We, in the ages lying
    In the buried past of the earth,
Built Nineveh with our sighing,
    And Babel itself with our mirth;
And o'erthrew them with prophesying
    To the old of the new world's worth;
For each age is a dream that is dying,
    Or one that is coming to birth.

ARTHUR O'SHAUGHNESSY

☙ • ❧

## *If I Can Stop One Heart From Breaking*

If I can stop one heart from breaking,
    I shall not live in vain;
If I can ease one life the aching,
    Or cool one pain,
Or help one fainting robin
    Unto his nest again,
I shall not live in vain.

EMILY DICKINSON

☙ • ❧

## *Laus Deo*

It is done!
Clang of bell and roar of gun
Send the tidings up and down.
How the belfries rock and reel!
How the great guns, peal on peal,
Fling the joy from town to town!

Ring, O bells!
Every stroke exulting tells
Of the burial hour of crime.
Loud and long, that all may hear,
Ring for every listening ear
Of Eternity and Time!

Let us kneel:
God's own voice is in that peal,
And this spot is holy ground.
Lord, forgive us! What are we
That our eyes this glory see,
That our ears have heard this sound!

For the Lord
On the whirlwind is abroad;
In the earthquake He has spoken;
He has smitten with His thunder
The iron walls asunder,
And the gates of brass are broken!

Loud and long
Lift the old exulting song;
Sing with Miriam by the sea,
He has cast the mighty down;
Horse and rider sink and drown;
'He hath triumphed gloriously!'

Did we dare,
In our agony of prayer,
Ask for more than He has done?
When was ever His right hand
Over any time or land
Stretched as now beneath the sun?

How they pale,
Ancient myth and song and tale,
In this wonder of our days
When the cruel rod of war

Blossoms white with righteous law,
And the wrath of man is praise!

Blotted out!
All within and all about
Shall a fresher life begin;
Freer breathe the universe
As it rolls its heavy curse
On the dead and buried sin!

It is done!
In the circuit of the sun
Shall the sound thereof go forth.
It shall bid the sad rejoice,
It shall give the dumb a voice,
It shall belt with joy the earth!

Ring and swing,
Bells of joy! On morning's wing
Send the song of praise abroad!
With a sound of broken chains
Tell the nations that He reigns,
Who alone is Lord and God!

JOHN GREENLEAF WHITTIER

## *Forbearance*

Hast thou named all the birds without a gun;
Loved the wood-rose, and left it on its stalk;
At rich men's tables eaten bread and pulse;
Unarmed, faced danger with a heart of trust;
And loved so well a high behavior,
In man or maid, that thou from speech refrained,
Nobility more nobly to repay?
O be my friend, and teach me to be thine!

RALPH WALDO EMERSON

❦ • ❧

## *Persistence*

My hopes retire; my wishes as before
Struggle to find their resting-place in vain:
The ebbing sea thus beats against the shore;
The shore repels it; it returns again.

WALTER SAVAGE LANDOR

❦ • ❧

## *A Song For A Sleigh Drive*

Hurrah for the forest! the dark pine wood forest!
The sleigh bells are jingling in musical chimes;
>> The woods are still ringing,
>> As gaily we're singing —
Oh, merry it is in the cold winter time.

Hurrah for the forest! the dark pine wood forest!
With the moon stealing down on the cold frozen snow.
>> With eyes beaming brightly,
>> And hearts beating lightly,
Through the wild forest by moonlight we go.

Hurrah for the forest! the dark pine wood forest!
Where silence and stillness for ages have been.
>> We'll rouse the grim bear,
>> And the wolf from his lair,
And the deer shall start up from the thick cedar screen.

Oh, wail for the forest! the green shady forest!
No more its depths may the hunter explore;
>> For the bright golden grain
>> Shall wave free o'er the plain.
Oh! wail for the forest, its glories are o'er!

CATHARINE PARR TRAILL

# *A Song*

There is ever a song somewhere, my dear,
There is ever a something sings alway:
There's the song of the lark when the skies are clear,
And the song of the thrush when the skies are gray.
The sunshine showers across the grain,
And the bluebird trills in the orchard tree;
And in and out, when the eaves drip rain,
The swallows are twittering ceaselessly.

There is ever a song somewhere, my dear,
Be the skies above or dark or fair;
There is ever a song that our hearts may hear —
There is ever a song somewhere, my dear —
There is ever a song somewhere!

There is ever a song somewhere, my dear,
In the midnight black or the midday blue:
The robin pipes when the sun is here,
And the cricket chirrups the whole night through;
The buds may blow and the fruit may grow,
And the autumn leaves drop crisp and sere:
But whether the sun or the rain or the snow,
There is ever a song somewhere, my dear.

There is ever a song somewhere, my dear,
Be the skies above or dark or fair;
There is ever a song that our hearts may hear —
There is ever a song somewhere, my dear —
There is ever a song somewhere!

JAMES WHITCOMB RILEY

## Tears, Idle Tears

Tears, idle tears, I know not what they mean,
Tears from the depth of some divine despair
Rise in the heart, and gather to the eyes,
In looking on the happy autumn-fields,
And thinking of the days that are no more.

Fresh as the first beam glittering on a sail,
That brings our friends up from the underworld,
Sad as the last which reddens over one
That sinks with all we love below the verge;
So sad, so fresh, the days that are no more.

Ah, sad and strange as in dark summer dawns
The earliest pipe of half-awaken'd birds
To dying ears, when unto dying eyes
The casement slowly grows a glimmering square;
So sad, so strange, the days that are no more.

Dear as remember'd kisses after death,
And sweet as those by hopeless fancy feign'd
On lips that are for others; deep as love,
Deep as first love, and wild with all regret;
O Death in Life, the days that are no more!

ALFRED, LORD TENNYSON

𝒜 • ℬ

# Spirit

AND

# Faith

# *And Did Those Feet In Ancient Time*

And did those feet in ancient time
Walk upon England's mountains green?
And was the holy Lamb of God
On England's pleasant pastures seen?
And did the countenance divine
Shine forth upon our clouded hills?
And was Jerusalem builded here
Among those dark satanic mills?

Bring me my bow of burning gold!
Bring me my arrows of desire!
Bring me my spear! O clouds, unfold!
Bring me my chariot of fire!
I will not cease from mental fight,
Nor shall my sword sleep in my hand,
Till we have built Jerusalem
In England's green and pleasant land.

WILLIAM BLAKE

## No Coward Soul Is Mine

No coward soul is mine,
No trembler in the world's storm-troubled sphere:
I see Heaven's glories shine,
And faith shines equal, arming me from fear.

O God within my breast,
Almighty, ever-present Deity!
Life, that in me has rest,
As I, undying Life, have power in thee!

Vain are the thousand creeds
That move men's hearts: unutterably vain;
Worthless as withered weeds,
Or idlest froth amid the boundless main,

To waken doubt in one
Holding so fast by Thy infinity;
So surely anchored on
The steadfast rock of immortality.

With wide-embracing love
Thy spirit animates eternal years,
Pervades and broods above,
Changes, sustains, dissolves, creates and rears.

Though earth and moon were gone,
And suns and universes ceased to be,
And Thou were left alone,
Every existence would exist in Thee.

There is not room for Death,
Nor atom that his might could render void:
Thou — THOU art Being and Breath,
And what THOU art may never be destroyed.

EMILY BRONTË

## *None Other Lamb*

None other Lamb, none other Name,
None other hope in Heav'n or earth or sea,
None other hiding place from guilt and shame,
None beside Thee!

My faith burns low, my hope burns low;
Only my heart's desire cries out in me
By the deep thunder of its want and woe,
Cries out to Thee.

Lord, Thou art Life, though I be dead;
Love's fire Thou art, however cold I be:
Nor Heav'n have I, nor place to lay my head,
Nor home, but Thee.

CHRISTINA GEORGINA ROSSETTI

ℰ • ℬ

## *Chartless*

I never saw a moor,
I never saw the sea;
Yet now know I how the heather looks,
And what a wave must be.

I never spoke with God,
Nor visited in Heaven;
Yet certain am I of the spot
As if the chart were given.

EMILY DICKINSON

ℰ • ℬ

# *The Lamb*

Little Lamb, who make thee?
Dost thou know who made thee,
Gave thee life, and bade thee feed
By the stream and o'er the mead;
Gave thee clothing of delight,
Softest clothing, woolly, bright;
Gave thee such a tender voice,
Making all the vales rejoice?
  Little Lamb, who made thee?
  Dost thou know who made thee?

Little Lamb, I'll tell thee;
Little Lamb, I'll tell thee,
He is callèd by thy name,
For He calls himself a Lamb
He is meek, and He is mild,
He became a little child.
I a child, and thou a lamb,
We are callèd by His name.
  Little Lamb, God bless thee!
  Little Lamb, God bless thee!

WILLIAM BLAKE

# *Death*

Death is a road our dearest friends have gone;
Why with such leaders, fear to say, 'Lead on?'
Its gate repels, lest it too soon be tried,
But turns in balm on the immortal side.
Mothers have passed it: fathers, children; men
Whose like we look not to behold again;
Women that smiled away their loving breath;
Soft is the travelling on the road to death!
But guilt has passed it? men not fit to die?
O, hush — for He that made us all is by!
Human we're all — all men, all born of mothers;
All our own selves in the worn-out shape of others;
Our used, and oh, be sure, not to be ill-used brothers!

LEIGH HUNT

## Flower In The Crannied Wall

Flower in the crannied wall,

I pluck you out of the crannies,

I hold you here, root and all, in my hand,

Little flower—but if I could understand

What you are, root and all, and all in all,

I should know what God and man is.

ALFRED, LORD TENNYSON

𝒜 • ℬ

## Lucifer In Starlight

On a starr'd night Prince Lucifer uprose.

Tired of his dark dominion swung the fiend

Above the rolling ball in cloud part screen'd,

Where sinners hugg'd their spectre of repose.

Poor prey to his hot fit of pride were those.

And now upon his western wing he lean'd,

Now his huge bulk o'er Afric's sands careen'd,

Now the black planet shadow'd Arctic snows.

Soaring through wider zones that prick'd his scars

With memory of the old revolt from Awe,

He reach'd a middle height, and at the stars,

Which are the brain of heaven, he look'd, and sank.
Around the ancient track march'd, rank on rank,
    The army of unalterable law.

GEORGE MEREDITH

*G • B*

# *A Hymn To God The Father*

Wilt thou forgive that sin where I begun,
    Which was my sin, though it were done before?
Wilt thou forgive that sin, through which I run,
    And do run still, though still I do deplore?
When thou hast done, thou hast not done,
      For I have more.

Wilt thou forgive that sin which I have won
    Others to sin, and made my sin their door?
Wilt thou forgive that sin which I did shun
    A year or two, but wallow'd in, a score?
When thou hast done, thou hast not done,
      For I have more.

I have a sin of fear, that when I've spun
      My last thread, I shall perish on the shore;
But swear by thyself, that at my death thy Son
      Shall shine as He shines now, and heretofore;
And, having done that, thou hast done;
      I fear no more.

JOHN DONNE

*ℰ • ℬ*

## *Invictus*

Out of the night that covers me,
Black as the Pit from pole to pole,
I thank whatever gods may be
For my unconquerable soul.

In the fell clutch of circumstance
I have not winced nor cried aloud.
Under the bludgeonings of chance
My head is bloody, but unbowed.

Beyond this place of wrath and tears
Looms but the Horror of the shade,
And yet the menace of the years
Finds, and shall find me, unafraid.

It matters not how strait the gate,
How charged with punishments the scroll,
I am the master of my fate:
I am the captain of my soul.

WILLIAM ERNEST HENLEY

𝒟 • ℬ

## *On His Blindness*

When I consider how my light is spent
Ere half my days in this dark world and wide,
And that one Talent which is death to hide,
Lodged with me useless, though my Soul more bent
To serve therewith my Maker, and present
My true account, lest he returning chide,
'Doth God exact day-labour, light denied?
I fondly ask. But Patience, to prevent
That murmur, soon replies, 'God doth not need
Either man's work or his own gifts. Who best
Bear his mild yoke, they serve him best. His State
Is kingly: thousands at his bidding speed
And post o'er land and ocean without rest;
They also serve who only stand and wait.'

JOHN MILTON

𝒟 • ℬ

## *The Oxen*

Christmas Eve, and twelve of the clock,
    'Now they are all on their knees',
An elder said as we sat in a flock
    By the embers in hearthside ease.

We pictured the meek mild creatures where
    They dwelt in their strawy pen,
Nor did it occur to one of us there
    To doubt they were kneeling then.

So fair a fancy few would weave
    In these years! Yet, I feel,
If someone said on Christmas Eve,
    'Come; see the oxen kneel

'In the lonely barton by yonder coomb
    Our childhood used to know'
I should go with him in the gloom,
    Hoping it might be so.

THOMAS HARDY

# The Donkey

When fishes flew and forests walked
    And figs grew upon thorn,
Some moment when the moon was blood
    Then surely I was born;

With monstrous head and sickening cry
    And ears like errant wings,
The devil's walking parody
    On all four-footed things.

The tattered outlaw of the earth,
    Of ancient crooked will;
Starve, scourge, deride me: I am dumb,
    I keep my secret still.

Fools! For I also had my hour;
    One far fierce hour and sweet:
There was a shout about my ears,
    And palms before my feet.

G. K. CHESTERTON

## *Death Be Not Proud, Though Some Have Called Thee*

Death be not proud, though some have called thee
Mighty and dreadfull, for, thou art not so,
For, those, whom thou think'st, thou dost overthrow,
Die not, poore death, nor yet canst thou kill me.
From rest and sleepe, which but thy pictures bee,
Much pleasure, then from thee, much more must flow,
And soonest our best men with thee doe goe,
Rest of their bones, and soules deliverie.
Thou art slave to Fate, Chance, kings, and desperate men,
And dost with poyson, warre, and sicknesse dwell,
And poppie, or charmes can make us sleepe as well,
And better then thy stroake; why swell'st thou then;
One short sleepe past, wee wake eternally,
And death shall be no more; death, thou shalt die.

JOHN DONNE

*∂ · ℬ*

## *The Village Blacksmith*

Under a spreading chestnut-tree
The village smithy stands;
The smith, a mighty man is he,
With large and sinewy hands;
And the muscles of his brawny arms
Are as strong as iron bands.

His hair is crisp, and black, and long,
His face is like the tan;
His brow is wet with honest sweat,
He earns whate'er he can,
And looks the whole world in the face,
For he owes not any man.

Week in, week out, from morn till night,
You can hear his bellows blow;
You can hear him swing his heavy sledge,
With measured beat and slow,
Like a sexton ringing the village bell,
When the evening sun is low.

And children coming home from school
Look in at the open door;

They love to see the flaming forge,
And hear the bellows roar,
And catch the burning sparks that fly
Like chaff from a threshing-floor.

He goes on Sunday to the church,
And sits among his boys;
He hears the parson pray and preach,
He hears his daughter's voice,
Singing in the village choir,
And makes his heart rejoice.

It sounds to him like her mother's voice,
Singing in Paradise!
He needs must think of her once more,
How in the grave she lies;
And with his hard, rough hand he wipes
A tear out of his eyes.

Toiling, — rejoicing, — sorrowing,
Onward through life he goes;
Each morning sees some task begin,
Each evening sees it close!
Something attempted, something done,
Has earned a night's repose.

Thanks, thanks to thee, my worthy friend,
For the lesson thou hast taught!
Thus at the flaming forge of life
Our fortunes must be wrought;
Thus on its sounding anvil shaped
Each burning deed and thought.

HENRY WADSWORTH LONGFELLOW

⊘ • ℛ

## *Lord Of My Heart's Elation*

Lord of my heart's elation,
Spirit of things unseen,
Be thou my aspiration
Consuming and serene!

Bear up, bear out, bear onward
This mortal soul alone,
To selfhood or oblivion,
Incredibly thine own, —

As the foamheads are loosened
And blown along the sea,

Or sink and merge forever
In that which bids them be.

I, too, must climb in wonder,
Uplift at thy command, —
Be one with my frail fellows
Beneath the wind's strong hand,

A fleet and shadowy column
Of dust or mountain rain,
To walk the earth a moment
And be dissolved again.

Be thou my exaltation
Or fortitude of mien,
Lord of the world's elation,
Thou breath of things unseen!

BLISS CARMAN

## *A Prayer In Darkness*

This much, O heaven—if I should brood or rave,
Pity me not; but let the world be fed,
Yea, in my madness if I strike me dead,
Heed you the grass that grows upon my grave.


If I dare snarl between this sun and sod,
Whimper and clamour, give me grace to own,
In sun and rain and fruit in season shown,
The shining silence of the scorn of God.


Thank God the stars are set beyond my power,
If I must travail in a night of wrath,
Thank God my tears will never vex a moth,
Nor any curse of mine cut down a flower.


Men say the sun was darkened: yet I had
Thought it beat brightly, even on — Calvary:
And He that hung upon the Torturing Tree
Heard all the crickets singing, and was glad.


G. K. CHESTERTON

## *Destiny*

Somewhere there waiteth in this world of ours

For one lone soul another lonely soul

Each choosing each through all the weary hours

And meeting strangely at one sudden goal.

Then blend they, like green leaves with golden flowers,

Into one beautiful and perfect whole;

And life's long night is ended, and the way

Lies open onward to eternal day.

SIR EDWIN ARNOLD

*ℐ · ℬ*

## *The Shepherd Boy Sings In The Valley Of Humiliation*

He that is down needs fear no fall,

He that is low, no pride;

He that is humble ever shall

Have God to be his guide.

I am content with what I have,

Little be it or much:

And, Lord, contentment still I crave,

Because Thou savest such.

Fullness to such a burden is
    That go on pilgrimage:
Here little, and hereafter bliss,
    Is best from age to age.

JOHN BUNYAN

_ • _

## *The Dying Christian To His Soul*

Vital spark of heav'nly flame!
    Quit, O quit this mortal frame:
Trembling, hoping, ling'ring, flying,
    O the pain, the bliss of dying!
Cease, fond Nature, cease thy strife,
    And let me languish into life.

Hark! they whisper; angels say,
    Sister Spirit, come away!
What is this absorbs me quite?
    Steals my senses, shuts my sight,
Drowns my spirits, draws my breath?
    Tell me, my soul, can this be death?

The world recedes; it disappears!
  Heav'n opens on my eyes! my ears
With sounds seraphic ring!
  Lend, lend your wings! I mount! I fly!
O Grave! where is thy victory?
  O Death! where is thy sting?


ALEXANDER POPE

## Hurrahing In Harvest

Summer ends now; now, barbarous in beauty, the stooks rise
 Around; up above, what wind-walks! what lovely behaviour
 Of silk-sack clouds! has wilder, wilful-wavier
Meal-drift moulded ever and melted across skies?

I walk, I lift up, I lift up heart, eyes,
 Down all that glory in the heavens to glean our Saviour;
 And eyes, heart, what looks, what lips yet give you a
Rapturous love's greeting of realer, of rounder replies?

And the azurous hung hills are his world-wielding shoulder
 Majestic — as a stallion stalwart, very-violet-sweet! —

These things, these things were here and but the beholder
Wanting; which two when they once meet,
   The heart rears wings bold and bolder
And hurls for him, O half hurls earth for him off under his feet.

GERARD MANLEY HOPKINS

*E · B*

## *The Whispers Of Time*

What does time whisper, youth gay and light,
   While thinning thy locks, silken and bright,
   While paling thy soft cheek's roseate dye,
      Dimming the light of thy flashing eye,
   Stealing thy bloom and freshness away —
      Is he not hinting at death — decay?

Man, in the wane of thy stately prime,
   Hear'st thou the silent warnings of Time?
Look at thy brow ploughed by anxious care,
   The silver hue of thy once dark hair; —
What boot thine honors, thy treasures bright,
When Time tells of coming gloom and night?

Sad age, dost thou note thy strength nigh, spent,
How slow thy footstep — thy form how bent?
Yet on looking back how short doth seem
The checkered course of thy life's brief dream.
Time, daily weakening each link and tie,
Doth whisper how soon thou art to die.

O! what a weary world were ours
With that thought to cloud our brightest hours,
Did we not know that beyond the skies
A land of beauty and promise lies,
Where peaceful and blessed we will love — adore —
When Time itself shall be no more!

ROSANNA LEPROHON

*ℐ • ℬ*

## The Resignation

O God, whose thunder shakes the sky,
Whose eye this atom globe surveys,
To thee, my only rock, I fly,
Thy mercy in thy justice praise.

The mystic mazes of thy will,
The shadows of celestial light,
Are past the pow'r of human skill, —
But what th' Eternal acts is right.

O teach me in the trying hour,
When anguish swells the dewy tear,
To still my sorrows, own thy pow'r,
Thy goodness love, thy justice fear.

If in this bosom aught but Thee
Encroaching sought a boundless sway,
Omniscience could the danger see,
And Mercy look the cause away.

Then why, my soul, dost thou complain?
Why drooping seek the dark recess?
Shake off the melancholy chain.
For God created all to bless.

But ah! my breast is human still;
The rising sigh, the falling tear,
My languid vitals' feeble rill,
The sickness of my soul declare.

But yet, with fortitude resigned,
I'll thank th' inflicter of the blow;
Forbid the sigh, compose my mind,
Nor let the gush of mis'ry flow.

The gloomy mantle of the night,
Which on my sinking spirit steals,
Will vanish at the morning light,
Which God, my East, my sun reveals.

THOMAS CHATTERTON

## Love Came Down At Christmas

Love came down at Christmas,
Love all lovely, love divine;
Love was born at Christmas,
Star and angels gave the sign.

Worship we the Godhead,
Love incarnate, love divine;
Worship we our Jesus:
But wherewith for sacred sign?

Love shall be our token,
Love shall be yours and love be mine,
Love to God and to all men,
Love for plea and gift and sign.

CHRISTINA GEORGINA ROSSETTI

☙ • ❧

## The Retreat

Happy those early days, when I
Shined in my Angel-infancy!
Before I understood this place
Appointed for my second race,
Or taught my soul to fancy aught
But a white, celestial thought;
When yet I had not walked above
A mile or two from my first Love,
And looking back, at that short space
Could see a glimpse of His bright face;
When on some gilded cloud or flower
My gazing soul would dwell an hour,
And in those weaker glories spy
Some shadows of eternity;

Before I taught my tongue to wound
My conscience with a sinful sound,
Or had the black art to dispense
A several sin to every sense,
But felt through all this fleshly dress
Bright shoots of everlastingness.

O how I long to travel back
And tread again that ancient track!
That I might once more reach that plain
Where first I felt my glorious train;
From whence th' enlightened spirit sees
That shady City of palm trees!
But ah! my soul with too much stay
Is drunk, and staggers in the way.
Some men a forward motion love,
But I by backward steps would move;
And when this dust falls to the urn,
In that state I came, return.

HENRY VAUGHAN

*ℰ • ℬ*

## *Even Such Is Time*

Even such is time, that takes in trust
Our youth, our joys, our all we have,
And pays us but with earth and dust;
Who, in the dark and silent grave,
When we have wandered all our ways,
Shuts up the story of our days:
But from this earth, this grave, this dust,
My God shall raise me up, I trust.

SIR WALTER RALEIGH

ℰ · ℬ

## *I Am*

I am: yet what I am none cares or knows,
My friends forsake me like a memory lost;
I am the self-consumer of my woes,
They rise and vanish in oblivious host,
Like shades in love and death's oblivion lost;
And yet I am, and live — like vapours tossed

Into the nothingness of scorn and noise,
Into the living sea of waking dreams,
Where there is neither sense of life nor joys,

But the vast shipwreck of my life's esteems;
Even the dearest, that I loved the best,
Are strange — nay, rather stranger than the rest.

I long for scenes where man has never trod;
A place where woman never smiled or wept;
There to abide with my creator, God,
And sleep as I in childhood sweetly slept:
Untroubling, and untroubled where I lie,
The grass below — above the vaulted sky.

JOHN CLARE

## Eternity

O years! and age! farewell:
Behold I go,
Where I do know
Infinity to dwell.

And these mine eyes shall see
All times, how they
Are lost i' th' sea
Of vast eternity: —

Where never moon shall sway
The stars; but she,
And night, shall be
Drown'd in one endless day.

ROBERT HERRICK

## A Good-Night

Close now thine eyes and rest secure;
Thy soul is safe enough, thy body sure;
He that loves thee, he that keeps
And guards thee, never slumbers, never sleeps.
The smiling conscience in a sleeping breast
Has only peace, has only rest;
The music and the mirth of kings
Are all but very discords, when she sings;
Then close thine eyes and rest secure;
No sleep so sweet as thine, no rest so sure.

FRANCIS QUARLES

# *Virtue*

Sweet day, so cool, so calm, so bright!
The bridal of the earth and sky—
The dew shall weep thy fall to-night;
For thou must die.

Sweet rose, whose hue angry and brave
Bids the rash gazer wipe his eye,
Thy root is ever in its grave,
And thou must die.

Sweet spring, full of sweet days and roses,
A box where sweets compacted lie,
My music shows ye have your closes,
And all must die.

Only a sweet and virtuous soul,
Like season'd timber, never gives;
But though the whole world turn to coal,
Then chiefly lives.

GEORGE HERBERT

$\mathcal{V} \cdot \mathcal{B}$

# *On Time*

Fly, envious Time, till thou run out thy race,
Call on the lazy leaden-stepping hours,
Whose speed is but the heavy Plummet's pace;
And glut thy self with what thy womb devours,
Which is no more than what is false and vain,
And merely mortal dross;
So little is our loss,
So little is thy gain.
For when as each thing bad thou hast entomb'd,
And last of all, thy greedy self consum'd,
Then long Eternity shall greet our bliss
With an individual kiss;
And Joy shall overtake us as a flood,
When every thing that is sincerely good
And perfectly divine,
With Truth, and Peace, and Love shall ever shine
About the supreme Throne
Of Him, t'whose happy-making sight alone,
When once our heav'nly-guided soul shall climb,
Then all this earthy grossness quit,
Attir'd with Stars, we shall for ever sit,
Triumphing over Death, and Chance, and thee O Time.

JOHN MILTON

$\mathscr{E} \cdot \mathscr{B}$

## *God's Grandeur*

The world is charged with the grandeur of God.
    It will flame out, like shining from shook foil;
    It gathers to a greatness, like the ooze of oil
Crushed. Why do men then now not reck his rod?
Generations have trod, have trod, have trod;
    And all is seared with trade; bleared, smeared with toil;
    And wears man's smudge and shares man's smell: the soil
Is bare now, nor can foot feel, being shod.

And for all this, nature is never spent;
    There lives the dearest freshness deep down things;
And though the last lights off the black West went
    Oh, morning, at the brown brink eastward, springs —
Because the Holy Ghost over the bent
    World broods with warm breast and with ah! bright
        wings.

GERARD MANLEY HOPKINS

## *Peace*

My soul, there is a country
  Far beyond the stars,
Where stands a winged sentry
  All skilful in the wars:
There, above noise and danger,
  Sweet Peace sits crown'd with smiles,
And One born in a manger
  Commands the beauteous files.
He is thy gracious Friend,
  And—O my soul, awake!—
Did in pure love descend
  To die here for thy sake.
If thou canst get but thither,
  There grows the flower of Peace,
The Rose that cannot wither,
  Thy fortress, and thy ease.
Leave then thy foolish ranges;
  For none can thee secure
But One who never changes—
  Thy God, thy life, thy cure.

HENRY VAUGHAN

## Light Shining Out Of Darkness

God moves in a mysterious way,
His wonders to perform;
He plants his footsteps in the sea,
And rides upon the storm.

Deep in unfathomable mines
Of never failing skill
He treasures up his bright designs,
And works his sovereign will.

Ye fearful saints, fresh courage take,
The clouds ye so much dread
Are big with mercy, and shall break
In blessings on your head.

Judge not the Lord by feeble sense,
But trust him for his grace;
Behind a frowning providence,
He hides a smiling face.

His purposes will ripen fast,
Unfolding every hour;

The bud may have a bitter taste,
But sweet will be the flower.

Blind unbelief is sure to err,
And scan his work in vain;
God is his own interpreter,
And he will make it plain.

WILLIAM COWPER
✍ • ✍

## *A Slumber Did My Spirit Seal*

A slumber did my spirit seal;
I had no human fears;
She seemed a thing that could not feel
The touch of earthly years.

No motion has she now, no force;
She neither hears nor sees;
Rolled round in earth's diurnal course,
With rocks, and stones, and trees.

WILLIAM WORDSWORTH
✍ • ✍

## *Pied Beauty*

Glory be to God for dappled things—
>> For skies of couple-colour as a brinded cow;
>>> For rose-moles all in stipple upon trout that
>>> swim;
Fresh-firecoal chestnut-falls; finches' wings;
>> Landscape plotted and pieced — fold, fallow, and
>> plough;
>>> And all trades, their gear and tackle and trim.

All things counter, original, spare, strange;
>> Whatever is fickle, freckled (who knows how?)
>>> With swift, slow; sweet, sour; adazzle, dim;
He fathers-forth whose beauty is past change:
>> Praise Him.

GERARD MANLEY HOPKINS

*G • B*

## *Blessed Are They That Mourn*

Oh, deem not they are blest alone
>> Whose lives a peaceful tenor keep;
The Power who pities man, has shown
>> A blessing for the eyes that weep.

The light of smiles shall fill again
    The lids that overflow with tears;
And weary hours of woe and pain
    Are promises of happier years.

There is a day of sunny rest
    For every dark and troubled night;
And grief may bide an evening guest,
    But joy shall come with early light.

And thou, who, o'er thy friend's low bier,
    Sheddest the bitter drops like rain,
Hope that a brighter, happier sphere
    Will give him to thy arms again.

Nor let the good man's trust depart,
    Though life its common gifts deny, —
Though with a pierced and broken heart,
    And spurned of men, he goes to die.

For God has marked each sorrowing day
    And numbered every secret tear,
And heaven's long age of bliss shall pay
    For all his children suffer here.

WILLIAM CULLEN BRYANT

## *Love Bade Me Welcome*

Love bade me welcome, yet my soul drew back,
  Guilty of dust and sin.
But quick-ey'd Love, observing me grow slack
  From my first entrance in,
Drew nearer to me, sweetly questioning
  If I lack'd anything.

'A guest,' I answer'd, 'worthy to be here';
  Love said, 'You shall be he.'
'I, the unkind, ungrateful? Ah, my dear,
  I cannot look on thee.'
Love took my hand and smiling did reply,
  'Who made the eyes but I?'

'Truth, Lord, but I have marr'd them; let my shame
  Go where it doth deserve.'
'And know you not,' says Love, 'who bore the blame?'
  'My dear, then I will serve.'
'You must sit down,' says Love, 'and taste my meat.'
  So I did sit and eat.

GEORGE HERBERT

# A Psalm Of Life

Tell me not, in mournful numbers,
    Life is but an empty dream! —
For the soul is dead that slumbers,
    And things are not what they seem.

Life is real! Life is earnest!
    And the grave is not its goal;
Dust thou art, to dust returnest,
    Was not spoken of the soul.

Not enjoyment, and not sorrow,
    Is our destined end or way;
But to act, that each to-morrow
    Find us farther than to-day.

Art is long, and Time is fleeting,
    And our hearts, though stout and brave,
Still, like muffled drums, are beating
    Funeral marches to the grave.

In the world's broad field of battle,
    In the bivouac of Life,
Be not like dumb, driven cattle!
    Be a hero in the strife!

Trust no Future, howe'er pleasant!
　　Let the dead Past bury its dead!
Act, — act in the living Present!
　　Heart within, and God o'erhead!

Lives of great men all remind us
　　We can make our lives sublime,
And, departing, leave behind us
　　Footprints on the sands of time;

Footprints, that perhaps another,
　　Sailing o'er life's solemn main,
A forlorn and shipwrecked brother,
　　Seeing, shall take heart again.

Let us, then, be up and doing,
　　With a heart for any fate;
Still achieving, still pursuing,
　　Learn to labor and to wait.

HENRY WADSWORTH LONGFELLOW

*C* • *B*

## The Camper

Night 'neath the northern skies, lone, black and grim:
Naught but the starlight lies 'twixt heaven and him.

Of man no need has he, of God, no prayer;
He and his Deity are brothers there.

Above his bivouac the firs fling down
Through branches gaunt and black, their needles brown.

Afar some mountain streams, rockbound and fleet,
Sing themselves through his dreams in cadence sweet,

The pine trees whispering, the heron's cry,
The plover's passing wing, his lullaby.

And blinking overhead the white stars keep
Watch o'er his hemlock bed — his sinless sleep.

E. PAULINE JOHNSON

## *Evolution*

Out of the dusk a shadow,
Then, a spark;
Out of the cloud a silence,
Then, a lark;
Out of the heart a rapture,
Then, a pain;
Out of the dead, cold ashes,
Life again.

JOHN BANISTER TABB

## *To The Fringed Gentian*

Thou blossom bright with autumn dew,
And colored with the heaven's own blue,
That openest when the quiet light
Succeeds the keen and frosty night.

Thou comest not when violets lean
O'er wandering brooks and springs unseen,
Or columbines, in purple dressed,
Nod o'er the ground-bird's hidden nest.

Thou waitest late and com'st alone,
When woods are bare and birds are flown,
And frosts and shortening days portend
The aged year is near his end.

Then doth thy sweet and quiet eye
Look through its fringes to the sky,
Blue—blue—as if that sky let fall
A flower from its cerulean wall.

I would that thus, when I shall see
The hour of death draw near to me,
Hope, blossoming within my heart,
May look to heaven as I depart.

WILLIAM CULLEN BRYANT

*❦ • ❦*

## *The Lie*

Go, soul, the body's guest,
Upon a thankless errand;
Fear not to touch the best;
The truth shall be thy warrant:
Go, since I needs must die,
And give the world the lie.

Say to the court, it glows
And shines like rotten wood;
Say to the church, it shows
What's good, and doth no good:
If church and court reply,
Then give them both the lie.

Tell potentates, they live
Acting by others' action;
Not loved unless they give,
Not strong but by a faction.
If potentates reply,
Give potentates the lie.

Tell men of high condition,
That manage the estate,
Their purpose is ambition,
Their practice only hate:
And if they once reply,
Then give them all the lie.

Tell them that brave it most,
They beg for more by spending,
Who, in their greatest cost,
Seek nothing but commending.

And if they make reply,
Then give them all the lie.

Tell zeal it wants devotion;
Tell love it is but lust;
Tell time it is but motion;
Tell flesh it is but dust:
And wish them not reply,
For thou must give the lie.

Tell age it daily wasteth;
Tell honour how it alters;
Tell beauty how she blasteth;
Tell favour how it falters:
And as they shall reply,
Give every one the lie.

Tell wit how much it wrangles
In tickle-points of niceness;
Tell wisdom she entangles
Herself in over-wiseness:
And when they do reply,
Straight give them both the lie.

Tell physic of her boldness;
Tell skill it is pretension;

Tell charity of coldness;
Tell law it is contention:
And as they do reply,
So give them still the lie.

Tell fortune of her blindness;
Tell nature of decay;
Tell friendship of unkindness;
Tell justice of delay:
And if they will reply,
Then give them all the lie.

Tell arts they have no soundness,
But vary by esteeming;
Tell schools they want profoundness,
And stand too much on seeming:
If arts and schools reply,
Give arts and schools the lie.

Tell faith it's fled the city;
Tell how the country erreth;
Tell manhood shakes off pity
Tell virtue least preferreth:
And if they do reply,
Spare not to give the lie.

So when thou hast, as I
Commanded thee, done blabbing—
Although to give the lie
Deserves no less than stabbing—
Stab at thee he that will,
No stab thy soul can kill.

SIR WALTER RALEIGH

$\mathscr{A} \cdot \mathscr{B}$

## *Death Stands Above Me*

Death stands above me, whispering low
I know not what into my ear:
Of his strange language all I know
Is, there is not a word of fear.

WALTER SAVAGE LANDOR

$\mathscr{A} \cdot \mathscr{B}$

## Poor Soul, The Centre
## Of My Sinful Earth

Poor soul, the centre of my sinful earth,
Pressed by those rebel powers that thee array,
Why dost thou pine within and suffer dearth,
Painting thy outward walls so costly gay?
Why so large cost, having so short a lease,
Dost thou upon thy fading mansion spend?
Shall worms, inheritors of this excess,
Eat up thy charge? Is this thy body's end?
Then soul, live thou upon thy servant's loss
And let that pine to aggravate thy store;
Buy terms divine in selling hours of dross;
Within be fed, without be rich no more.

    So shalt thou feed on Death, that feeds on men,
    And, Death once dead, there's no more dying then.

WILLIAM SHAKESPEARE

&#9827; • &#9827;

# Adieu, Farewell Earth's Bliss

Adieu, farewell earth's bliss,
This world uncertain is;
Fond are life's lustful joys,
Death proves them all but toys,
None from his darts can fly:
I am sick, I must die.
Lord, have mercy on us!

Rich men, trust not in wealth,
Gold cannot buy your health;
Physic himself must fade;
All things to end are made;
The plague full swift goes by:
I am sick, I must die.
Lord, have mercy on us!

Beauty is but a flower
Which wrinkles will devour;
Brightness falls from the air,
Queens have died young and fair,
Dust hath clos'd Helen's eye:
I am sick, I must die.
Lord, have mercy on us!

Strength stoops unto the grave,
Worms feed on Hector brave,
Swords may not fight with fate,
Earth still holds ope her gate;
Come, come, the bells do cry.
I am sick, I must die.
Lord, have mercy on us!

Wit with his wantonness
Tasteth death's bitterness:
Hell's executioner
Hath no ears for to hear
What vain art can reply:
I am sick, I must die.
Lord, have mercy on us!

Haste, therefore, each degree
To welcome destiny:
Heaven is our heritage,
Earth but a player's stage:
Mount we unto the sky.
I am sick, I must die.
Lord, have mercy on us!

THOMAS NASHE

*ƍ • Ƃ*

# Not Yet, My Soul

Not yet, my soul, these friendly fields desert,
Where thou with grass, and rivers, and the breeze,
And the bright face of day, thy dalliance hadst;
Where to thine ear first sang the enraptured birds;
Where love and thou that lasting bargain made.
The ship rides trimmed, and from the eternal shore
Thou hearest airy voices; but not yet
Depart, my soul, not yet awhile depart.

Freedom is far, rest far. Thou art with life
Too closely woven, nerve with nerve intwined;
Service still craving service, love for love,
Love for dear love, still suppliant with tears.
Alas, not yet thy human task is done!
A bond at birth is forged; a debt doth lie
Immortal on immortality. It grows —
By vast rebound it grows, unceasing growth;
Gift upon gift, alms upon alms, upreared,
From man, from God, from nature, till the soul
At that so huge indulgence stands amazed.

Leave not, my soul, the unfoughten field, nor leave
Thy debts dishonoured, nor thy place desert
Without due service rendered. For thy life,

Up, spirit, and defend that fort of clay.

Thy body, now beleaguered; whether soon

Or late she fall; whether to-day thy friends

Bewail thee dead, or, after years, a man

Grown old in honour and the friend of peace.

Contend, my soul, for moments and for hours;

Each is with service pregnant; each reclaimed

Is as a kingdom conquered, where to reign.

As when a captain rallies to the fight

His scattered legions, and beats ruin back,

He, on the field, encamps, well pleased in mind.

Yet surely him shall fortune overtake,

Him smite in turn, headlong his ensigns drive;

And that dear land, now safe, to-morrow fall.

But he, unthinking, in the present good

Solely delights, and all the camps rejoice.

ROBERT LOUIS STEVENSON

## *Crossing The Bar*

Sunset and evening star,
    And one clear call for me!
And may there be no moaning of the bar,
    When I put out to sea,

But such a tide as moving seems asleep,
    Too full for sound and foam,
When that which drew from out the boundless deep
    Turns again home.

Twilight and evening bell,
    And after that the dark!
And may there be no sadness of farewell,
    When I embark;

For tho' from out our bourne of Time and Place
    The flood may bear me far,
I hope to see my Pilot face to face
    When I have crossed the bar.

ALFRED, LORD TENNYSON

## *The Prism Of Life*

All that began with God, in God must end:
All lives are garnered in His final bliss:
All wills hereafter shall be one with His:
When in the sea we sought, our spirits blend.
Rays of pure light, which one frail prism may rend
Into conflicting colours, meet and kiss
With manifold attraction, yet still miss
Contentment, while their kindred hues contend.
Break but that three-edged glass:—inviolate
The sundered beams resume their primal state,
Weaving pure light in flawless harmony.
Thus decomposed, subject to love and strife,
God's thought, made conscious through man's mortal life,
Resumes through death the eternal unity.

JOHN ADDINGTON SYMONDS

# Longer Works

# *The Raven*

ONCE upon a midnight dreary, while I pondered, weak and
weary,
Over many a quaint and curious volume of forgotten lore, —
While I nodded, nearly napping, suddenly there came a tapping,
As of some one gently rapping, rapping at my chamber door.
'T is some visitor,' I muttered, 'tapping at my chamber door;
  Only this and nothing more.'

Ah, distinctly I remember it was in the bleak December
And each separate dying ember wrought its ghost upon the floor.
Eagerly I wished the morrow; — vainly I had sought to borrow
From my books surcease of sorrow — sorrow for the lost Lenore,
For the rare and radiant maiden whom the angels name Lenore:
  Nameless here for evermore.

And the silken sad uncertain rustling of each purple curtain
Thrilled me — filled me with fantastic terrors never felt before;
So that now, to still the beating of my heart, I stood repeating
'T is some visitor entreating entrance at my chamber door,
Some late visitor entreating entrance at my chamber door:
  This it is and nothing more.'

Presently my soul grew stronger; hesitating then no longer,
'Sir,' said I, 'or Madam, truly your forgiveness I implore;
But the fact is I was napping, and so gently you came rapping,
And so faintly you came tapping, tapping at my chamber door,

That I scarce was sure I heard you' — here I opened wide the
door: —
  Darkness there and nothing more.

Deep into that darkness peering, long I stood there wondering,
fearing,
Doubting, dreaming dreams no mortals ever dared to dream
before;
But the silence was unbroken, and the stillness gave no token,
And the only word there spoken was the whispered word,
'Lenore?'
This I whispered, and an echo murmured back the word,
'Lenore:'
  Merely this and nothing more.

Back into the chamber turning, all my soul within me burning,
Soon again I heard a tapping somewhat louder than before.
'Surely,' said I, 'surely that is something at my window lattice;
Let me see, then, what thereat is, and this mystery explore;
Let my heart be still a moment and this mystery explore:
  'Tis the wind and nothing more.'

Open here I flung the shutter, when, with many a flirt and
flutter,
In there stepped a stately Raven of the saintly days of yore.
 Not the least obeisance made he; not a minute stopped or
stayed he;
But, with mien of lord or lady, perched above my chamber door,

Perched upon a bust of Pallas just above my chamber door:
    Perched, and sat, and nothing more.

Then this ebony bird beguiling my sad fancy into smiling
By the grave and stern decorum of the countenance it wore, —
'Though thy crest be shorn and shaven, thou,' I said, 'art sure
no craven,
Ghastly grim and ancient Raven wandering from the Nightly
shore:
Tell me what thy lordly name is on the Night's Plutonian shore!'
    Quoth the Raven, 'Nevermore.'

Much I marvelled this ungainly fowl to hear discourse so
plainly,
Though its answer little meaning — little relevancy bore;
For we cannot help agreeing that no living human being
Ever yet was blessed with seeing bird above his chamber door,
Bird or beast upon the sculptured bust above his chamber door,
    With such name as 'Nevermore.'

But the Raven, sitting lonely on the placid bust, spoke only
That one word, as if his soul in that one word he did outpour.
Nothing further then he uttered, not a feather then he fluttered,
Till I scarcely more than muttered, — 'Other friends have
flown before;
On the morrow he will leave me, as my Hopes have flown
before.'
    Then the bird said, 'Nevermore.'

Startled at the stillness broken by reply so aptly spoken,
'Doubtless,' said I, 'what it utters is its only stock and store,
Caught from some unhappy master whom unmerciful Disaster
Followed fast and followed faster till his songs one burden bore:
Till the dirges of his Hope that melancholy burden bore
    Of 'Never — nevermore.'

But the Raven still beguiling all my fancy into smiling,
Straight I wheeled a cushioned seat in front of bird and bust and door;
Then, upon the velvet sinking, I betook myself to linking
Fancy unto fancy, thinking what this ominous bird of yore,
What this grim, ungainly, ghastly, gaunt, and ominous bird of yore
    Meant in croaking 'Nevermore.'

This I sat engaged in guessing, but no syllable expressing
To the fowl whose fiery eyes now burned into my bosom's core;
This and more I sat divining, with my head at ease reclining
On the cushion's velvet lining that the lamplight gloated o'er,
  But whose velvet violet lining with the lamp-light gloating o'er
    She shall press, ah, nevermore!

Then, methought, the air grew denser, perfumed from an unseen censer
Swung by seraphim whose foot-falls tinkled on the tufted floor.
'Wretch,' I cried, 'thy God hath lent thee — by these angels he hath sent thee

Respite—respite and nepenthe from thy memories of Lenore!'
Quaff, oh quaff this kind nepenthe, and forget this lost Lenore.'
 Quoth the Raven, 'Nevermore.'

'Prophet!' said I, 'thing of evil! prophet still, if bird or devil!
Whether Tempter sent, or whether tempest tossed thee here
ashore,
Desolate yet all undaunted, on this desert land enchanted —
On this home by Horror haunted — tell me truly, I implore:
Is there—is there balm in Gilead? — tell me — tell me, I implore!'
 Quoth the Raven, 'Nevermore.'

'Prophet!' said I, 'thing of evil — prophet still, if bird or devil!
By that Heaven that bends above us, by that God we both
adore,
Tell this soul with sorrow laden if, within the distant Aidenn,
It shall clasp a sainted maiden whom the angels name Lenore:
Clasp a rare and radiant maiden whom the angels name
Lenore!'
 Quoth the Raven, 'Nevermore.'

'Be that word our sign of parting, bird or fiend!' I shrieked,
upstarting:
'Get thee back into the tempest and the Night's Plutonian
shore!
Leave no black plume as a token of that lie thy soul hath
spoken!
Leave my loneliness unbroken! quit the bust above my door!

Take thy beak from out my heart, and take thy form from off
my door!'
    Quoth the Raven, 'Nevermore.'

And the Raven, never flitting, still is sitting, still is sitting
On the pallid bust of Pallas just above my chamber door;
And his eyes have all the seeming of a demon's that is
dreaming,
And the lamp-light o'er him streaming throws his shadow on
the floor:
And my soul from out that shadow that lies floating on the
floor
    Shall be lifted — nevermore!

EDGAR ALLEN POE

*E* • *B*

## *The Lady Of Shalott*

On either side the river lie
Long fields of barley and of rye,
That clothe the wold and meet the sky;
And through the field the road run by
To many-tower'd Camelot;
And up and down the people go,
Gazing where the lilies blow
Round an island there below,
The island of Shalott.

Willows whiten, aspens quiver,
Little breezes dusk and shiver
Through the wave that runs for ever
By the island in the river
Flowing down to Camelot.
Four grey walls, and four grey towers,
Overlook a space of flowers,
And the silent isle imbowers
The Lady of Shalott.

By the margin, willow veil'd,
Slide the heavy barges trail'd
By slow horses; and unhail'd
The shallop flitteth silken-sail'd
Skimming down to Camelot:

But who hath seen her wave her hand?
Or at the casement seen her stand?
Or is she known in all the land,
The Lady of Shalott?

Only reapers, reaping early,
In among the bearded barley
Hear a song that echoes cheerly
From the river winding clearly;
Down to tower'd Camelot;
And by the moon the reaper weary,
Piling sheaves in uplands airy,
Listening, whispers, 'Tis the fairy
The Lady of Shalott.'

There she weaves by night and day
A magic web with colours gay.
She has heard a whisper say,
A curse is on her if she stay
To look down to Camelot.
She knows not what the curse may be,
And so she weaveth steadily,
And little other care hath she,
The Lady of Shalott.

And moving through a mirror clear
That hangs before her all the year,
　　Shadows of the world appear.
There she sees the highway near
　　Winding down to Camelot;
There the river eddy whirls,
And there the surly village churls,
And the red cloaks of market girls
　　Pass onward from Shalott.

Sometimes a troop of damsels glad,
　　An abbot on an ambling pad,
Sometimes a curly shepherd lad,
Or long-hair'd page in crimson clad
　　Goes by to tower'd Camelot;
And sometimes through the mirror blue
The knights come riding two and two.
She hath no loyal Knight and true,
　　The Lady of Shalott.

But in her web she still delights
To weave the mirror's magic sights,
For often through the silent nights
A funeral, with plumes and lights
　　And music, went to Camelot;

Or when the Moon was overhead,
Came two young lovers lately wed.
'I am half sick of shadows,' said
    The Lady of Shalott.


A bow-shot from her bower-eaves,
He rode between the barley sheaves,
The sun came dazzling thro' the leaves,
And flamed upon the brazen greaves
    Of bold Sir Lancelot.
A red-cross knight for ever kneel'd
    To a lady in his shield,
That sparkled on the yellow field,
    Beside remote Shalott.


The gemmy bridle glitter'd free,
Like to some branch of stars we see
    Hung in the golden Galaxy.
    The bridle bells rang merrily
    As he rode down to Camelot:
And from his blazon'd baldric slung
    A mighty silver bugle hung,
And as he rode his armour rung
    Beside remote Shalott.

All in the blue unclouded weather
Thick-jewell'd shone the saddle-leather,
The helmet and the helmet-feather
Burn'd like one burning flame together,
As he rode down to Camelot.
As often thro' the purple night,
Below the starry clusters bright,
Some bearded meteor, burning bright,
Moves over still Shalott.

His broad clear brow in sunlight glow'd;
On burnish'd hooves his war-horse trode;
From underneath his helmet flow'd
His coal-black curls as on he rode,
As he rode down to Camelot.
From the bank and from the river
He flashed into the crystal mirror,
'Tirra lirra,' by the river
Sang Sir Lancelot.

She left the web, she left the loom,
She made three paces through the room,
She saw the water-lily bloom,
She saw the helmet and the plume,
She look'd down to Camelot.

Out flew the web and floated wide;
The mirror crack'd from side to side;
'The curse is come upon me,' cried
　　The Lady of Shalott.

In the stormy east-wind straining,
The pale yellow woods were waning,
The broad stream in his banks complaining.
Heavily the low sky raining
Over tower'd Camelot;
Down she came and found a boat
Beneath a willow left afloat,
And around about the prow she wrote
　　The Lady of Shalott.

And down the river's dim expanse
Like some bold seer in a trance,
Seeing all his own mischance —
With a glassy countenance
Did she look to Camelot.
And at the closing of the day
She loosed the chain, and down she lay;
The broad stream bore her far away,
　　The Lady of Shalott.

Lying, robed in snowy white
That loosely flew to left and right —
The leaves upon her falling light —
Thro' the noises of the night,
She floated down to Camelot:
And as the boat-head wound along
The willowy hills and fields among,
They heard her singing her last song,
The Lady of Shalott.

Heard a carol, mournful, holy,
Chanted loudly, chanted lowly,
Till her blood was frozen slowly,
And her eyes were darkened wholly,
Turn'd to tower'd Camelot.
For ere she reach'd upon the tide
The first house by the water-side,
Singing in her song she died,
The Lady of Shalott.

Under tower and balcony,
By garden-wall and gallery,
A gleaming shape she floated by,
Dead-pale between the houses high,
Silent into Camelot.

Out upon the wharfs they came,
Knight and Burgher, Lord and Dame,
And around the prow they read her name,
The Lady of Shalott.

Who is this? And what is here?
And in the lighted palace near
Died the sound of royal cheer;
And they crossed themselves for fear,
All the Knights at Camelot;
But Lancelot mused a little space
He said, 'She has a lovely face;
God in his mercy lend her grace,
The Lady of Shalott.'

ALFRED, LORD TENNYSON

* • *

# *The Old Vicarage, Grantchester*

Just now the lilac is in bloom,
All before my little room;
And in my flower-beds, I think,
Smile the carnation and the pink;
And down the borders, well I know,
The poppy and the pansy blow . . .

Oh! there the chestnuts, summer through,

Beside the river make for you

A tunnel of green gloom, and sleep

Deeply above; and green and deep

The stream mysterious glides beneath,

Green as a dream and deep as death.

— Oh, damn! I know it! and I know

How the May fields all golden show,

And when the day is young and sweet,

Gild gloriously the bare feet

That run to bathe . . .

*Du lieber Gott!*


Here am I, sweating, sick, and hot,

And there the shadowed waters fresh

Lean up to embrace the naked flesh.

*Temperanmentvoll* German Jews

Drink beer around; — and *there* the dews

Are soft beneath a morn of gold.

Here tulips bloom as they are told;

Unkempt about those hedges blows

An English unofficial rose;

And there the unregulated sun

Slopes down to rest when day is done,

And wakes a vague unpunctual star,
A slippered Hesper; and there are
Meads towards Haslingfield and Coton
Where *das Betreten's* not verboten.

εἴθε γενοίμην ... would I were
In Grantchester, in Grantchester! –
Some, it may be, can get in touch
With Nature there, or Earth, or such.
And clever modern men have seen
A Faun a-peeping through the green,
And felt the Classics were not dead,
To glimpse a Naiad's reedy head,
Or hear the Goat-foot piping low: . . .
But these are things I do not know.
I only know that you may lie
Day-long and watch the Cambridge sky,
And, flower-lulled in sleepy grass,
Hear the cool lapse of hours pass,
Until the centuries blend and blur
In Grantchester, in Grantchester . . .
Still in the dawnlit waters cool
His ghostly Lordship swims his pool,
And tries the strokes, essays the tricks,

Long learnt on Hellespont, or Styx.
Dan Chaucer hears his river still
Chatter beneath a phantom mill.
Tennyson notes, with studious eye,
How Cambridge waters hurry by . . .
And in that garden, black and white,
Creep whispers through the grass all night;
And spectral dance, before the dawn,
A hundred Vicars down the lawn;
Curates, long dust, will come and go
On lissom, clerical, printless toe;
And oft between the boughs is seen
The sly shade of a Rural Dean . . .
Till, at a shiver in the skies,
Vanishing with Satanic cries,
The prim ecclesiastic rout
Leaves but a startled sleeper-out,
Grey heavens, the first bird's drowsy calls,
The falling house that never falls.

God! I will pack, and take a train,
And get me to England once again!
For England's the one land, I know,
Where men with Splendid Hearts may go;
And Cambridgeshire, of all England,

The shire for Men who Understand;
And of *that* district I prefer
The lovely hamlet Grantchester.
For Cambridge people rarely smile,
Being urban, swaut, and packed with guile;
And Royston men in the far South
Are black and fierce and strange of mouth;
At Over they fling oaths at one,
And worse than oaths at Trumpington,
And Ditton girls are mean and dirty,
And there's none in Harston under thirty,
And folks in Shelford and those parts
Have twisted lips and twisted hearts.
And Barton men make Cockney rhymes,
And Coton's full of nameless crimes,
And things are done you'd not believe
At Madingley, on Christmas Eve.
Strong men have run for miles and miles,
When one from Cherry Hinton smiles;
Strong men have blanched, and shot their wives,
Rather than send them to St. Ives;
Strong men have cried like babes, bydam,
To hear what happened at Babraham.
But Grantchester! ah, Grantchester!

There's peace and holy quiet there,
Great clouds along pacific skies,
And men and women with straight eyes,
Lithe children lovelier than a dream,
A bosky wood, a slumberous stream,
And little kindly winds that creep
Round twilight corners, half asleep.
In Grantchester their skins are white;
They bathe by day, they bathe by night;
The women there do all they ought;
The men observe the Rules of Thought.
They love the Good; they worship Truth;
They laugh uproariously in youth;
(And when they get to feeling old,
They up and shoot themselves, I'm told) . . .

Ah God! to see the branches stir
Across the moon at Grantchester!
To smell the thrilling-sweet and rotten
Unforgettable, unforgotten
River-smell, and hear the breeze
Sobbing in the little trees.
Say, do the elm-clumps greatly stand
Still guardians of that holy land?
The chestnuts shade, in reverend dream,

The yet unacademic stream?
Is dawn a secret shy and cold
Anadyomene, silver-gold?
And sunset still a golden sea
From Haslingfield to Madingley?
And after, ere the night is born,
Do hares come out about the corn?
Oh, is the water sweet and cool,
Gentle and brown, above the pool?
And laughs the immortal river still
Under the mill, under the mill?
Say, is there Beauty yet to find?
And Certainty? and Quiet kind?
Deep meadows yet, for to forget
The lies, and truths, and pain? . . . oh! yet
Stands the Church clock at ten to three?
And is there honey still for tea?

RUPERT BROOKE

*♉ • ℛ*

# Song Of The Open Road

1

Afoot and light-hearted, I take to the open road,
Healthy, free, the world before me,

The long brown path before me, leading wherever I
    choose.
Henceforth I ask not good-fortune — I myself am good
    fortune;
Henceforth I whimper no more, postpone no more, need
    nothing,
Strong and content, I travel the open road.

The earth — that is sufficient;
I do not want the constellations any nearer;
I know they are very well where they are;
I know they suffice for those who belong to them.

(Still here I carry my old delicious burdens;
I carry them, men and women — I carry them with me
    wherever I go;
I swear it is impossible for me to get rid of them;
I am fill'd with them, and I will fill them in return.)

2

You road I enter upon and look around! I believe you
    are not all that is here;
I believe that much unseen is also here.

Here the profound lesson of reception, neither preference
    or denial;
The black with his woolly head, the felon, the diseas'd,

the illiterate person, are not denied;

The birth, the hasting after the physician, the beggar's
tramp, the drunkard's stagger, the laughing party of
mechanics,

The escaped youth, the rich person's carriage, the fop,
the eloping couple,

The early market-man, the hearse, the moving of
furniture into the town, the return back from the town,

They pass — I also pass — anything passes — none
can be interdicted;

None but are accepted — none but are dear to me.


### 3

You air that serves me with breath to speak!

You objects that call from diffusion my meanings, and
give them shape!

You light that wraps me and all things in delicate
equable showers!

You paths worn in the irregular hollows by the
roadsides!

I think you are latent with unseen existences — you are
so dear to me.


You flagg'd walks of the cities! you strong curbs at the
edges!

You ferries! you planks and posts of wharves! you
timber-lined sides! you distant ships!

You rows of houses! you window-pierc'd façades! you
   roofs!
You porches and entrances! you copings and iron
   guards!
You windows whose transparent shells might expose so
   much!
You doors and ascending steps! you arches!
You gray stones of interminable pavements! you trodden
   crossings!
From all that has been near you, I believe you have
   imparted to yourselves, and now would impart the
   same secretly to me;
From the living and the dead I think you have peopled
   your impassive surfaces, and the spirits thereof would
   be evident and amicable with me.

4

The earth expanding right hand and left hand,
The picture alive, every part in its best light,
The music falling in where it is wanted, and stopping
   where it is not wanted,
The cheerful voice of the public road — the gay fresh
   sentiment of the road.

O highway I travel! O public road! do you say to me,
   *Do not leave me?*
*Do you say, Venture not? If you leave me, you are lost?*

*Do you say, I am already prepared — I am well-beaten and*
   *undenied — adhere to me?*
*O public road! I say back, I am not afraid to leave you — yet I*
   *love you;*
You express me better than I can express myself;
You shall be more to me than my poem.

I think heroic deeds were all conceiv'd in the open air,
   and all great poems also;
I think I could stop here myself, and do miracles;
(My judgments, thoughts, I henceforth try by the open
   air, the road;)
I think whatever I shall meet on the road I shall like,
   and whoever beholds me shall like me;
I think whoever I see must be happy.

5

From this hour, freedom!
From this hour I ordain myself loos'd of limits and
   imaginary lines,
Going where I list, my own master, total and absolute,
Listening to others, and considering well what they say,
Pausing, searching, receiving, contemplating,
Gently, but with undeniable will, divesting myself of the
   holds that would hold me.

I inhale great draughts of space;
The east and the west are mine, and the north and the
   south are mine.

I am larger, better than I thought;
I did not know I held so much goodness.
All seems beautiful to me;
I can repeat over to men and women, You have done
   such good to me, I would do the same to you.

I will recruit for myself and you as I go;
I will scatter myself among men and women as I go;
I will toss the new gladness and roughness among them;
Whoever denies me, it shall not trouble me;
Whoever accepts me, he or she shall be blessed, and
   shall bless me.

6

Now if a thousand perfect men were to appear, it would
   not amaze me;
Now if a thousand beautiful forms of women appear'd, it
   would not astonish me.

Now I see the secret of the making of the best persons,
It is to grow in the open air, and to eat and sleep with
   the earth.

Here a great personal deed has room;
A great deed seizes upon the hearts of the whole race of
   men,

Its effusion of strength and will overwhelms law, and
    mocks all authority and all argument against it.

Here is the test of wisdom;
Wisdom is not finally tested in schools;
Wisdom cannot be pass'd from one having it, to another
    not having it;
Wisdom is of the Soul, is not susceptible of proof, is its
    own proof,
Applies to all stages and objects and qualities, and is
    content,
Is the certainty of the reality and immortality of things,
    and the excellence of things;
Something there is in the float of the sight of things that
    provokes it out of the Soul.

Now I reexamine philosophies and religions,
They may prove well in lecture-rooms, yet not prove at
    all under the spacious clouds, and along the landscape
    and flowing currents.

Here is realization;
Here is a man tallied — he realizes here what he has in
    him;
The past, the future, majesty, love — if they are vacant
    of you, you are vacant of them.

Only the kernel of every object nourishes;

Where is he who tears off the husks for you and me?

Where is he that undoes stratagems and envelopes for
you and me?

Here is adhesiveness — it is not previously fashion'd —
it is apropos;

Do you know what it is, as you pass, to be loved by
strangers?

Do you know the talk of those turning eye-balls?


## 7

Here is the efflux of the Soul;

The efflux of the Soul comes from within, through
embower'd gates, ever provoking questions:

These yearnings, why are they? These thoughts in the
darkness, why are they?

Why are there men and women that while they are nigh
me, the sun-light expands my blood?

Why, when they leave me, do my pennants of joy sink
flat and lank?

Why are there trees I never walk under, but large and
melodious thoughts descend upon me?

(I think they hang there winter and summer on those
trees, and always drop fruit as I pass;)

What is it I interchange so suddenly with strangers?

What with some driver, as I ride on the seat by his side?

What with some fisherman, drawing his seine by the
    shore, as I walk by, and pause?
What gives me to be free to a woman's or man's good-
    will? What gives them to be free to mine?

### 8

The efflux of the Soul is happiness — here is happiness;
I think it pervades the open air, waiting at all times;
Now it flows unto us — we are rightly charged.


Here rises the fluid and attaching character;
The fluid and attaching character is the freshness and
    sweetness of man and woman;
(The herbs of the morning sprout no fresher and sweeter
    every day out of the roots of themselves, than it
    sprouts fresh and sweet continually out of itself).


Toward the fluid and attaching character exudes the
    sweat of the love of young and old;
From it falls distill'd the charm that mocks beauty and
    attainments;
Toward it heaves the shuddering longing ache of contact.

### 9

Allons! whoever you are, come travel with me!
Traveling with me, you find what never tires.

The earth never tires;

The earth is rude, silent, incomprehensible at first —
  Nature is rude and incomprehensible at first;

Be not discouraged — keep on — there are divine
  things, well envelop'd;

I swear to you there are divine things more beautiful
  than words can tell.


Allons! we must not stop here!

However sweet these laid-up stores — however
  convenient this dwelling, we cannot remain here;

However shelter'd this port, and however calm these
  waters, we must not anchor here;

However welcome the hospitality that surrounds us, we
  are permitted to receive it but a little while.


## 10

Allons! the inducements shall be greater;

We will sail pathless and wild seas;

We will go where winds blow, waves dash, and the
  Yankee clipper speeds by under full sail.


Allons! with power, liberty, the earth, the elements!

Health, defiance, gayety, self-esteem, curiosity;

Allons! from all formules!
From your formules, O bat-eyed and materialistic priests!

The stale cadaver blocks up the passage — the burial
    waits no longer.

Allons! yet take warning!
He traveling with me needs the best blood, thews,
    endurance;
None may come to the trial, till he or she bring courage
    and health.

Come not here if you have already spent the best of
    yourself;
Only those may come, who come in sweet and
    determin'd bodies;
No diseas'd person — no rum-drinker or venereal taint
    is permitted here.

I and mine do not convince by arguments, similes,
    rhymes;
We convince by our presence.

11

Listen! I will be honest with you;

I do not offer the old smooth prizes, but offer rough new
    prizes;
These are the days that must happen to you:
You shall not heap up what is call'd riches,
You shall scatter with lavish hand all that you earn or
    achieve,
You but arrive at the city to which you were destin'd —
    you hardly settle yourself to satisfaction, before you
    are call'd by an irresistible call to depart,
You shall be treated to the ironical smiles and mockings
    of those who remain behind you;
What beckonings of love you receive, you shall only
    answer with passionate kisses of parting,
You shall not allow the hold of those who spread their
    reach'd hands toward you.

12

Allons! after the GREAT COMPANIONS! and to
    belong to them!
They too are on the road! they are the swift and majestic
    men; they are the greatest women.
Over that which hinder'd them — over that which
    retarded — passing impediments large or small,
Committers of crimes, committers of many beautiful virtues,
Enjoyers of calms of seas, and storms of seas,
Sailors of many a ship, walkers of many a mile of land,
Habitués of many distant countries, habitués of
    far-distant dwellings,

Trusters of men and women, observers of cities, solitary
    toilers,
Pausers and contemplators of tufts, blossoms, shells of
    the shore,
Dancers at wedding-dances, kissers of brides, tender
    helpers of children, bearers of children,
Soldiers of revolts, standers by gaping graves, lowerers
    down of coffins,
Journeyers over consecutive seasons, over the years — the
    curious years, each emerging from that which preceded it,
Journeyers as with companions, namely, their own
    diverse phases,
Forth-steppers from the latent unrealized baby-days,
Journeyers gayly with their own youth — Journeyers
    with their bearded and well-grain'd manhood,
Journeyers with their womanhood, ample, unsurpass'd,
    content,
Journeyers with their own sublime old age of manhood
    or womanhood,
Old age, calm, expanded, broad with the haughty
    breadth of the universe,
Old age, flowing free with the delicious near-by freedom
    of death.

### 13

Allons! to that which is endless, as it was beginningless,
To undergo much, tramps of days, rests of nights,

To merge all in the travel they tend to, and the days and
nights they tend to,

Again to merge them in the start of superior journeys;

To see nothing anywhere but what you may reach it and
pass it,

To conceive no time, however distant, but what you may
reach it and pass it,

To look up or down no road but it stretches and waits
for you — however long, but it stretches and waits for
you;

To see no being, not God's or any, but you also go thither,

To see no possession but you may possess it — enjoying
all without labor or purchase — abstracting the feast,
yet not abstracting one particle of it;

To take the best of the farmer's farm and the rich man's
elegant villa, and the chaste blessings of the
well-married couple, and the fruits of orchards and
flowers of gardens,

To take to your use out of the compact cities as you pass
through,

To carry buildings and streets with you afterward
wherever you go,

To gather the minds of men out of their brains as you
encounter them — to gather the love out of their
hearts,

To take your lovers on the road with you, for all that

you leave them behind you,
To know the universe itself as a road — as many roads
  — as roads for traveling souls.

14

The Soul travels;
The body does not travel as much as the soul;
The body has just as great a work as the soul, and parts
  away at last for the journeys of the soul.

All parts away for the progress of souls;
All religion, all solid things, arts, governments, — all that
  was or is apparent upon this globe or any globe, falls
  into niches and corners before the procession of Souls
  along the grand roads of the universe.

Of the progress of the souls of men and women along
  the grand roads of the universe, all other progress is
  the needed emblem and sustenance.

Forever alive, forever forward,
Stately, solemn, sad, withdrawn, baffled, mad, turbulent,
  feeble, dissatisfied,
Desperate, proud, fond, sick, accepted by men, rejected
  by men,
They go! they go! I know that they go, but I know not
  where they go;

But I know that they go toward the best — toward
    something great.


               15

Allons! whoever you are! come forth!
You must not stay sleeping and dallying there in the
    house, though you built it, or though it has been built
    for you.


Allons! out of the dark confinement!
It is useless to protest — I know all, and expose it.


Behold, through you as bad as the rest,
Through the laughter, dancing, dining, supping, of people, 200
Inside of dresses and ornaments, inside of those wash'd
    and trimm'd faces,
Behold a secret silent loathing and despair.


No husband, no wife, no friend, trusted to hear the
    confession;
Another self, a duplicate of every one, skulking and
    hiding it goes,
Formless and wordless through the streets of the cities,
    polite and bland in the parlors,
In the cars of rail-roads, in steamboats, in the public assembly,

Home to the houses of men and women, at the table, in
    the bed-room, everywhere,
Smartly attired, countenance smiling, form upright, death
    under the breast-bones, hell under the skull-bones,
Under the broadcloth and gloves, under the ribbons and
    artificial flowers,
Keeping fair with the customs, speaking not a syllable of
    itself,
Speaking of anything else, but never of itself.

## 16

Allons! through struggles and wars!
The goal that was named cannot be countermanded.


Have the past struggles succeeded?
What has succeeded? yourself? your nation? nature?
Now understand me well — It is provided in the essence
    of things, that from any fruition of success, no matter
    what, shall come forth something to make a greater
    struggle necessary.
My call is the call of battle — I nourish active rebellion;
He going with me must go well arm'd;
He going with me goes often with spare diet, poverty,
    angry enemies, desertions.

## 17

Allons! the road is before us!

It is safe — I have tried it — my own feet have tried it
well.

Allons! be not detain'd!

Let the paper remain on the desk unwritten, and the
book on the shelf unopen'd!

Let the tools remain in the workshop! let the money
remain unearn'd!

Let the school stand! mind not the cry of the teacher!

Let the preacher preach in his pulpit! let the lawyer
plead in the court, and the judge expound the law.

Mon enfant! I give you my hand!

I give you my love, more precious than money,

I give you myself, before preaching or law;

Will you give me yourself? will you come travel with me?

Shall we stick by each other as long as we live?

WALT WHITMAN

*S • B*

# BIOGRAPHICAL NOTES

MAX ADELER was the pseudonym of CHARLES HEBER CLARK (1841–1915) a Philadelphia journalist and author. His first book, *Out of the Hurly-Burly* (1874), helped establish him as one of the most popular American humourists of the late 19th century.

WILLIAM ALLINGHAM (*c.* 1824–1889) was born in Ballyshannon, Ireland. He worked as a customs officer in Ireland and England, during which time his first books were published, beginning with *Poems* (1850). After retirement he served as an editor at *Fraser's Magazine*.

SIR EDWIN ARNOLD (1832–1904) was born at Gravesend, Kent, the son of a magistrate. A schoolmaster and journalist, he is often credited with having been the first to propose a Cape to Cairo railway traversing the African continent. He was the father of Edwin Lester Arnold, author of the escapist novel *Lieutenant Gullivar Jones: His Vacation* (1905), popularly known as *Gullivar of Mars*.

MATTHEW ARNOLD (1822–1888) was born in Laleham, Middlesex, the son of schoolmaster and historian Thomas Arnold. His first volume of poetry, *The Strayed Reveller*, was published in 1849. Eight years later he was appointed Professor of Poetry, Oxford.

HAROLD BECKH (1984–1916) was born on New Year's Day at Great Amwell, Hertfordshire. Educated at Cambridge, intending to become a clergyman, his studies were interrupted by the First World War. He was killed while on patrol in the Robecq area of France. *Swallows in Storm and Sunlight* (1917), his only collection of verse, was published posthumously.

AMBROSE BIERCE (1842–?1914) was born to a farming couple near Horse Cave Creek, Ohio. After receiving a head wound while serving on the Union side in the American Civil War, he embarked on a series of careers, the most successful of which was as a newspaperman. Bierce disappeared while reporting on the Mexican Revolution.

WILLIAM BLAKE (1757–1827) was born into a middle-class family in London. A poet, painter and printmaker, he was educated by his mother and, later, at a drawing school and the Royal Academy. Blake is best remembered for his illuminated books, beginning with *All Religions Are One* (*c.* 1788).

JEAN BLEWETT (1862–1934) was born Jean McKishnie in Scotia, Canada West (Ontario). Educated at St Thomas Collegiate Institute, she began contributing to newspapers and periodicals while in her teens. Her first volume of verse, *Heart Songs*, was published in 1897.

FRANCIS WILLIAM BOURDILLON (1852–1921) was born in Buddington, Sussex. Educated at Cambridge, Bourdillon was a tutor by profession. Thirteen volumes of verse were published during his lifetime, the first being *Among the Flowers and Other Poems*. (1878).

ANNE BRADSTREET (*c.* 1612–1672) was born Anne Dudley, in Northampton, England. She emigrated to North America in 1630, where both her father and husband would serve as governors of the Massachusetts Bay Colony. Highly educated, she wrote on history, politics, theology and medicine. Her *The Tenth Muse Lately Sprung Up in America, by a Gentlewoman in such Parts* (1650) is considered the first volume of verse by an American woman.

CHRISTOPHER BRENNAN (1870–1921) was born in Sydney, Australia. He studied in Australia and, after winning a travelling scholarship, Germany. His first volume of verse, *XXI poems*, was published in 1897.

EMILY BRONTË (1818–1848) was born in Thornton, Yorkshire, the fifth of six children who included the novelists Charlotte and Anne Brontë. Her only volume of verse, *Poems of Currer, Ellis and Acton Bell* (1846), sold only two copies. She is best remembered for the novel *Wuthering Heights* (1847).

RUPERT BROOKE (1887–1915) was born at Rugby, Warwickshire. A graduate of Cambridge, his first collection of verse, *Poems*, was published in 1911. He died of blood poisoning while serving in the First World War.

ELIZABETH BARRETT BROWNING (1806–1861) was born Elizabeth Barrett Moulton-Barrett at Coixhoe Hall, near Durham, England. Her first book, *The Battle of Marathon*, a work of juvenilia, was published at the age of fourteen by her father. An accomplished and popular poet, she was thought of as a possible successor to William Wordsworth as England's poet laureate. She was married to the poet Robert Browning.

ROBERT BROWNING (1812–1889) was born in Camberwell, south London, the son of a well-paid clerk with the Bank of England. His education is said to have come primarily through his father's 6,000-volume library. Browning received little notice until the publication of his second volume of verse, *Paracelsus* (1835). He was married to the poet Elizabeth Barrett Browning.

WILLIAM CULLEN BRYANT (1794–1878) was born in Cummington, Massachusetts. Educated at Williams College, he was admitted to the bar and worked for a time as a lawyer. He later relocated to New York City, where he worked as a journalist for *The New York Review* and *The New York Evening Post*. He used his position as editor of the latter publication in the fight against slavery.

JOHN BUNYAN (1628–1688) was born in Harrowden, Elstow. A man with little schooling, he served briefly in the Parliamentary army. In 1653, he was received into the Baptist Church and two years later became a deacon. He is best remembered for his allegorical novel *The Pilgrim's Progress* (1678), composed while he was imprisoned for preaching without a licence.

ROBERT BURNS (1759–1796) was born in Alloway, South Ayrshire, Scotland, the son of a farming couple. His childhood was spent in poverty and much of his education came through his father who supplemented his modest income through tutoring. In 1783, he began composing poetry, employing the Ayrshire dialect. The publication three years later of his first volume of verse, *Poems, Chiefly in the Scottish Dialect*, established his reputation as national poet of Scotland.

SAMUEL BUTLER (1835–1902) was born into a family of Anglican clerics at Langar Rectory, near Bingham, Nottinghamshire. Following his studies at Cambridge, in preparation for entering the clergy, he abandoned the church, and emigrated to New Zealand where he worked as a sheep farmer. Five years later, he returned to England. He settled into a literary life, writing the classic novels *Erewhon* (1872) and *The Way of All Flesh* (1902), among others.

GEORGE GORDON, LORD BYRON (1788–1824) was born in London. At the age of ten he inherited the title and estates of his great-uncle, the 5th Baron Byron. In 1806, the year after he began studies at Cambridge, he published *Fugitive Pieces*, his first collection of verse. A prolific poet and one of the leading figures in Romanticism, his accomplished works are often overshadowed by an extravagant life of scandal, intrigue and sexual adventure.

THOMAS CAMPBELL (1777–1844) was born in Glasgow. He was educated at the University of Glasgow, where he was awarded prizes for his verse. Although he had contemplated a career in law, the early success of his long poem, *The Pleasures of Hope* (1799), encouraged a career in letters. As a professional writer, he contributed to newspapers, magazines and encyclopaedias, and served for over a decade as the editor of *The New Monthly Review*.

WILFRED CAMPBELL (1858–1918) was born in Newmarket, Canada West (Ontario), the son of an Anglican minister. After an education received at a number of institutions, including the University of Toronto, University College, in 1884 Campbell was ordained into the Anglican priesthood. Seven years later, he suffered a crisis of faith, resigned from the church, and accepted a civil service position in Ottawa. He wrote six collections of verse and served as the editor of *The Oxford Book of Canadian Verse* (1913).

THOMAS CAMPION (1567–1620) was born in London. A poet, composer and physician, Campion studied at Cambridge. His earliest published poetry appears in Sir Philip Sidley's *Astrophel and Stella* (1591). Campion's early study of verse, *Observations in the Art of English Poesie* (1602), contains criticism of rhyming in poetry.

THOMAS CAREW (1595–1640), the son of Sir Thomas Carew, was born in West Wickham, Kent. Educated at Oxford, he served in a variety of diplomatic positions in Europe, before being appointed to the court of Charles I.

HENRY CAREY (1687–1743), rumoured to be the illegitimate son of George Savile, 1st Marquess of Halifax, was born in London to a teaching couple. A dramatist, psalmist, songwriter and poet, much of Carey's work was published anonymously, and is likely to remain unidentified. His earliest known verse appears in *Poems on Several Occasions* (1703).

BLISS CARMAN (1861–1929), a first cousin of Sir Charles G. D. Roberts, was born in Fredericton, New Brunswick. Though in his time he was Canada's best-known poet, his adult life was largely spent in the United States. There, he worked as a contributor and editor for a number of magazines, including *The Atlantic Monthly* and *Cosmopolitan*.

LEWIS CARROLL was the pseudonym of CHARLES LUTWIDGE DODGSON (1832–1898). An author, mathematician and photographer, he was born in Daresbury, Cheshire, the son of an Anglican clergyman. After studies at Oxford, Dodgson followed his father into the church. He is best remembered as the author of *Alice's Adventures in Wonderland* (1865) and its sequel *Through the Looking Glass* (1871).

PHOEBE CARY (1824–1871) was born to a farming couple near Cincinnati, Ohio. Her education was received from her elder sister Alice. Following the modest success of their first collection of verse, *Poems of Alice and Phoebe Carey* [*sic*], published in 1850, the sisters relocated to New York City, where they became regular contributors to *Harper's*, *The Atlantic Monthly* and other popular periodicals.

THOMAS CHATTERTON (1752–1770) was born in Bristol, England to a widowed mother. Educated at a charity school, Chatterton struggled greatly in an attempt to support himself through writing. Ulltimately, impoverished, he chose arsenic over starvation, committing suicide at the age of seventeen. He is often considered the first Romantic poet writing in the English language.

G. K. CHESTERTON (1874–1936) was born in London. He studied at Slade School of Art and University College, before embarking on a career that encompassed journalism, criticism, biography, detective fiction and verse. A prolific writer, sixty-nine Chesterton titles were published during his lifetime.

JOHN CLARE (1793–1864) was born in Helpston, Cambridgeshire. The son of a farm labourer, his first verse was written in an attempt to prevent the eviction of his parents from their home. His highly praised first collection of verse, *Poems Descriptive of Rural Life and Scenery* (1820), led to his title 'the Northamptonshire Peasant Poet'.

ARTHUR HUGH CLOUGH (1819–1861) was born on New Year's Day in Liverpool. At the age of three, his father, a cotton merchant, relocated the family to Charleston, South Carolina. Clough returned to England to take up studies at Rugby School and later continued his education at Oxford. After graduation he held several positions as an educator and worked as an unpaid assistant to his wife's cousin, Florence Nightingale.

SAMUEL TAYLOR COLERIDGE (1772–1834) was born in Ottery St Mary, Devonshire, the youngest of 16 children. He was educated at

Jesus College and Cambridge. A poet, critic and philosopher, he was a key figure in the Romantic movement and counted Robert Southey and William Wordsworth among his closest friends. Coleridge's literary output was both aided and hindered by an addiction to opium.

WILLIAM CONGREVE (1670–1729) was born in Bardsey, west Yorkshire. His youth was spent in Ireland. He was educated at Trinity College, Dublin, where he met Jonathan Swift, who would become a lifelong friend. Primarily a dramatist, he wrote five successful plays between 1693 and 1700, before abandoning the craft. He was supported for the remainder of his life by the residuals.

WILLIAM COWPER (1731–1800) was born in Berkhamstead, Hertfordshire. After studying at Westminster School, his training for a career in law ended with the first of many bouts of mental illness. He sought strength through evangelical Christianity and, collaborating with John Newton, became one of the foremost composer of hymns.

HART CRANE (1899–1932) was born in Garrettsville, Ohio. His father had made a fortune in the confectionery business as the inventor of the Life Saver. A high-school drop out, Crane worked periods as an advertising copywriter and on the floor in his father's factory. The poor reception of his greatest work, *The Bridge* (1930), may have been one of the contributing factors to his suicide, the result of jumping off a ship in the Gulf of Mexico.

STEPHEN CRANE (1871–1900) was born in Newark, New Jersey, the fourteenth child of a Methodist minister. He began writing for *The New York Tribune* and local newspapers while in his teens. After being expelled from Lafayette College and Syracuse University, he moved to New York, where he began a career as a freelance writer. He is best remembered for his novel of the American Civil War, *The Red Badge of Courage* (1895).

RICHARD CRASHAW (*c.* 1613–1649) was born in London and educated at Charterhouse School, Cambridge and, briefly, Oxford. Though the son of an anti-Catholic theologian, he converted to the faith and was made a canon shortly before his death. A collection of religious verse, *Carmen Deo Nostro*, was published three years after his death.

ISABELLA VALANCY CRAWFORD (1850–1887) was born in Dublin and, with her family, emigrated to Canada at the age of six. In her twenties, she attempted to support herself and her mother by contributing novels, short stories and poems to a variety of Canadian newspapers and magazines. One book, *Old Spookses' Pass, Malcolm's Katie and Other Poems* (1884) was published during her lifetime.

THOMAS DEKKER (*c.* 1572–1632) is believed to have been born in London. Principally a dramatist, most of his plays are lost. Much that survives of Dekker's work is in the form of pamphlets he wrote on such diverse subjects as the plague and the death of Elizabeth I.

RICHARD DENNYS (1884–1916) was born in London. Though schooled in medicine, he pursued a career in the arts as a painter, actor, writer and poet. He enlisted at the outbreak of the First World War and was mortally wounded at the Battle of the Somme. His poetry is collected in *There Is No Death* (1917).

EMILY DICKINSON (1832–1886) was born in Amherst, Massachusetts. Though one of the great American poets, only seven of her poems saw print during her lifetime – all anonymously. The first collection of her poetry, *Poems*, was published four years after her death.

JOHN DONNE (1572–1631) was born in London. Educated at Oxford and Cambridge, he served as a Member of Parliament and was ordained into the Church of England. His collection of verse, *Poems*, was published in 1633.

ERNEST DOWSON (1867–1900) was born in Lee, south east London. Associated with the Decadent movement, Dowson's life was one of tragedy and loss. He died of alcoholism or tuberculosis – perhaps a combination of the two. After his death, Dowson's verse was collected and published with a memoir by Arthur Symons as *The Poems of Ernest Dowson* (1902).

JOHN DRYDEN (1631–1700) was born in Aldwinkle, Northamptonshire. He studied as a King's Scholar under Richard Busby at Westminster School and at Trinity College, Cambridge. His talents as a poet and critic overshadowed somewhat his career as a playwright. In 1668 he was appointed Poet Laureate, a position he held for more than two decades.

PAUL LAURENCE DUNBAR (1872–1906) was born in Dayton, Ohio, the son of former slaves. His father was a veteran of the American Civil War. His first poetic recital was made at the age of nine. Dunbar's verse first saw print as a high-school student in a newspaper printed by his friends Wilbur and Orville Wright. *Oak and Ivy*, the first of his 12 collections of verse, was published in 1892. His wife was the poet and short-story writer Alice Dunbar-Nelson.

RALPH WALDO EMERSON (1803–1882) was born in Boston. After attending Harvard, he worked as an educator, before returning to become a Unitarian minister like his father. After three years, in 1832, he resigned from the church. An essayist and poet, Emerson derived much of his income through his skills as a public orator.

EUGENE FIELD (1850–1895) was born in St Louis, Missouri. After studies at Williams College and the University of Missouri, he embarked on a career as a journalist, columnist and newspaper editor. His poetry, written for children, first appeared in his book *Christmas Treasures* (1879).

FRANCIS MILES FINCH (1827–1907) was born in Ithica, New York. A Yale graduate, he practised law, served on the bench, and lectured at Cornell University, an institution he had helped to establish.

MARJORY FLEMING (1803–1811) was born in Kirkaldy, Scotland. A child writer and poet, she died of meningitis at the age of eight. Her writing was first published as *Pet Marjorie: A Story of Child Life Fifty Years Ago* (1858).

MARY WESTON FORDHAM (*c.* 1862–unknown) was most likely born in Charleston, South Carolina. An African-American, her only collection of poetry, *Magnolia Leaves* (1897), includes an introduction by Booker T. Washington.

CHARLOTTE PERKINS GILMAN (1860–1935) was born Charlotte Anne Perkins in Hartford, Connecticut. She was the niece of Harriet Beecher Stowe. Gilman studied at the Rhode Island school of Design and for two years worked as a greeting card artist. A writer of fiction, non-fiction and poetry Gilman is best remembered for her short story, 'The Yellow Wallpaper', which was inspired by her struggles with mental illness.

OLIVER GOLDSMITH (1728–1774) was born in Pallas, near Ballymahon, Ireland, the son of an Anglican curate. He studied theology, law and medicine, eventually becoming a physician and apothecary's assistant. A gambler, perennially in debt, he supplemented his income by freelance writing for a number of London publishers and is thought to have been the author of *The History of Little Goody Two-Shoes* (1765). He is best remembered for his novel *The Vicar of Wakefield* (1766) and the play *She Stoops to Conquer* (1771).

ADAM LINDSAY GORDON (1833–1870) was born at Fayal in the Azores, the son of an English Army officer. Raised in Cheltenham, England, he rejected the family tradition of military service, and, in 1853, emigrated to Australia. For a brief period he served in the South Australian mounted police, before taking up horse-breaking and racing. His first book of verse, *Ashtaroth, a Dramatic Lyric*, was published in 1867.

HARRY GRAHAM (1874–1936) was born in England, the son of wealthy parents. He was educated at Eton and Sandhurst and later became an officer in the Coldstream Guards. After a stay in Canada as aide-de-camp to the Governor General, Lord Minto, he returned to England and worked as a journalist and writer of popular fiction.

THOMAS GRAY (1716–1771) was born in London. Educated at Eton and Cambridge, he spent most of his life in study. Anything but prolific, fewer than 1,000 lines of verse were published during his lifetime. In 1757, he became the first person to refuse the position of Poet Laureate.

THOMAS HARDY (1840–1928) was born in Higher Bockhampton, Dorset, the son of a stonemason. Trained as an architect, in 1862 he moved to London where he was awarded prizes from the Royal Institute of British Architects and the architectural association. The author of several classic novels, including *Tess of the d'Ubervilles* (1891), *Far from the Madding Crowd* (1874) and *Jude the Obscure* (1895), Hardy turned his talents increasingly toward verse in later life.

W. S. HAWKINS (1837–1865) was born in Madison County, Alabama. A student at the outbreak of the American Civil War, he enlisted and quickly rose to the rank of colonel. In January, 1864, Hawkins was captured and imprisoned for the remainder of the war. He died mere months after his release.

CHARLES HEAVYSEGE (1816–1876) was probably born in Huddersfield, England. A woodcarver, he emigrated to Canada in 1853, and soon found work as a reporter for *The Montreal Transcript* and *The Montreal Daily Witness*. Heavysege asserted that there was some claim to nobility in his background. After his death, personal material was stolen from several different collections of his papers.

WILLIAM ERNEST HENLEY (1849–1902) was born in Gloucester, England, the son of a bookseller. As a child, he developed what was probably tubercular arthritis, a condition that interrupted his schooling, and resulted in the amputation of part of his left leg. His earliest published poems were written while undergoing treatment at an Edinburgh hospital After his recovery, Henley worked as an editor for *London* and *The Scots Observer*.

GEORGE HERBERT (1593–1633) was born in Montgomery, Wales. He studied at Trinity College, Cambridge, where he later taught, and served as a Member of Parliament. All of his surviving poems are religious in nature. His only collection, *The Temple: Sacred Poems and Private Ejaculations* (1633), was published posthumously.

ROBERT HERRICK (1591–1674) was born in London, the son of a wealthy goldsmith who committed suicide when the future poet was one year old. He attended Cambridge, took religious orders and became chaplain to the Duke of Buckingham.

OLIVER WENDELL HOLMES SR (1809–1894) was born at Cambridge, Massachusetts, and educated in Andover, Boston and Paris. His prominence as a physician and professor of anatomy was overshadowed by greater fame as a poet of national prominence. His son, Oliver Wendell Holmes Jr, was a hero of the American Civil War and served as Justice of the Supreme Court.

THOMAS HOOD (1799–1845) was born in London, the son of a bookseller. He served in a number of editorial positions with *London Magazine*, *The Gem* and *The New Monthly Magazine*, and was a part-owner of the literary journal *The Athenaeum*.

GERARD MANLEY HOPKINS (1844–1889) was born in Stratford, Essex, the son of an insurance agent and amateur poet. During his studies at Oxford, he converted from Anglicanism to Roman Catholicism and eventually became a Jesuit priest. It wasn't until nearly three decades after Hopkins' death that the first volume of his verse was published.

A. E. HOUSMAN (1859–1936) was born in Fockbury, Worcestershire. He was awarded a scholarship to Oxford, where he studied classics. For most of his life he taught Latin at Cambridge. Housman's masterpiece, *The Shropshire Lad* (1896), was rejected by several publishers and was eventually published at his own expense. His siblings, Laurence and Clemence Housman, were also writers.

LEIGH HUNT (1784–1859) was born in London to loyalist parents from Philadelphia. His first collection of poems, *Juvenalia*, was published in 1801. As a young man he embarked on a career as a critic, which involved his editorship of *The Examiner*, a newspaper founded by his brother, John Hunt.

HELEN HUNT JACKSON (1831–1885) was born Helen Maria Fiske in Amherst, Massachusetts. A writer of poetry, children's stories, novels and essays, her book, *Mercy Philbrick's Choice* (1876), is said to be a fictional portrait of her friend Emily Dickinson.

SOAME JENYNS (1704–1787) was born in London, the son of Sir Roger Jenyns. Educated at Cambridge, he served as a Member of Parliament for Cambridgeshire. His first published work was the mock-heroic poem *The Art of Dancing* (1729).

E. PAULINE JOHNSON (Tekahionwake) (1861–1914) was born on the Six Nations Indian Reserve in Canada West (Ontario), the daughter of an Englishwoman and a Mohawk chief. In her day, a popular poet, she toured the Canada, the United Kingdom and the United States giving poetry readings. Her best-known collection of verse is *Flint and Feather* (1912).

BEN JONSON (1572–1637) was born in London. After graduating from Westminster School, he worked as a bricklayer, a soldier and an actor. In 1597, he was imprisoned for his roles as playwright and player in a satire, *The Isle of Dogs*. The following year he was again imprisoned after killing a fellow actor in a duel. The first folio collection of his works was printed in 1616.

JOHN KEATS (1795–1821) was born in London. He was apprenticed to an apothecary-surgeon. His first volume of verse, *Poems*, published in 1817, was poorly received. Four years later, he died of tuberculosis while visiting Italy. He was soon recognized as one of the great poets of the English Romantic movement.

T. M. KETTLE (1880–1916) was born in Artane, Ireland. A Member of Parliament, lawyer, professor and journalist, he was killed at the battle of the Somme. His wartime prose and verse is collected in *The Ways of War* (1917).

JOYCE KILMER (1886–1918) was born in New Brunswick, New Jersey. After graduating from Columbia University, he worked as an editor, journalist and writer of popular poetry. He enlisted in the National Guard shortly after the United States entered the First World War. Kilmer was killed by a sniper outside Ourcq, France.

BEN KING (1857–1884) was born in St Joseph, Michigan. His verse was published in newspapers and magazine, often employing the pseudonym Bow Hackley. His only collection of poetry, *Ben King's Verse* (1894), was published posthumously.

CHARLES KINGSLEY (1819–1875) was born in Holne, Devon, the son of a clergyman. He studied at Cambridge and was ordained into the Church of England. His best-known work is the children's novel, *The Water-Babies* (1863).

RUDYARD KIPLING (1865–1936) was born in Bombay (now Mumbai), India. He is best remembered for his books for children, *The Jungle Book* (1894), *The Second Jungle Book* (1895) and *Just So Stories* (1902). He wrote two collections of poetry, *Barrack-Room Ballads and Other Verses* (1893) and *Rudyard Kipling's Verse* (1923).

RAYMOND KNISTER (1899–1932) was born in Ruscom, Ontario. He studied at Victoria College, the University of Toronto and Iowa State University. Primarily a writer of poetry and short stories, only his first novel, *White Narcissus* (1929), was published during his lifetime. Knister drowned while swimming in Ontario's Lake St Clair.

CHARLES LAMB (1775–1834) was born in London. An essayist and poet, Lamb spent much of his life as a clerk with the British East India Company. He is best known for the children's book, *Tales from Shakespeare* (1807), which he wrote with his sister Mary Lamb.

ARCHIBALD LAMPMAN (1861–1899) was born in Morpeth, Canada West (Ontario). While studying at Trinity College, Toronto, he contributed his first poems to the literary magazine *Rouge et Noir*. After an unsuccessful attempt at teaching, he obtained a job with the Post Office in Ottawa. Two collections of verse, *Among the Millet and Other Poems* (1888) and *Lyrics of Earth* (1895) were published before his death.

WILLIAM SAVAGE LANDOR (1775–1864) was born at Ipsley Court, Warwick, the son of a wealthy couple. He was expelled from both Rugby School and Oxford, being sent down from Oxford for firing a shotgun inside his rooms. His first collection of verse, *Poems*, was published in 1795. Landor twice fled England to avoid being sued for libel, and was staying in Florence with Robert Browning and Elizabeth Barrett Browning at the time of his death.

D. H. LAWRENCE (1885–1930) was born in Eastwood, Nottinghamshire. He attended University College, Nottingham, from which he received a teaching certificate in 1908. A key figure in 20th-century literature, he is best remembered for his novel, *Lady Chatterley's Lover* (1928), which on publication caused a scandal due to its explicit sex scenes and use of four-letter words.

EDWARD LEAR (1812–1888) was born in the London suburb of Highgate. An accomplished illustrator, he is best remembered for his nonsense verse which he began publishing with *A Book of Nonsense* (1846).

HENRY SAMBROOKE LEIGH (1837–1883) was an English author. He published several volumes of verse, the most popular of which is *Carols of Cockayne* (1869).

ROSANNA LEPROHON (1829–1879) was born Rosanna Eleanor Mullins in Montreal. Her first published poetry appeared in *The Literary Garland* at the age of 17. Primarily a writer of fiction, her best-known work is *Antoinette de Mirecourt* (1864).

STUART LIVINGSTONE was a Canadian. 'December', his only known poem, was published in *A Century of Canadian Sonnets* (1910), an anthology edited by Lawrence J. Burpee.

FREDERICK LOCKER-LAMPSON (1821–1895) was born Frederick Locker in London. Employed in the Civil Service, he left upon marrying Lady Charlotte Bruce, daughter of Lord Elgin. Following her death, he again married, this time adopting his wife's surname. His first collection of verse, *London Lyrics*, was published in 1857.

HENRY WADSWORTH LONGFELLOW (1807–1882) was born in Portland, Maine. Educated at Bowdoin College, he taught there and at Harvard. Among his more popular works are *Evangeline: A Tale of Acadie* (1847) and *The Song of Hiawatha* (1855).

RICHARD LOVELACE (1618–1659) was born at Lovelace Palace, Kent. A member of the nobility, he was imprisoned briefly for his support of the Royalists. All his poetry was published posthumously.

JAMES RUSSELL LOWELL (1819–1891) was born in Cambridge, Massachusetts. He studied law at Harvard, but after graduation chose to pursue a life in letters. His first collection of verse, *A Fable for Critics*, was published in 1848. He served as the first editor of *The Atlantic Monthly*.

WALTER SCOTT STEWART LYON (1886–1915) was a member of the 9th Royal Scots at the outbreak of the First World War. He served in France and Belgium and was killed by shellfire near Ypres. His only book, *Easter at Ypres 1915 and Other Poems*, was published in 1916.

AGNES MAULE MACHAR (1837–1927) was born in Kingston, Upper Canada (Ontario), the daughter of a Presbyterian minister and future principal of Queen's University, Canada. A novelist, poet and historian, she was a key figure in the literary life of Victorian Canada. She often published under the pseudonym 'Fidelis'.

CHARLES MAIR (1838–1927) was born in Lanark, Upper Canada (Ontario). He studied medicine at Queen's University, Canada but left to work in his family's lumber business. His first book, *Dreamland and Other Poems*, was published in 1868. He was a participant in the Red River Rebellion and was briefly imprisoned by the freedom fighter, Louis Riel. He is best remembered for the verse play *Tecumseh: A Drama* (1886).

KATHERINE MANSFIELD (1888–1923) was born Katherine Mansfield Beauchamp in Wellington, New Zealand. She studied at Queen's College, London, during which time she began to write sketches and prose poems. Although she returned to New Zealand, much of the rest of her life was spent moving around the literary circles of Europe. Her debut collection of verse, *Poems*, was published in 1923.

CHRISTOPHER MARLOWE (1564–1593) was most probably born in Canterbury, England. Marlowe was educated at Cambridge, during which time he wrote his first known drama, *Dido, Queen of Carthage* (1594), possibly in collaboration with Thomas Nashe. Considered the foremost Elizabethan playwright before William Shakespeare, he was murdered in mysterious circumstances.

ANDREW MARVELL (1621–1678) was born in Winestead-in-Holderness, East Yorkshire, the son of a clergyman. He attended Cambridge and served many years as a Member of Parliament.

JOHN McCRAE (1872–1918) was born in Guelph, Ontario. He studied medicine at the University of Toronto and McGill. McCrae's earliest war poetry was written while serving in the Boer War. He died of pneumonia complicated by meningitis at a hospital in Boulogne, France during the First World War. His only volume of poetry, *In Flanders Fields and Other Poems* (1919), was published posthumously.

THOMAS D'ARCY McGEE (1825–1868) was born in Carlingford, Ireland. A participant in the rebellion of 1848, he worked for a number of Irish newspapers in Ireland and the United States. In 1857, he settled in Montreal where, as a journalist and Member of Parliament, he sought a united British North America. His death, probably the result of a Fenian conspiracy, remains the only assassination of a federal politician in Canada.

ALEXANDER McLACHLAN (1818–1896) was born in Johnstone, Scotland. In 1840, he emigrated to Caldon, Upper Canada (Ontario). He farmed and worked as a civil servant, a position he obtained through his friendship with Thomas d'Arcy McGee. He wrote five volumes of verse, the first of which was *The Spirit of Love and Other Poems* (1846).

HERMAN MELVILLE (1819–1891) was born in New York City. After an education that suffered due to the financial situation of his father, he found employment as a sailor, a schoolteacher and, ultimately, as a customs inspector. His masterpiece, *Moby-Dick* (1851), is often cited as 'The Great American Novel'.

GEORGE MEREDITH (1828–1909) was born in Portsmouth, England. He studied law, but ultimately chose to pursue a career in journalism. Although he is best remembered as a novelist, his first book was a collection of verse entitled *Poems* (1851). His first wife was the daughter of Thomas Love Peacock.

ALICE MEYNELL (1847–1922) was born in London. An editor and critic, her first collection of poetry, *Preludes*, was published in 1875.

JOHN MILTON (1608–1674) was born in London, the son of a composer. He studied at Cambridge, during which time he wrote some of his finest poetry. His masterpiece, *Paradise Lost*, was published in 1667.

HAROLD MONRO (1879–1932) was born in Brussels to Scottish parents. Educated at Cambridge, his first volume of verse, *Poems*, was published in 1906. As the proprietor of the Poetry Bookshop in London, he helped bring the work of many poets to public attention.

L. M. MONTGOMERY (1874–1942) was born in Clifton (now New London), Prince Edward Island. She attended Prince of Wales College and Dalhousie University. She is best known as the author of the children's novel *Anne of Green Gables* (1908), considered the best-selling work in Canadian literature.

SUSANNA MOODIE (1803–1885) was born Susanna Strickland in Bungay, England. The younger sister of Catharine Parr Traill, she was one of a family of writers. Her first book, *Spartacus*, was published in 1822. In 1832, she relocated with her husband and daughter, emigrating to Upper Canada. Her early pioneer experiences are recorded in her best-known work, *Roughing It in the Bush* (1852).

CLEMENT C. MOORE (1779–1863) was born in New York City. A professor of Oriental and Greek literature at Columbia College, he is best known as the author of 'A Visit from St Nicholas'.

THOMAS MOORE (1779–1852) was born in Dublin and educated at Trinity College. A poet, novelist, translator and balladeer, Moore also served as literary executor for Lord Byron.

WILLIAM MORRIS (1834–1896) was born in Walthamstow, England. He was educated at Oxford, where he became friends with Edward Burne-Jones and Dante Gabriel Rossetti, Although he is remembered today for his designs in furniture, decoration and architecture, Morris, was also a prolific writer. His first book of verse, *The Defence of Guenevere and Other Poems*, was published in 1858.

THOMAS NASHE (1567–?1601) was probably born in Lowestoft, Suffolk. He began studies at Cambridge, but left for an unknown reason. By 1589, he was living in London, where he pursued a life in letters as a poet, playwright, pamphleteer and satirist. Although he is memorialized in Charles Fitzjeoffry's *Affaniae* (1601), his death is otherwise unrecorded.

CHARLES, LORD NEAVES (1800–1876) was born in Edinburgh. A lawyer, theologian and judge, he served as Lord of Justiciary and Rector of the University of St Andrews. He was a frequent contributor to *Blackwood's Magazine*.

EDITH NESBIT (1858–1924) was born in London. A writer of poetry, novels and short stories, she received commercial and critical success for her children's novels, including *The Railway Children* (1906).

STANDISH O'GRADY (*c.* 1793–*c.*1841), born in Ireland, was a graduate of Trinity College, Dublin. An Anglican minister, he emigrated to Lower Canada (Quebec) in 1836, settling on a farm on the south bank of the St Lawrence River near the town of Sorel. Only one of his works, *The Emigrant: A Poem in Four Cantos* (1840), was published during his lifetime.

ARTHUR O'SHAUGHNESSY (1844–1881) was born in London. Employed from a young age at the British Museum, his true interests lay in literature. O'Shaughnessy's first collection of verse, *Epic of Women*, was published in 1870.

WILFRED OWEN (1893–1918) was born in Oswestry, Shropshire. Educated at the Birkenhead Institute and the University of London, he worked as a teacher before enlisting to fight in the First World War. He was killed by German machine-gun fire seven days before the Armistice. The first collection of his verse, *Poems* (1920), was published posthumously.

COVENTRY PATMORE (1823–1896) was born in Woodford, Essex, the son of author Peter George Patmore. Privately educated, and very much under his father's influence, he immersed himself in literary life. After the lukewarm reception given to his first book, *Poems* (1844), he bought the remaining stock and had it destroyed. His most accomplished work is *The Unknown Eros* (1877).

THOMAS LOVE PEACOCK (1785–1866) was born in Melcombe Regis, now Weymouth, Dorset. He moved to London at the age of sixteen, where he took up independent study in the British Museum. In 1804, he self-published his first volume of verse, *The Monks of St Mark*. Twenty volumes, consisting of his novels, verse and essays, were published before his death at the age of 90.

MARJORIE PICKTHALL (1883–1922) was born in Middlesex, England. In 1889, with her family she emigrated to Canada, settling in Toronto. Her first writing was sold as a student attending Bishop Strachan School. She divided her adult years between England and Canada, during which time her poetry and short stories appeared in dozens of magazines and newspapers.

EDGAR ALLAN POE (1809–1849) was born in Boston. His brief studies at the University of Virginia were followed by a short stint in the United States Army. He eventually took up an extremely successful career in letters as an editor and author of 'The Fall of the House of Usher', 'The Tell-Tale Heart' and other classic short stories. Poe's first collection of verse, *Tamerlane and Other Poems* (1827), published anonymously as the work of 'a Bostonian', is one of the most sought after books by bibliophiles.

ALEXANDER POPE (1688–1744) was born in London. His first published verse appeared in *Poetical Miscellanies* (1709), an anthology published by Jacob Tonson. His most famous poem, 'The Rape of the Lock', was published in 1712.

MATTHEW PRIOR (1664–1721) was born in Wimborne Minster, east Dorset. He was educated under Richard Busby at Westminster School and at Cambridge. A poet and diplomat, he served as a Member of Parliament for East Grinstead.

FRANCIS QUARLES (1592–1644) was born in Romford, Essex. He was educated at Cambridge and studied law at Lincoln's Inn. He served in a number of public positions including City Chronologer of London. During the English Civil War, he wrote pamphlets in support of Charles I.

SIR WALTER RALEIGH (*c.* 1552–1618) was born near Budleigh Salterton, Devon. He was the half-brother of Sir Humphrey Gilbert. A soldier and explorer, he was responsible for establishing the first English colony in North America. Accused of conspiring against James I, he was sentenced to death. For 13 years he was imprisoned in the Tower of London, but was released. In 1618, the death sentence was reinstated and he was executed.

JAMES WHITCOMB RILEY (1849–1916) was born in Greenfield, Indiana, the son of a well-to-do lawyer. He left school at an early age and soon began contributing verse to *The Indianapolis Saturday Mirror* under the name 'Jay Whit', the first step on a path that would lead him to becoming a popular, nationally recognized poet. In his native country he was often dubbed the 'People's Laureate'.

EDWIN ARLINGTON ROBINSON (1869–1935) was born to a wealthy family in Alna, Maine. Robinson's studies at Harvard were interrupted by the death of his father, an event that seemed to trigger a series of tragedies culminating in poverty. Dedicated to his craft, but unable to make a living through his writing, he spent much of his life as an inspector for the New York subway and later worked at a United States Customs House.

ISAAC ROSENBERG (1890–1918) was born in Bristol, England to Russian immigrants. Though he considered himself first and foremost a portrait artist, Rosenberg was a talented poet. His first collection of verse, *Night and Day*, was published in 1912. He was killed near the French village of Frampoux during the First World War.

CHRISTINA GEORGINA ROSSETTI (1830–1894) was born into a literary household in London. Her siblings included Dante Gabriel Rossetti, Michael Rossetti and Maria Francesca Rossetti. Her first collection of verse, *Goblin Market and Other Poems*, was published in 1862.

DANTE GABRIEL ROSSETTI (1828–1882) was born Gabriel Charles Dante Rossetti in London. A talented artist, he was at the forefront of the Pre-Raphaelite movement. His sister was Christina Georgina Rossetti.

CHARLES SANGSTER (1822–1893) was born in Kingston, Upper Canada (Ontario). As a young man, he held a variety of newspaper positions, before settling into a career in mid-life with the Ottawa Post Office. Two volumes of verse, *The St Lawrence and the Saguenay and Other Poems* (1856) and *Hesperus and Other Poems and Lyrics* (1860), were published during his lifetime.

H. SMALLEY SARSON (1890–unknown) was born in London, England. A farmer, he enlisted in the Canadian Expeditionary Force at the beginning of the First World War. Sarson wrote two slim volumes of verse, *From Field and Hospital* (1916) and *A Reliquary of War* (date unknown).

SIR CHARLES SEDLEY (1639–1701) was probably born in Aylesford, Kent, the son of Sir John Sedley. Educated at Oxford, he left without obtaining a degree. A Member of Parliament, he is best known as a playwright. *The Mulberry Garden*, his first piece for the theatre, was performed in 1668.

ALAN SEEGER (1888–1916) was born in New York City and spent much of his early childhood in Mexico. Educated at Harvard, he was conducting research in London when the First World War began. He served in the French Foreign Legion and was killed at Belloy-en-Santerre. A collection of his verse, *Poems*, was published a few months later.

WILLIAM SHAKESPEARE (1564–1616) was born in England at Stratford-on-Avon. A poet and playwright, he is widely considered the greatest writer in the English language.

PERCY BYSSHE SHELLEY (1792–1822), the son of Sir Timothy Shelley, was raised in Sussex, England. A graduate of Eton, he enrolled at Oxford in 1810, only to be expelled the following year as the author of the pamphlet, *The Necessity of Atheism* (1811). His first published poetry was *Queen Mab* (1813). Shelley drowned the month before his thirtieth birthday. His second wife was Mary Shelley.

FRANCIS SHERMAN (1871–1926) was born in Fredericton, New Brunswick. He studied at the University of New Brunswick, but his poor financial situation forced him to leave. He began what would become an extremely successful career in banking. Sherman's first collection of poems, *Matins*, was published in 1896. Although other volumes followed, within five years he had ceased writing verse.

SIR PHILIP SIDNEY (1554–1586) was born in Penshurst, Kent, the eldest son of Sir Henry Sidney. Educated at Oxford, he served as Governor of Flushing in the Netherlands. He died from a fatal wound received in the Battle of Zutphen.

CHARLES HAMILTON SORLEY (1895–1915) was born in Aberdeen, Scotland, the son of a university professor. He deferred a scholarship to Oxford to serve in the First World War and was killed in the battle of Loos. A collection of verse, *Marlborough and Other Poems*, was published the year after his death.

ROBERT SOUTHEY (1774–1843) was born in Bristol, England. Educated at Oxford, he was a literary scholar and biographer. In 1813, he was made Poet Laureate, a position offered after Sir Walter Scott refused it.

EDMUND SPENSER (*c.* 1552–1599) was born in London. Educated at Cambridge, his most famous work is *The Faerie Queen*, written in praise of Elizabeth I.

J. K. STEPHEN (1859–1892) was born in London. He studied at Eton and Cambridge and was tutor to Prince Edward of Wales. He is one of many suspects posited as Jack the Ripper.

ROBERT LOUIS STEVENSON (1850–1894) was born in Edinburgh. He studied law at the University of Edinburgh, though he never practised. He travelled widely and wrote some of the greatest classics of the Victorian era, including *Treasure Island* (1883), *The Strange Case of Dr Jekyll and Mr Hyde* (1886) and *Kidnapped* (1886).

SIR JOHN SUCKLING (1609–1642) was born in Whitton, Middlesex. He attended Cambridge, but left before earning a degree. A soldier, ambassador, playwright and poet, he is credited with having invented the game of cribbage.

ALGERNON CHARLES SWINBURNE (1837–1909) was born in London. A graduate of Eton and Oxford, he was one of England's foremost Decadent poets. His early work led some to believe that he might one day be named Poet Laureate.

JONATHAN SWIFT (1667–1745) was born in Dublin and educated at Trinity College. A satirist, essayist and pamphleteer, he is best known for his novel *Gulliver's Travels* (1726).

JOHN ADDINGTON SYMONDS (1840–1893) was born in Bristol, England, the son of a physician who was also the author of several books on health. He was educated at Oxford, and became a leading literary critic of his day.

JOHN BANISTER TABB (1845–1909) was born to a wealthy Episcopalian family near Richmond, Virginia. After a private education, he served in the Confederate Navy during the American Civil War. Following the war, he converted to Catholicism and became a priest. He taught at St Charles's College until he was overcome by blindness.

BERT LESTON TAYLOR (1866–1921) was an American humourist and journalist from the Midwest. He was the author of ten books, including *Line-o'-type Lyrics* (1902).

SARA TEASDALE (1884–1933) was born SARAH TEASDALE in St Louis, Missouri. A sickly child, until the age of nine she was unable to attend school. Her first volume of verse, *Helen of Troy and Other Poems*, was published in 1911. Teasdale committed suicide at the age of 48.

E. WYNDHAM TENNANT (1897–1916) was born in Wiltshire, England, the son of Baron Glenconnor. His younger brother was Stephen Tennant. At the age of 17, during the First World War, he enlisted in the army and was killed by a sniper at the battle of the Somme.

ALFRED, LORD TENNYSON (1809–1892) was born in Somersby, Lincolnshire, the son of a clergyman. He was educated at Cambridge, during which time his first book, *Poems, Chiefly Lyrical* (1830), was published. He was forced to abandon his studies following the death of his father. In 1850, he was appointed Poet Laureate, a position he held for over four decades.

WILLIAM MAKEPEACE THACKERAY (1811–1863) was born in Calcutta, India, the son of an official with the British East India Company. From the age of five, he lived most of his life in England. Once considered a rival of Dickens, he is remembered today primarily for his novel *Vanity Fair* (1847–1848).

EDWARD THOMAS (1878–1917) was born in London. After studying at Oxford, he began a life in letters as an author, editor and critic. He did not begin writing verse until 1914, the year before he joined up for the First World War. He was killed by a shell at Arras, France.

HENRY DAVID THOREAU (1817–1862) was born in Concord, Massachusetts. Educated at Harvard, he is best known for the essay *Civil Disobedience* (1849) and *Walden* (1854), his reflection upon simple living.

HENRY TIMROD (1829–1867) was born in Charleston, South Carolina, the son of a minor poet. The younger Timrod's first collection of verse, *Poems*, was published in 1860. He found work as a tutor and as a journalist and editor for a number of newspapers, including *The Daily South Carolinian*. After his home was destroyed during the American Civil War, he was reduced to a level of poverty from which he was unable to escape. He died of tuberculosis.

CATHARINE PARR TRAILL (1802–1899) was born Catharine Strickland in London. In 1832, with her husband she emigrated to Upper

Canada, settling near Peterborough on a farm adjacent to that of her sister, Susannna Moodie. Her best-known book, *The Backwoods of Canada* (1836), is an account of her first three years in the colony.

BERNARD FREEMAN TROTTER (1890–1917) was born in Toronto and spent much of his youth in Wolfville, Nova Scotia. He was killed while serving as a transport officer during the First World War. His only collection of verse, *A Canadian Twilight and Other Poems of War and Peace*, was published the month of the Armistice.

HENRY VAUGHAN (1622–1695) was born in Newton-upon-Usk, Wales. His studies in law at Oxford were interrupted by the English Civil War. He eventually became a physician and published his first book of verse, *Poems with the Tenth Satire of Juvenile Englished*, in 1646. He was the twin brother of philosopher and alchemist Thomas Vaughan.

EDMUND WALLER (1606–1687) was born in Buckinghamshire, England, the son of a wealthy landowner. Educated at Eton and Cambridge, he studied law at Lincoln's Inn. At 16, he was elected to Parliament, where he developed a reputation as a skilful orator. A Royalist, he was imprisoned and, in 1643, exiled for his involvement in a plot to secure London for Charles I. After nearly a decade travelling throughout Europe, he was permitted to return to England in 1652.

WILLIAM WALSH (1663–1708) was born in Abberley, Worcestershire. He studied at Oxford, without taking a degree. Four times a Member of Parliament, he served as Gentleman of the Horse for Queen Anne. He wrote a number of essays and poems, but it is likely that his greatest contribution to letters came as a mentor to the young Alexander Pope.

ARTHUR GRAHAM WEST (1891–1917) was born in Norfolk, England and spent his childhood in London. A graduate of Oxford, he enlisted as a private in the First World War. He was killed by a sniper outside Bapaume, France.

WALT WHITMAN (1819–1892) was born in West Hills, New York. After leaving school he undertook a variety of occupations, including printer, carpenter, teacher and newspaper editor. Whitman's key work, *Leaves of Grass*, was first published in 1855 as a slim volume containing 12 long poems. He spent much of the remainder of his life revising the work, adding and, on occasion, removing verse. The last edition, published the year before his death, featured nearly 400 poems.

JOHN GREENLEAF WHITTIER (1807–1892) was born in Haverhill, Massachusetts. Though he had little in the way of schooling, he made his literary debut at the age of 19. A dedicated abolitionist, he promoted the cause through his editorship of a number of influential publications. His greatest success came with the publication of his long narrative poem, *Snow-Bound*, in 1866.

ELLA WHEELER WILCOX (1850–1919) was born in Jonestown, Wisconsin. An extremely prolific and popular poet, she wrote dozens of volumes of poetry.

OSCAR WILDE (1854–1900) was born in Dublin. An outstanding student, he studied classics at Trinity College, Dublin and was granted a scholarship to Oxford. A graduate of Oxford, he was known for his satirical verse. An accomplished playwright, novelist, short story writer and poet, he is known as much for his wit as for his art.

JOHN WILMOT, EARL OF ROCHESTER (1647–1680) was born in Ditchley, Oxfordshire. A graduate of Oxford, he was known for his bawdy verse. Such was its bite, that he was banned from the court of Charles II.

CHARLES WOLFE (1791–1823) was born in Blackhall, Ireland. He studied at Trinity College, Dublin and was ordained as a minister in the Church of Ireland. His only volume of verse, *Poetical Remains*, appeared two years after his death from tuberculosis.

WILLIAM WORDSWORTH (1770–1850) was born in Cockermouth on the River Derwent, England. He graduated from Cambridge in 1791 and two years later published his first two collections of verse, *An Evening Walk* and *Descriptive Sketches*. In 1843, he was made Poet Laureate, a position he held until his death. His sister was the poet and diarist Dorothy Wordsworth.

SIR THOMAS WYATT (1503–1542) was born at Allington Castle, Kent. Educated at Cambridge, he spent most of his life in the service of Henry VII. He was twice imprisoned in the Tower of London, once under suspicion of being one of Anne Boleyn's lovers.

# INDEX OF POETS

# INDEX OF TITLES

# INDEX OF FIRST LINES

Go and catch a falling star, 66
Go, lovely rose! 40
Go, soul, the body's guest, 567
God bless our good and gracious King, 158
God moves in a mysterious way 558
God! How I hate you, you young cheerful men, 464
Golden slumbers kiss your eyes, 4
Good-bye, good-bye to Summer! 336
Good people all, of every sort, 397
Good reader, if you e'er have seen 185

Had he and I but met 443
Had we but world enough, and time, 57
Hail to thee, blithe Spirit! 329
Half a league, half a league 420
Halted against the shade of a last hill, 468
Happy the man, whose wish and care 264
Happy those early days!, when I 549
Hast thou named all the birds without a gun; 518
He fought like those who've nought to lose 430
He sang of life, serenely sweet, 263
He sat in a wheeled chair, waiting for dark, 474
He that is down needs fear no fall, 542
Heavy with haze that merges and melts free 198

Helen, thy beauty is to me 222
Here dead we lie 451
Here lies poor Johnson. Reader! have a care: 174
Here sparrows build upon the trees, 9
Here the dead sleep—the quiet dead. No sound 281
High grew the snow beneath the low-hung sky, 510
His Grace! impossible! what dead! 173
How best can I serve thee, my child! My child! 17
How delicious is the winning 254
How do I love thee? Let me count the ways. 37
How doth the little crocodile 400
How great unto the living seem the dead! 294
How like a winter hath my absence been 225
How many dawns, chill from his rippling rest 211
How old may Phyllis be, you ask, 399
'How pleasant to know Mr Lear!' 386
How shall we please this Age? If in a song 134
Hurrah for the forest! the dark pine wood forest! 519
Hushed in a calm beyond mine utterance, 363
I am: yet what I am none cares or knows, 551
I chose the place where I would rest 191
I had written to Aunt Maud, 138